The Changing Fights and Fighters of Contemporary War

Marie Robin · Amelie Theussen ·
Kerstin Bree Carlson
Editors

The Changing Fights and Fighters of Contemporary War

From the Margins to the Middle

palgrave
macmillan

Editors
Marie Robin
Leiden University
The Hague, The Netherlands

Amelie Theussen
Royal Danish Defence College
Copenhagen, Denmark

Kerstin Bree Carlson
Roskilde University
Roskilde, Denmark

ISBN 978-3-032-05517-0 ISBN 978-3-032-05518-7 (eBook)
https://doi.org/10.1007/978-3-032-05518-7

This Palgrave Macmillan imprint is published by the registered company Springer Nature Switzerland AG
The registered company address is: Gewerbestrasse 11, 6330 Cham, Switzerland

Acknowledgments

This book began at the University of Southern Denmark (SDU), as the topic of the annual Center for War Studies (CWS) conference in 2020. The Covid-19 pandemic forced us online, and so dozens of scholars and students in SDU's Master of International Security and Law (MOISL) program convened to talk about the changing nature of battlefields and fighters over Zoom, from our living rooms. The interdisciplinary conference crossed several traditional fields, including at least war studies, military studies, political science, and international law. Even stuck behind our screens, we managed that most elusive of interdisciplinary feats: breaking out of silos to discuss a common object, how the center and periphery of war and warriors might be changing, how we might discuss it, and what consequences this fluidity might have.

These fruitful and fascinating conversations convinced we three editors, who were all working at SDU and affiliated with CWS and MOISL, though all in different fields and not working together directly, that we should collaborate and try to bottle some of the conference's interdisciplinary lightning. We began working on bringing the ideas from that conference into the world. This book is the result.

The book emerges in a world much changed from where it started. War in 2020 felt arguably more distant and theoretical for three academics working in Denmark than it does today. Yet the task the book set itself, charting, theorizing, and examining the meaning of movement as observed is only more urgent in the current bellicose moment.

A book accrues debts, and this one is no different. Our first collective debt is to SDU and CWS, the institutions that brought us into each other's orbit, as well as providing an intellectual home for this and so many other projects. In the long gestation between conference and the book you hold in your hands, we lost some chapters and gained some others. Each of us moved to new institutions, complete with the changing priorities this implies. One of us had a baby! In the crowded press of dissertations, moves, new programs, and other projects, we kept pushing this project forward. Our second collective debt, therefore, is to our contributors and each other, for perseverance, creativity, generosity, and gumption. Our third collective debt is to Palgrave Macmillan, Lucy Everitt, Uma Vinesh and the rest of the team, and series editor Trine Flockhart, for shepherding this project to completion with support and grace.

Finally, individually Marie Robin thanks her coeditors for their trust, mentorship, and most importantly, for their invaluable kindness. This book was thought and carried on in France, Denmark, and the Netherlands, but it also traveled to Scotland, the United States, Canada, Turkey, and many places—my warmest thanks to all those who, voluntarily or not, heard about it and gave it their time and attention. Karel heard about wars and violence a lot these past few years; yet he still manages to bring peace, laughter, and gnocchi at home.

Amelie Theussen thanks her coeditors for being the most unwavering cheerleaders one could hope for, and for believing in this project, and in its eventual completion, through the many twists and turns of life over the past five years. What a truly remarkable team we have been, lifting one another and the work itself every step of the way. Mark listened to every idea, read every draft, and shouldered the load at home on the busiest days. And Adrian, thank you for reminding me to step away from the screen and for teaching me how to find a new rhythm between work and life.

Kerstin Bree Carlson thanks her coeditors for smarts, generosity, and tenacity; you are a dream team of war studies women! Claudio checked all the equations. Love and gratitude to Lolo and Niamh for patience, curiosity, and (more and more frequently as the years go by) making dinner without even being asked.

Contents

Notes on Contributors

Jacqueline G. Burns is Senior Policy Analyst at RAND and currently working on her doctoral degree in political science at the University California—Irvine.

Kerstin Bree Carlson is Associate Professor of Law & Society at Roskilde University researching transitional justice, criminal law, terror law, and trials.

Troels Burchall Henningsen is Associate Professor at the Institute for Strategy and War Studies at the Royal Danish Defence College specializing in proxy warfare and special operation forces.

Vicky Karyoti is Assistant Professor at the Institute of Leadership and Organization at the Royal Danish Defence College studying changes to the military profession, new technologies, and innovation.

Arthur P. B. Laudrain is Research Associate in Cyber Diplomacy at the Department of War Studies and holds a Doctorate in Cybersecurity from the University of Oxford.

Chiara Libiseller is Lecturer at the Institute of History at Leiden University working on the history of concepts and distinctions in war studies.

Patrick A. Mello is Assistant Professor of International Security at the Department of Political Science and Public Administration of the Vrije

Universiteit Amsterdam focusing on comparative politics, foreign policy, and participation in armed conflicts.

Lukas Milevski is Assistant Professor at the Institute of History at Leiden University working on strategy and grey zone threats.

Marie Robin is Assistant Professor at the Institute of Security and Global Affairs at Leiden University studying revenge and emotions in conflict, disinformation, as well as the ethics of war.

Amelie Theussen is Associate Professor at the Institute for Strategy and War Studies at the Royal Danish Defence College specializing in changes to war and warfare, Arctic and Baltic security, as well as German and Danish defence and security policy.

List of Figures

List of Tables

CHAPTER 1

Introduction: From Margins to Middle: Introducing Movement in Our Understanding of Wars

Marie Robin, Amelie Theussen, and Kerstin Bree Carlson

As Ukrainian forces re-entered the suburban streets of Bucha, a once-peaceful town of 28,500 residents located 50 km northwest of Kyiv, they uncovered extensive evidence of mass killings and abuses against civilians. Dozens of bodies lay in the streets, some with their hands bound behind their backs, while mass graves near churches contained over 280 victims. Three days after retaking the city, Ukrainian authorities discovered 18

M. Robin (✉)
Institute of Security and Global Affairs, Leiden University, The Hague, The Netherlands
e-mail: m.p.c.e.robin@fgga.leidenuniv.nl

A. Theussen
Royal Danish Defence College, København, Denmark
e-mail: amth@fak.dk

K. B. Carlson
Roskilde University, Roskilde, Denmark
e-mail: carlson@ruc.dk

M. Robin et al. (eds.), *The Changing Fights and Fighters of Contemporary War*, https://doi.org/10.1007/978-3-032-05518-7_1

bodies—men, women, and children—in a basement, many showing signs of mutilation. Buildings bore traces of forced entry and looting. Satellite imagery and eyewitness accounts later confirmed that these atrocities occurred during the month-long Russian occupation (27 February–31 March 2022), pointing to arbitrary executions and systematic violations of international humanitarian law. On 9 August 2022, the municipal authorities reported a total of 458 bodies recovered following the occupation, including 366 men, 86 women, 12 children under the age of 21, and five individuals whose remains were unidentifiable. A bag of body parts was also found, further underscoring the scale of the violence. The Bucha massacre became a defining episode of Russia's invasion, emblematic of both the brutality of conventional warfare and the evolving nature of modern conflict.

The occupation itself reflected traditional military engagements. Russian forces used infantry units, mechanized troops, and artillery to establish control (Sabbagh, 2023). Military logistics were key to sustaining the occupation, with supply convoys, command posts, and structured troop deployments ensuring operational effectiveness. Uniformed soldiers set up checkpoints, conducted patrols, as well as engaged in direct confrontations with Ukrainian defenders. The use of state-supplied weaponry, including armored vehicles and artillery, reinforced the conventional aspect of the conflict, leading some to see in Russia's invasion of Ukraine a "return of war in Europe" (Le dessous des cartes, 2023; Minassian, 2023). These elements underscore the continued relevance of traditional warfare, where state actors employ organized military strategies to seize and hold territory.

At the same time, the occupation of Bucha and broader invasion of Ukraine demonstrated the changing character of warfare. Drones were widely used for reconnaissance and targeting, assisting in battlefield coordination and artillery precision (Kunertova, 2025). The involvement of irregular forces, including private military personnel and auxiliary security units, blurred the lines between conventional and unconventional combatants (Minic, 2023; Pattison, 2024). Information warfare played a critical role, as Russian state media denied and reframed reports of war crimes insisting that the bodies were planted following the departure of Russian troops (Representation in Ireland, 2023). Open-source intelligence (OSINT) analysts and journalists—Bellingcat among others—used satellite imagery and forensic evidence to challenge disinformation and document human rights violations (EU vs Disinfo, 2025; Higgins, 2022; Jankowicz, 2020; Viginum, 2025).

Russia's war against Ukraine—and the Bucha massacre as one of its most tragic manifestations—have been described as both a revival of traditional inter-state warfare, reminding of the importance of classical elements of war, such as ammunition stockpiles and logistics, and a harbinger of future war where drone technology, private enterprises, and information operations take on a leading role (Kormych & Malyarenko, 2023). In conventional interstate wars, infantry-based confrontations typically unfold on geographically defined battlefields, where soldiers in uniform, aligned with their respective states, engage using state-supplied weapons and strategies. This is also partly the case in the Russo-Ukrainian war. But the boundaries of war have also shifted. In Ukraine as in Gaza and other conflicts, the introduction of new domains of warfare, new technologies, and evolving forms of conflict—drones, private companies, and information warfare being only but a few examples—means that battlefields are arguably no longer strictly geographically limited; combatants are not always in uniform; non-state actors play increasingly prominent roles; while, locally produced improvised lethal devices—often crafted from seemingly innocuous everyday objects such as cars, oil canisters (Zohar, 2023), or pagers (Le Monde, 2024)— coexist with and actively engage high-value, technologically superior targets, enabling remote operations and facilitating combat from afar (Shashank, 2023). In this context, doubts and debates emerge as to what constitutes warfare, including where and how it is waged, and by whom.

"Nothing Is Lost, Nothing Is Created, Everything Is Transformed": Introducing Movement in Our Analysis of Wars.

The Changing Identities of Fighters and Battlefields

Contemporary war studies scholarship has long interrogated the blurring boundaries between war and peace, combatants and noncombatants, and conventional and unconventional tactics. Various disciplines—including international politics, law, history, culture, and geography—have examined these transformations, analyzing changes in battlefields, actors, and practices of war. For instance, scholarship has widely explored how technological advancements, such as drones, have *expanded the battlespace* to a global scale (Akhter, 2019; Bergen & Rothenberg, 2014; Hantke, 2018; Lewis, 2012; Lubell & Derejko, 2013). Cyberspace has emerged as a domain of warfare, according to some, shifting conflict into the realm of information operations—the so-called "Infowars"—and cyberattacks (Allhoff et al., 2016; Andress & Winterfeld, 2013; Kello, 2017; Lucas, 2017; Oakley, 2019; Ramírez & García-Segura, 2017; Rid, 2013). The early twenty-first-century revival of counterinsurgency doctrine declared the "hearts and minds" of populations to be the primary battlefield (Bolt, 2020; Kilcullen et al., 2009; Petersen, 2011), while widely debated concepts of hybrid and grey zone warfare have sought to highlight the fusion of conventional conflict with political warfare, leveraging all elements of national power to achieve strategic objectives (Atkinson, 2018; Livermore, 2018; NATO 2024; Theussen & Jakobsen, 2021).

When it comes to defining the *boundaries of combatancy*, the use of surrogate actors—such as insurgents, unmanned drones, or private military companies—has been increasingly documented as shaping contemporary conflict dynamics (Krieg & Rickli, 2019). Others have examined the emergence of so-called "lone wolf" terrorists (Della Porta, 2013; Hamm & Spaaij, 2017), the legal and operational challenges posed by foreign (de Guttry et al., 2016), and unlawful fighters (Robin, 2024; Scheipers, 2015), the increasing role of women in combatancy (Goldstein, 2001; Kinsella, 2011; Matfess, 2017), as well the incorporation of nonhuman combatants, such as artificial intelligence and military animals (Forsyth, 2017; Gardiner, 2006; Heintschel von Heinegg et al., 2018; Kosek, 2010; Scharre, 2018). Crucially, Chinkin and Kaldor (2017) have argued that these transformations in where the battlefield happens and who it contains must be understood in relation to evolving norms of international law and humanitarian principles.

Building on these foundational works and on the prudent, multidisciplinary approach that characterizes war studies (Howard, 1964; Rynning, 2017), this volume critically examines how actors, battlefields, and practices that once existed on the margins of war have frequently moved to its center, while elements that we socially constructed as "traditional"—such as geographically bounded battlefields and uniformed soldiers engaging in conventional combat—have also regularly been relegated to the periphery. This phenomenon is evidenced by the increasing involvement of civilian actors, the normalization of targeting children and humanitarian workers, and the expanded role of private military companies, as seen in the ongoing war in Gaza. Simultaneously, strategic norms governing the conduct of war, including the rules of engagement and jus in bello principles, are being stretched and reinterpreted.

This Book's Contribution: Introducing Movements in How We Understand the Changing Character of War

Documenting how war is changing and how fundamental such changes are is nothing new. As early as the nineteenth century, Prussian general Carl von Clausewitz depicted war as a true chameleon, changing its character throughout the ages. Yet, for Clausewitz, the nature of war remained the same: it is the continuation of politics by other means; a form of duel, where each side tries to compel the other to act according to its will. War, in his view, is guided by chance, influenced by emotion, and controlled by reason—at least in its ideal form. Over the past three decades, as exemplified above, much has been written about the changing character of war—including whether these changes extend to its nature.

This book, however, does not do the same. While it speaks to this literature and situates itself among the remarkable works within this tradition, we propose a different analytical framework to analyze questions of changes in war and warfare. In this book, we conceptualize change as a movement from the "middle" of war to its "margins," and vice versa, from the margins to the middle. The middle of war encompasses what the armed forces generally consider their core tasks, and everything related to said core tasks: engaging and defeating enemy forces on the battlefield, with all the related training, equipment, and suitable normative framework to succeed at this core task. The margins of war then is everything not generally associated with war and warfare: the broader society, other societal functions unrelated to the management of violence, industry and its private companies, nature, neutral states, and other actors not generally involved in war fighting. Put simply—and borrowing from another field of social sciences—war and warfare consist of a core and a periphery. But what is part of the core, and what is part of the periphery is not static; it changes throughout time, shaped by societal, technological, political, and other developments.

We believe that, in the growing literature on war evolutions, conceptualizing the changes to war and warfare as movements from the middle of warfare to the margins and vice versa has a number of advantages over the traditional debate over changes to the character or nature of war:

First, it allows us to capture the changes in actors, technologies, and battlefields that make up the changing character of war throughout the ages, without the need to argue that these changes are new. We do not argue that movement between middle and margins is new. Rather, we argue that what is seen as the middle and what is seen as the margins of war depends on the characteristics of the age under investigation, and the margins/middle analytical framework in fact allows for comparison between different ages to uncover similarities and differences as well as patterns of what was (is) seen as the core of war and warfare, and its periphery.

Second, the middle/margins analytical framework should be seen as independent of the content of the middle or the margins. This allows the framework to be applied across time and different cultures, because it gives a tool to investigate how understandings of war and warfare change based on what is seen to be the middle/core and what is relegated to the margins/periphery. It also allows its users to uncover more holistic approaches to war and warfare, which might resist such categorization, and the underlying dynamics for that.

Third, understanding change as movement from the margins to the middle and the middle to the margins also allows an investigation into why some of these changes leave states and their armed forces surprised and unprepared. If core tasks need to be adjusted, self-understandings modified, and new actors or technologies accommodated, adjusting to such changes can be lengthy and difficult.

This volume, in so doing, does not merely catalog change. Warfare has always evolved in response to technological advancements, shifts in political power, and normative developments. In war, middle and margins are fluid, constantly moving and contesting each other. The nine chapters in this volume therefore adopt an interdisciplinary approach to examine the dynamic interplay between continuity and change, drawing on the analytical lens of "movement"—from margins to middle, and middle to margins—as a means of conceptualizing shifts in war. By examining and theorizing this movement, the book provides critical examples and paradigmatic (but fluid) categories to investigate conflicts that appear to represent more traditional contestations, such as Russia's invasion of Ukraine or the war in Tigray. By drawing on these seemingly more conventional cases of interstate warfare, the book highlights the relevance of thinking about war in terms of fluid boundaries.

Using movement to analyze how conflicts evolve matters all the more when the most recent scholarship on war has sought to challenge dominant narratives about contemporary conflicts. The notion that war is in decline (Mueller, 1989; Pinker, 2011) is now widely contested both by everyday news as well as by scholars who emphasize the persistence of geopolitical rivalries (Renz, 2019) and the enduring political nature of war, despite its changing modalities (Strachan & Scheipers, 2011). The increasing fusion of war and information operations, as highlighted in Russian strategic doctrine (Renz, 2019), underscores how non-kinetic dimensions of conflict—cyber warfare, propaganda, and strategic deterrence—are now increasingly analyzed within what we coin as the "middle of the battlefield," rather than at its peripheries. Similarly, the erosion of clear distinctions between war and peace (Whetham, 2016) challenges traditional frameworks of just war theory, necessitating new ethical and legal considerations.

By analyzing war through movement—as a fluid and continuous dialogue between the middle and margins of the battlefield—this volume offers a conceptual framework that not only captures the transformations in how wars are fought but also interrogates the contested dimension of what makes a battlefield or a fighter, depending on time and space.

Outline of This Volume

The book is divided into three sections, each comprised of three chapters. The first section conceptualizes the middle and the margins of warfare. The book opens with Chiara Libiseller and Lukas Milevski's chapter on the values and constraints that arise in using concepts as mental shortcuts, with a focus on what this means for the study of war. Libiseller and Milevski argue that concepts related to war are often developed and applied unsystematically. Even more problematically, specific biases—Libiseller and Milevski examine the conventional war and structure biases—create false prototypes that obscure a more productive focus, which would be on agency and intentions. Libiseller and Milevski examine the dominant concepts obtaining in war studies, and conclude that resistance to these concepts in favor of greater focus on actors' intentions and actions could facilitate more productive understandings of war. Libiseller and Milevski argue for greater focus on empirical data, rather than ideological or conceptual pre-fabricated ideas, as a necessary means to study war.

In Chapter 3, Troels Burchall Henningsen considers a war studies shibboleth, the notion that great power theory explains proxy warfare. Around the globe, proxy wars are increasing in prevalence, moving from the margins to the mainstream of contemporary warfare. Proxy wars are longer and bloodier than other wars. They are also particularly destabilizing due to their creation of sponsor-proxy relationships. While great power theory can go part of the way in explaining proxy warfare, it cannot explain its rising incidence. To understand this movement, focus on regional and in some cases local drivers is necessary. In his chapter, Henningsen examines regional drivers in Africa and the Middle East that concretize our understanding of the rise in proxy warfare, making empirical and theoretical contributions to our understanding of the changing role of proxy wars in war.

Chapter 4 ends the section with an investigation into the movements between the margins and middle of warfare that leave their mark on the conceptualization of the battlefield and where it is located in contemporary conflicts. Amelie Theussen argues that changes in actors and means and methods of warfare have created a globalized battlefield, where spaces often considered peaceful suddenly become potential battlefields, such as urban centers located at substantial distance to the traditional battlefield. This includes the increasingly geographically unbounded battlefield in the cyber domain, which targets individuals' political opinions, conversations, and emotions. An analysis of the Russia-Ukraine war reveals that, where traditional war took place on a geographically constrained battlefield, supported by operations targeting support structures and the hearts and minds of populations, today the population and support structures are an integral part of a multi-layered battlefield, at least as decisive as the physical clash of armed forces on the frontlines, if that even exists at all.

The second section of the book examines practices moving from the margins to the middle. In Chapter 5, Arthur P.B. Laudrain examines how cyber warfare is redefining power dynamics and combat strategies. The chapter focuses on three "middle ground states": Israel, India, and North Korea. For each of these states, Laudrain examines empirical examples to demonstrate the specific tactics and methods middle ground states have employed to leverage cyber capabilities. These states' use of cyber ranges from attacks that are economic in nature (North Korea's theft from Bangladesh's Central Bank and against cryptocurrencies) to technological meddling (Israel's Stuxnet malware attack on Iran's nuclear program) to social-media influence (India in Pakistan) to more traditional explosive capacities (Israel's pager attack on Hezbollah in Lebanon). Through his examination of specific tactics and events, Laudrain convincingly shows how cyber is offsetting traditional notions of power, autonomy, and influence for middle ground states.

Jacqueline G. Burns uses a gendered lens to examine how the changing nature of war is accompanied by new opportunities for women's participation in peace in Chapter 6. Focusing on the peace processes in Sudan and South Sudan, Gardner Burns shows how the increasingly informal practice of war, what Mary Kaldor defined as "new wars," has opened spaces for women's participation that have not been possible in the peace processes following more traditional forms of warfare. Gardner Burns shows how women in Sudan and South Sudan, historically excluded from political processes, have leveraged informal social networks, grassroots organizing, and informal economic participation to influence peace processes. She identifies three pathways through which women have sought to influence peace outcomes, theorizing that where formal institutions are weak or absent, space opens for actors working in informal networks and movements.

In Chapter 7, Marie Robin examines how the category of "fighter" is constructed by actors in terror organizations. Where international law seeks to make a firm distinction between combatant and civilian, attributing combatant status to armed, violent actors, terror groups have a broader conception of fighters that includes propaganda warriors. Through an examination of speeches, pamphlets, and terrorist violence, Robin shows how a Western definition of combatant does not obtain for Al Qaeda and the Islamic State. These groups conceptualize speech and ideology as important weapons of war, and those who practice them are warriors. Robin's chapter challenges the universalism of extant legal categories, with broad implications for how fighters and battlefields are defined.

The final section of the book considers practices and ideologies that have moved from the middle to the margins. The section begins with Vicky Karyoti's Chapter 8, which examines drone operators' status in relation to other military professionals. Using a sociological analysis of the makeup, inner workings, and boundaries of the concept of professionalism, Karyoti argues that drone operators exist in a grey zone because they are in many ways not recognized as military professionals. Karyoti examines what the relevant criteria for professionalism in the military is, before concluding that drone operators meet these criteria. Karyoti's chapter challenges our understanding of how we define military professionals especially as the tasks that a professional military performs evolve.

In Chapter 9, Patrick Mello examines the variance in countries' military responses to the Islamic State (IS). Focusing on EU states' involvement in the military coalition to defeat IS, Mello examines how variance is usually explained through five theories: threat perceptions, alliance considerations, political partisanship, institutional constraints, and public opinion. While each of these theories adds to our understanding, Mello finds that none of the five theories can fully explain variance in relation to the anti-IS coalition. Rather, he finds that countries with foreign fighters in Iraq and Syria, who also valued their alliance with the United States, were particularly prone to become involved militarily. Importantly, he identifies a structural component which also explains variance: the presence of parliamentary veto rights. These internal political structures proved to be an effective constraint on executive decision-making in relation to the coalition military response to IS, challenging and expanding our understanding of participation in military coalitions.

Finally, in Chapter 10, Kerstin Bree Carlson examines an increasing illiberalism in Europe being evidenced through European countries' treatment of their "foreign fighters." Many European countries have elected not to repatriate citizens trapped in Syria, including children; this excommunication includes citizenship revocation in some cases. Carlson's chapter contrasts this European illiberalism with a restorative justice experiment in Colombia. Carlson argues that transitional justice, including as practiced in Colombia, could provide a mechanism for Europeans to recenter liberalism in their treatment of unpopular populations.

In the book's conclusion, Kerstin Bree Carlson tests the middle/margins model on the case of the international rules-based order, which many scholars and pundits argue is in decline or even defeat. Carlson revisits the contributors' arguments in relation to the rules-based international order before applying the middle/margins model to recent jurisprudence initiated by countries in the global south (margins) that applies and seeks to shore up the rule-based international legal order (middle). To make the argument, the conclusion briefly visits cases brought before the International Court of Justice, as well as invocations of the jurisprudence from the International Criminal Court.

In Conclusion

War's means and methods have never been fixed, and movement, change, diversion and even sleight of hand have always enjoyed central billing in war. The many and varied attempts consistently made to order war's chaos exist in parallel with technologies, strategies, narratives, and politics designed to achieve war's aspirations.

The chapters in this book theorize what a focus on core/periphery, middle/margin, affords those who study war, its technologies, and its social, political, and legal consequences. By using movement as a starting focus, we gain different understandings of what is challenged, gained, and at stake in the means, methods, and narratives that surround war.

References

Akhter, M. (2019). The proliferation of peripheries: Militarized drones and the reconfiguration of global space. *Progress in Human Geography, 43*(1), 64–80.

Allhoff, F., et al. (Eds.). (2016). *Binary bullets: The ethics of cyberwarfare*. Oxford University Press.

Andress, J., & Winterfeld, S. (2013). *Cyber warfare: Techniques, tactics and tools for security practitioners*. Elsevier.

Atkinson, C. (2018). Hybrid warfare and societal resilience implications for democratic governance. *Information & Security, 39*(1), 63–76.

Bergen, P. L., & Rothenberg, D. (Eds.). (2014). *Drone Wars: Transforming conflict, law, and policy*. Cambridge University Press.

Bolt, N. (2020). *The violent image: Insurgent propaganda and the new revolutionaries*. Oxford University Press.

Chinkin, C., & Kaldor, M. (2017). *International law and new wars*. Cambridge University Press.

De Guttry, A., et al. (2016). *Foreign fighters under international law and beyond*. TMC Asser Press.

Della Porta, D. (2013). *Clandestine political violence*. Cambridge University Press.

EU vs Disinfo (2025, April 7). Disinfo: The so-called 'Bucha massacre' appears to have been fabricated. *Disinfo Review*. https://euvsdisinfo.eu/report/the-so-called-bucha-massacre-appears-to-have-been-fabricated/.

Forsyth, I. (2017). A bear's biography: Hybrid warfare and the more-than-human battlespace. *Environment and Planning d: Society and Space, 35*(3), 495–512. https://doi.org/10.1177/0263775816664098

Gardiner, J. (2006). *The animal's War: Animals in wartime from the First World War to the present day*. Portrait.

Goldstein, J. S. (2001). *War and gender: How gender shapes the war system and vice versa*. Cambridge University Press.
Hamm, M. S., & Spaaij, R. (2017). *The age of lone wolf terrorism*. Columbia University Press.
Hantke, S. (2018). Armchair adventurers: Technology on the global battlefield in films about drone warfare. *The Journal of Popular Culture, 51*(6), 1398–1414. https://doi.org/10.1111/jpcu.12740
Heintschel Von, W., et al. (2018). *Dehumanization of warfare*. Springer.
Higgins, E. (2022, April 4). Russia's Buch 'facts' versus the evidence. *Bellingcat*.
Howard, M. (1964). Military power and international order. *International Affairs, 40*(3), 397–408.
Jankowicz, N. (2020). *How to lose the information war: Russia, fake news, and the future of conflict*. I.B. Tauris.
Kello, L. (2017). *The virtual weapon and international order*. Yale University Press.
David, K. (2010). *Counterinsurgency*. Oxford University Press.
Kilcullen, D., et al. (2009). *US government counterinsurgency guide*. Department of State.
Kinsella, H. M. (2011). *The image before the weapon. A critical history of distinction between combatant and civilian*. Cornell University Press.
Kormych, B., & Malyarenko, T. (2023). From gray zone to conventional warfare: The Russia-Ukraine conflict in the Black Sea. *Small Wars & Insurgencies, 34*(7), 1235–1270.
Kosek, J. (2010). Ecologies of empire: On the new uses of the honeybee. *Cultural Anthropology, 25*(4), 650–678.
Krieg, A., & Rickli, J.-M. (2019). *Surrogate warfare: The transformation of war in the twenty-first century*. Georgetown University Press.
Kunertova, D. (2025, April). Embracing drone diversity: Five challenges to Western military adaptation in drone warfare. *Freeman Air & Space Institute, King's College London, Research Paper 29*.
Le dessous des cartes (2023, February 25). Ukraine, le retour de la guerre, *Arte.tv*.
Le Monde (2024, September 17). At least nine dead from exploding pagers across Lebanon, Hezbollah blames Israel. *Le Monde*. https://www.lemonde.fr/en/international/article/2024/09/17/hundreds-wounded-as-hezbollah-pagers-simultaneously-explode-across-lebanon_6726383_4.html
Lewis, M. W. (2012). Drones and the boundaries of the battlefield. *Texas International Law Journal, 47*(2), 293–314.

Livermore, D.A. (2018). A primer on understanding the threat—Russian, Iranian, and Chinese political warfare. *Small Wars Journal*. https://archive.smallwarsjournal.com/jrnl/art/primer-understanding-threat-russian-iranian-and-chinese-political-warfare.

Lubell, N., & Derejko, N. (2013). A global battlefield? Drones and the geographical scope of armed conflict. *Journal of International Criminal Justice, 11*(1), 65–88.

Lucas, G. R. (2017). *Ethics and cyber warfare: The quest for responsible security in the age of digital warfare*. Oxford University Press.

Matfess, H. (2017). *Women and the war on Boko Haram; Wives, weapons, witnesses*. Bloomsbury Publishing.

Minassian, G. (2023, February 27). François Heisbourg: 'Avec la guerre en Ukraine, nous changeons d'époque'. *Le Monde*. https://www.lemonde.fr/idees/article/2023/02/27/francois-heisbourg-avec-la-guerre-en-ukraine-nous-changeons-d-epoque_6163422_3232.html.

Minic, D. (2023). *Pensée et culture stratégiques russes. Du contournement de la lutte armée à la guerre en Ukraine*. Éditions de la Maison des sciences de l'homme.

Mueller, J. (1989). *Retreat from Doomsday. The Obsolescence of Major War*. Basic Books.

NATO (2024). *Countering hybrid threats*. https://www.nato.int/cps/en/natohq/topics156338.htm

Oakley, J. G. (2019). *Professional red teaming: Conducting successful cybersecurity engagements*. Apress.

Pattison, J. (2024). Ukraine, Wagner, and Russia's convict-soldiers. *Ethics & International Affairs, 38*(1), 17–30.

Petersen, R. D. (2011). *Western intervention in the Balkans: The strategic use of emotion in conflict*. Cambridge University Press.

Pinker, S. (2011). *The better angels of our nature: The decline of violence in history and its causes*. Penguin.

Ramírez, J. M., & García Segura, L. A. (Eds.). (2017). *Cyberspace: Risks and benefits for society, security and development*. Springer.

Renz, B. (2019). Russian responses to the changing character of war. *International Affairs, 95*(4), 817–834.

Representation in Ireland (2023, April 3). The Bucha massacre: mapping a year of Kremlin denial. *European Commission*. https://ireland.representation.ec.europa.eu/news-and-events/news/bucha-massacre-mapping-year-kremlin-denial-2023-04-03-0_en.

Rid, T. (2013). More attacks, less violence. *Journal of Strategic Studies, 36*(1), 139–142.

Robin, M. (2024). Are propagandists combatants? Analysing the ethical status of propagandists in warfare. *Review of International Studies, 50*(6), 1046–1065.

Rynning, S. (2017). War studies—en introduktion. *Økonomi & Politik*, *90*(1), 98.
Sabbagh, D. (2023, March 6). Traditional, heavy warfare has returned to Europe with Ukraine conflict. *The Guardian*. https://www.theguardian.com/world/2023/mar/06/traditional-heavy-warfare-has-returned-to-europe-with-ukraine-conflict.
Scharre, P. (2018). How swarming will change warfare. *Bulletin of the Atomic Scientists*, *74*(6), 385–389.
Scheipers, S. (2015). *Unlawful combatants: A genealogy of the irregular fighter*. Oxford University Press.
Shashank, J. (2023, July 3). The war in Ukraine shows how technology is changing the battlefield. *The Economist*. https://www.economist.com/special-report/2023/07/03/the-war-in-ukraine-shows-how-technology-is-changing-the-battlefield.
Strachan, H., & Scheipers, S. (Eds.). (2011). *The changing character of war*. Oxford University Press.
Theussen, A., & Jakobsen, P. V., et al. (2021). In the shadows: The challenge of Russian and Chinese gray zone conflict for the West. In S. Rynning (Ed.), *War time: Temporality and the decline of Western military power* (pp. 161–183). Brookins Institution Press.
Viginum. (2025, February). War in Ukraine. Three years of Russian information operations. *Secrétariat general de la défense et de la sécurité nationale*. https://www.sgdsn.gouv.fr/files/2025-02/20250224_TLP-CLEAR_NP_SGDSN_VIGINUM_War%20in%20Ukraine_Three%20years%20of%20Russian%20information%20operations_1.0_VF.pdf.
Whetham, D. (2016). 'Are we fighting yet?' Can traditional just war concepts cope with contemporary conflict and the changing character of war? *The Monist*, *99*, 55–69.
Zohar, E. (2023). *Understanding non-state actors: How rebels acquire their weapons*. De Gruyter.

CHAPTER 2

Not to Confuse Ourselves: The Changing Character of War and Conceptual Change

Chiara Libiseller and Lukas Milevski

Introduction

The changing character of war has become a cliché, it seems: scholars and practitioners of war see change and revolutions around every corner.[1] As a consequence, concepts of war and warfare have mushroomed, particularly after the end of the Cold War. New means, techniques, instances, and outcomes of war have continuously inspired new categories of war. To be clear, change in war and warfare is indeed ubiquitous; it arises from long-term trends, such as changes in technology and society, as well as immediate pressures, such as the dynamics of the interaction between adversaries. However, the flurry of concepts that aim to capture these

[1] See, for example, the Revolution in Military Affairs debate, which has already identified six waves of revolutionary change in warfare since the 1990s; cf. Raska (2020).

We want to thank Vladimir Rauta for very useful comments on an earlier draft.

C. Libiseller (✉) · L. Milevski
King's College London, London, United Kingdom
e-mail: chiara.3.libiseller@kcl.ac.uk

M. Robin et al. (eds.), *The Changing Fights and Fighters of Contemporary War*, https://doi.org/10.1007/978-3-032-05518-7_2

changes might have done more harm than good for our understanding of war. Given the many concepts used for the analysis of wars and their vague meanings and unspecified relations to related concepts, scholars working on similar issues are often talking past one another. There is little effort to systematize the different concepts. Neither is there much agreement on what the most useful or important concepts are, and few new concepts are widely accepted or appreciated. At the same time, in overemphasizing change, understanding the broader phenomenon of war has not been addressed sufficiently.

This is problematic because of the foundational role that concepts play in our ability to make sense of the world. Concepts fundamentally underlie and structure our thinking and actions; the concepts we use to make sense of war and warfare shape research, defense planning, strategies, and policies. Conceptual clarity is, therefore, an academic and practical necessity and obligation. Yet, as this chapter shows, concept formation on war and warfare in War and Strategic Studies has often lacked system and rigor.

Hence, the question this chapter aims to answer is: why are there so many concepts on war and warfare? The purpose of this chapter is to critically examine concept formation in relation to war and warfare over the past decades. Building on discussions on concept formation in political science as well as discussions on the concept of war, we discuss three mutually constitutive tendencies of concept formation on war and warfare that have led to fundamentally flawed concepts while encouraging further conceptual innovation. First, concepts have repeatedly been introduced without reference to their conceptual network. Instead, they are ad-hoc creations that are inherently linked to specific and recent instances of war. Second, underlying most of these concepts is a conventional war bias which considers full-scale interstate war as ideal type of war. This conventional war bias marginalizes all actors other than state militaries and erases them from memory and analysis of war. New concepts have brought these hitherto marginalized actors and means to the center, but did so in an unsystematic way, and, more problematically, even implicitly reproduced the underlying conventional war bias. Third, many of these concepts focus on capturing the character of war, meaning they lack an appreciation of agency of the actors involved in the war effort. Underlying conceptual innovation is a moral economy that privileges certain actors and experiences over others. As a consequence of these tendencies, many of our concepts are unfit to capture dynamics or changes within wars. At the same time, we argue that the solution to these problems exists already: a recourse to the broader, conventional-agnostic, and agency-respectful understanding of war that traditionally has underlain War and Strategic Studies.

Academic Concept Formation

Concepts, a form of ideas, are crucial tools for humans to interpret the world, act in it, and communicate about it. Their central function is to reduce complexity by 'deciding what is important about an entity' (Goertz, 2006, 27). Concepts thereby work as mental shortcuts, as abbreviations. Therefore, concept formation is about making fundamental ontological decisions about the phenomenon in question: what are its central characteristics? Concept formation determines the concept's definition (intension), its real-life instances (extension), and its relationships with other concepts within the overall system of knowledge. For example, the concept of a 'tree' includes a wooden trunk, branches growing from its upper part, and 'considerable height and size' (Oxford English Dictionary; Cambridge Dictionary). The latter two aspects set it apart from bushes and shrubs. Whether a tree has leaves, needles, or is bare, on the other hand, is not considered relevant to establish its 'treeness'.

The above definition of a tree exemplifies the 'classical model' of concepts, in which concepts are formed based on necessary and sufficient conditions, and empirical cases categorized clearly either inside or outside a specific concept. This model dominated philosophical discussions on concepts from Aristotle to Wittgenstein (Lakoff, 1987, 6), who discovered that humans also categorize based on what he called 'family resemblance'. The category of games may serve as an illustrative example: despite the fact that there is no one feature that all games share, they are still grouped together based on the fact that each 'game' is characterized by some, but not all, characteristics of a pool of characteristics attributed to 'games' (Wittgenstein, 2016[1984], paras. 66–71). For Wittgenstein, therefore, to understand the meaning of a concept we have to look at its use in language. New insights in Cognitive Psychology in the 1970s, too, threw into question the 'classical model' by suggesting that humans do not categorize by checking necessary criteria, but by comparing objects and ideas to the 'prototype' of a category. In contrast to the 'classical model', Rosch's prototype theory is a model of graded categorization in which some objects are more typical of a category than others (Lakoff,

1987, 7). Family resemblance and prototype theory show that human categorization does not follow strict criteria. This means that our concepts often are vague (their boundaries are not clearly demarcated), ambiguous (they have more than one meaning), and/or open-ended (their core is ill-defined) (Schaffer, 2005, 2).

In academia, however, vague, general, or ambiguous concepts can have major repercussions for the quality of research (cf. Libiseller, 2023, 2026). They may hamper effective communication among scholars and thus impede theoretical thinking, scientific progress, and accumulation (cf. Rauta, 2021, 545). They may also hamper communication between scholars and practitioners, impeding empirical understanding or translation and outreach opportunities. The reliance by practitioners upon inapt, misleading, or otherwise flawed concepts in contexts from battlefield tactics to policymaking may impede the quality and even ultimate success of practice by enabling or even legitimizing inferior courses of action, undue confidence in one's own intentions and plans, and downgrading the importance of the enemy's own perceptions and behavior.

In contrast to the Natural Sciences which have created neologisms to describe their research objects (ether, phlogiston, atom, electron, to give a few examples), the Social Sciences and Humanities (the two disciplines from which War and Strategic Studies primarily draw) rely on a vocabulary that primarily stems from 'ordinary' language use and is fundamentally entangled with the political and social phenomena it aims to analyze. Political Science, specifically, frequently deals with contested concepts such as democracy, human rights, terrorism, or war. In the field of Strategic Studies, the close connection between scholars and practitioners allows concepts to travel—usually from the latter to the former—meaning that concepts coined for their political utility have found their way into academic debates, masquerading as academic concepts (cf. Libiseller, 2023). As a consequence, concepts of war and warfare are often characterized by conceptual stretching—'the application of (often value-laden) concepts to cases that lack essential characteristics of these concepts' (Schedler, 2010, 7; cf. Sartori, 1970)—and conceptual masking—'the description of (morally relevant) cases through neutral concepts that disguise essential characteristics of these cases' (ibid.). However, as Schedler (2010, 5) has argued, social science concepts 'are often complex and contested, and we cannot take for granted that others comprehend them in the same manner as we do. Linguistic transparency is, therefore, our first obligation in the social scientific use of concepts'.

The difficulty of creating precise concepts has invited a lot of discussion in philosophy and the social sciences. In political science, especially in comparative politics, making concepts transferable to other contexts without stretching them encouraged detailed engagement with concept formation. If we were interested in only one war at one time, such debates would not matter as much. However, once we become interested in the phenomenon of war per se, and especially in how it changes across time and place, we need to identify a transferable definition of war. 'Concept formation' as Schedler (2010, 9) explained 'is the systematic development and explication of the core claims we commit ourselves to when applying a concept'. Concept formation is based on existing meanings, related concepts, and empirical cases. Good concepts are clearly defined, demarcated from related concepts, and useful to analyze empirics (cf. Gerring, 1999; Sartori, 1970; Schedler, 2010). Concept formation, therefore, has to start from the existing conceptual network: any form of conceptual innovation or change has implications for other elements of the conceptual network. As John Gerring (1999, 382) has argued, it is 'impossible [...] to redefine one term without redefining others, for the task of definition consists of establishing relationships with neighboring terms'. Neighboring concepts might be similar to another, but it is their 'semantic nuances that are relevant for our research purposes' (Schedler, 2010, 10). This assumes, however, that new concepts are clearly demarcated from existing ones.

Scholars have identified different approaches to concept formation. Proper neologisms are a rare occasion in political science according to Schaffer (2005, 3f.) who cites the concept of 'genocide' as an example. A more frequent type of conceptual innovation is the reconstruction of existing terms, which may include the privileging of one of the different existing meanings of a term; adding a new meaning; 'shifting the grammatical use of a term' ('transposition'); and 'spinning-off', i.e., adding a pre- or a suffix or creating a compound term (Schaffer 2005, 5f.).

To ensure that this process is structured and systematic, Sartori (1970) introduced the ladder of abstraction which allows scholars to adapt concepts to different contexts without losing specificity. By starting from a core understanding of a concept and climbing or descending the ladder of abstraction, a concept can be made more or less specific, respectively. One may climb the 'ladder of abstraction' by reducing the necessary characteristics of a concept to broaden the number of cases that fall under it.

In this way, the concept becomes more abstract and general, but a conceptual essence remains. Alternatively, one may descend the ladder by adding additional characteristics and creating subtypes. For example, by adding the characteristic 'has leaves' to our definition of a tree, we create the more specific category of deciduous trees. Similarly, by adding the characteristic 'fought between states' to our understanding of war, we create the more specific category of interstate wars. Notably, each subtype is a complete instance of the main concept—it shares all core attributes plus one or more additional ones (Collier & Levitsky, 1997, 435). Subtypes allow for differentiation by making the concept more specific.

An alternative way of creating subtypes was suggested by Collier and Levitsky (ibid.). Their 'diminished subtypes' are not full instances of the main concept; they come close but miss one or two key attributes and thus represent incomplete forms. A diminished subtype therefore has fewer attributes than the main type—this distinguishes the approach from Sartori's ladder of abstraction. By highlighting the missing attribute in their label, they too create differentiation from the main concept. For example, 'illiberal democracy' would be a diminished subtype of democracy that lacks a key definitional trait (liberal freedoms such as free speech and assembly; ibid., 434). Diminished subtypes are meant to overcome the issue posed by binary categories by allowing for the inclusion of hybrids. For example, regimes that are neither fully democratic nor fully authoritarian but close to either of these two categories can be grouped as such through the creation of a diminished subtype (ibid., 441). However, Collier and Levitsky (ibid., 450) also warned of the negative implications of creating diminished subtypes. Especially when it comes to loaded concepts such as democracy, the inclusion of an incomplete democracy as subtype thereof (rather than as a subtype of authoritarianism) might distort or hide key aspects of said regime. A second issue is the proliferation of terms that comes from the creation of such subtypes: many concepts are similar in meaning, creating confusion (ibid., 1997, 450).

These limitations of diminished subtypes point to more general power dynamics underlying concept formation. Since concept formation is about identifying what matters about an entity it is an act of power: it shapes and delimits future deliberations. People might have power over ideas, i.e., the 'capacity … to control and dominate the meaning of ideas' (Carstensen & Schmidt 2016, 323). But ideas can also become powerful by themselves if they are authoritative in 'structuring thought at the expense of other ideas' (ibid., 329). The use and formation of concepts can thus be used to 'affirm or challenge power' (Schaffer, 2016, 9). Acknowledging this, there is a tension in our argument between positivist and interpretivist approaches to concept formation and analysis. We are aware that conceptual innovation, preference, or confusion are not coincidental, but reflect power structures. Concepts serve interests and promoting one concept over another is to (implicitly) support certain interests and assumptions, highlight certain aspects while marginalizing others. At the same time, we consider a common vocabulary necessary to academic and practitioners' ability to make sense of war.

Conceptual Innovation in War Studies and Strategic Studies

Based on the theoretical insights of the previous section, this section looks at how concepts of war and warfare have been created in War and Strategic Studies. As many observers have already pointed out, the rate of conceptual (or rather: terminological) innovation is extremely high in War and Strategic Studies (e.g., Haug & Maaø, 2012; Libiseller, 2026; Rauta, 2021). There are plenty of plausible explanations for that, including the general appeal of introducing new concepts into academic debates, the impact of events on debates in the field (cf. Aron, 1969, 7; Baylis & Wirtz, 2016), and the close connection between scholars and practitioners that allows concepts to travel easily from practice to academia (rarely the other way; Libiseller, 2026). Additionally, the question of why new concepts are formed in the field is immediately linked to the question of how they are formed, which we deal with in the consecutive paragraphs. First, we argue that concepts of war and warfare are often created in an unsystematic manner without reference to their conceptual network. Second, we link this frequent and ad-hoc concept formation to two biases underlying Western thinking about war: a *conventional war bias* and a *structure bias*. The former promotes an idealized version of conventional war as prototype of war, while the latter focuses our attention on the character of war to the detriment of agency. As we will show, many concepts of war and warfare are diminished subtypes of the prototype of conventional war, focusing on deficiencies rather than helping us to understand the phenomenon of war.

Lack of Consideration for the Conceptual Network

True conceptual innovation is rare in War and Strategic Studies. Rather, we can witness different types of concept reconstruction. For example, 'spin-offs' are frequently created through the addition of affixes or the creation of compound terms. Examples include 'new wars' and 'new Cold War' (cf. Rauta, 2021, 554). Many concepts are also formed through the addition of new meaning. Information warfare, for example, used to refer to the manipulation of information channels and technologies of the adversary to limit their situational awareness (cf. Endsley & Jones, 1997). Today it refers to information campaigns more generally, usually those directed at the general population (cf. Whyte et al., 2021)—an idea that used to be labeled 'propaganda'. Another example is 'unconventional warfare', which used to refer to the use of nuclear weapons but has been reconceptualized in the context of the 'war on terror' to refer to the imbalance in conflicts between state and non-state actors (see below). Maybe most problematically, conceptual innovation often actually is thinly veiled terminological innovation or relabeling, where a new term is applied to existing concepts. The above-mentioned relabeling of propaganda as information warfare constitutes such a case.

In these examples, little consideration has been given to the existing conceptual network. If the meaning of concepts is changed, their relation to neighboring concepts becomes unclear. If the meaning of a concept (e.g., information warfare) is extended to subsume another concept (propaganda), the boundaries of the former concept are muddied, and the relevance of the latter concept becomes unclear. New concepts are added, unsettling the existing conceptual structure. Scholars have tried to bring structure into this chaos by offering *post-facto* meta analyses. Rauta (2021, 556) has divided existing concepts into several categories: outcome-focused notions, process-oriented notions, tool-centric terms, actor-centric terms, domain-focused notions, and context-affirming notions. Similarly, Angstrom and Widen (2015) distinguish between categories according to actors, purposes, intensity, methods, and generations. But such a systematic and reflective approach usually does not inform concept formation itself. Instead, concepts are created on an ad-hoc basis, often in response to specific events.

As a consequence, concepts are very similar to another, with differentiation hard to establish. For example, the concepts of 'irregular', 'unconventional', and 'asymmetric warfare' are almost synonymous in meaning; so are the most recent instantiations of 'hybrid warfare' and 'gray zone' challenges (both will be further addressed below). This makes communication between scholars and accumulation of knowledge difficult. Academic debates instead tend to happen in a compartmentalized manner, with little agreement on what the most useful or important concepts are.

The Conventional War Bias

Many concepts of war and warfare are diminished subtypes. To make this argument, we first need to look at how traditional subtypes of war are formed. For this purpose, we have to identify a core concept of war. Strachan and Scheipers (2013, 6f.) outline five criteria for the core concept of war: (1) use of force, (2) reciprocity thereof, (3) a degree of intensity and scale, (4) 'those who fight do not do so in a private capacity', and (5) 'war is fought for some aim beyond fighting itself'. This definition distinguishes war from non-violent types of coercion, one-directional forms of violence, and private violent fights. It also largely corresponds with International Humanitarian Law (cf. ICTY Appeals Chamber, 1995). Let us call this the 'traditional' understanding of war for the purposes of this chapter.

Moving up the ladder of abstraction, we can derive a more general understanding of war that is even better able to travel across time and space. For example, Heuser (2021, original in italics), in her *magnum opus* on the Western concept of war, defines war as 'the practice of organized violence between two groups', including one-directional violence. Moving down the ladder of abstraction, we add more necessary characteristics. For example, by specifying the actors conducting the war we get three commonly used subtypes: interstate war (fought exclusively between states); civil war (fought by non-state actors or non-state and state actors); internationalized civil war (fought by non-state actors or non-state and state actors with the support of external state actors). The demarcation of these subtypes is by no means undisputed, not least because it too reproduces the historical acknowledgment of only interstate wars being actual wars (as is also evident in International Humanitarian Law). The purpose here, however, is to show the logic of the ladder of abstraction: each subtype is a full instance of the concept of war, with further characteristics added for differentiation. It is systematic and arguably useful as state and non-state actors tend to have access to different resources which effectively shape the dynamics of the war. These three subtypes are also accepted in academic debates and—under slightly different labels and with the exception of 'internationalized civil war'—in legal debates.

The majority of 'novel' concepts in War/Strategic Studies, however, are neither broadly accepted nor were they derived systematically. Many of them can be considered diminished subtypes, but—importantly—they are diminished subtypes not of the above-defined concept of war, but of the ideal type of conventional war that pervades the Western imagination of war, past and present (Strachan, 2013). In fact, we argue that from the 'traditional' understanding of war (as exemplified by Strachan and Scheipers' definition) neither of these terms adds much to our understanding of war, either because they highlight the obvious or because they cannot be considered full instances of war. But realizing that these subtypes are based on the core concept of *conventional* war, we are able to understand their trajectory and criticize them more fruitfully. To support this argument, let us first look at the ideal type of conventional war, and then at some prominent concepts of the past few years.[2]

Conventional war is understood 'as state-on-state conflict between organized, uniformed, professional military forces using massed firepower in open space away from civilians with the aim of destroying each other to gain and hold ground' (Fabian, 2021). The United States defines it as '[a] violent struggle for domination between nation-states or coalitions and alliances of nation-states' (United States DoD, 2024, 43). The ways in which the First and Second World Wars are remembered in the West—primarily for their exhausting trench warfare and bloody battles respectively—showcase this bias (in reality, both wars were characterized by many 'irregular' elements such as partisan and guerrilla warfare).

This conventional war bias is especially strong in the United States. As Ucko and Marks (2018, 211f.) have noted:

> For cultural, financial, and psychological reasons, armed services see conventional campaigns as the real business of war and adapt only minimally to "lower-end contingencies," or what were once called "military

[2] Defining these concepts and locating them on the ladder of abstraction is no easy task as scholars have proposed vastly different, occasionally even contradicting definitions of these concepts. We aim to take this into account, but a full conceptual history which would be necessary to capture the journey of each of these concepts is not possible within the confines of this chapter.

> operations other than war" [...] This rank ordering was sustained even during the heights of the Iraq and Afghanistan wars, with changes in institutional prioritization accepted only on a temporary basis and in ways that would not disrupt pre-existing investment patterns.

This dominant understanding of war is passed on to new generations through military education. The history which the US military teaches itself often presents, emphasizes, reinforces, and justifies the military's conventional preferences. Victor Davis Hanson's *The Western Way of War* appears on military reading lists, although its inclusion has become contested due to how historically controversial it has become (Jackson et al., 2018, 138). Hanson's thesis encourages the conventional mindset, arguing that Western strategic culture since ancient Greece has been battle- and annihilation-centric: 'It is this Western desire for a single, magnificent collision of infantry, for brutal killing with edged weapons on a battlefield between free men, that has baffled and terrified our adversaries from the non-Western world for more than 2500 years' (Hanson, 1989, 9). This understanding of war is not exclusive to the United States, however. In a widely read book, UK General Rupert Smith (2006, 1) epitomizes the dominance of this mainstream understanding with his assertion that '[w]ar no longer exists', immediately qualified as 'war as cognitively known to most non combatants, war as battle in a field between men and machinery, war as a massive deciding event in dispute in international affairs: such war no longer exists'. War and conventional war are implicitly considered identical.

For many scholars and practitioners, conventional war—or more specifically and idealized version of it—thus serves as prototype for the category of war. Instances of war are compared to this prototype and categorized based on the similarity (or lack thereof) to it. Whatever is characterized by large-scale fighting between uniformed armies is considered war; when fighting takes other forms, scholars and practitioners invent new terms. This is particularly visible in concepts such as 'asymmetric', 'irregular', 'unconventional', 'guerrilla', 'ambiguous', or 'low-intensity' war(fare) as is outlined in more detail in the following paragraphs. What sets these types of war apart—i.e., why scholars or practitioners thought they needed to be captured with new terms—is their distinction from conventional war.

Asymmetric war(fare), for example, refers to a war in which the relationship between the two sides is asymmetric in terms of their power and/or the means they employ. The concept had been in use earlier but gained prominence and was redefined in the context of the war on terror (cf. Winter, 2011, 491). From the traditional perspective on war, asymmetry—more or less pronounced—is a feature of all wars (cf. Milevski, 2014, Metz & Johnson, 2001). It therefore does not make sense to distinguish between asymmetric and symmetric wars. From the perspective of conventional wars, however, which tend to be symmetric as they are fought between states, asymmetric war is a diminished subtype: it is not *conventional* war because it lacks a certain kind of symmetry.

The argument about irregular war is similar: the United States Department of Defense (2024, 98) defines irregular warfare as '[a] form of warfare where states and non-state actors campaign to assure or coerce states or other groups through indirect, non-attributable, or asymmetric activities'. Similarly, unconventional warfare is defined as '[a]ctivities conducted to enable a resistance movement or insurgency to coerce, disrupt, or overthrow a government or occupying power by operating through or with an underground, auxiliary, and guerrilla force in a denied area' (ibid., 195). What seems to set these types of warfare apart is firstly the inclusion of non-state actors and secondly the use of 'indirect' means. These diminished subtypes again are pitted in contrast to conventional war in which state actors openly engage one another on the battlefield. In the traditional understanding of war, on the other hand, there is no distinction between 'regular' and 'irregular' war. Indeed, quantitatively speaking, what is considered as 'irregular' war in the West has been the norm historically (Vacca & Davidson, 2011). Moreover, the fact that asymmetric, irregular, and unconventional wars point to the same phenomenon shows the issue with overlapping concepts in the field mentioned earlier.

Another instantiation of the conventional war bias, but not a diminished subtype, is the concept of 'hybrid war(fare)'. Indeed, the original conceptualization of 'hybrid warfare' quite clearly was coined in opposition to conventional war: Frank G. Hoffman originally developed the 'hybrid warfare' concept to challenge the focus on conventional war and the conceptual distinction between 'conventional' and 'irregular' challenges in US defense planning and strategic thought. According to Hoffman's (2007, 14, italics omitted) conceptualization, 'Hybrid Wars incorporate a range of different modes of warfare, including conventional capabilities, irregular tactics and formations, terrorist acts including indiscriminate violence and coercion, and criminal disorder'. These different modes 'are generally operationally and tactically directed and coordinated within the main battlespace to achieve synergistic effects'(ibid, 29). Hoffman (2009, 35) expected both state and non-state actors to mix a variety of different approaches to warfare from a 'menu' to suit their strategic culture and target US vulnerabilities. Hoffman thus chose to focus his concept on the convergence of different means in war, challenging the idea that threats could be categorized as either conventional or irregular, with a particular focus on the battlespace. His concept, therefore, is not a diminished subtype of conventional war, but a step up the ladder that reduces the number of necessary conditions and, in fact, brings it back closer to the traditional understanding of war. Hoffman also assessed existing concepts for their fit and clearly distinguished his new concept from them.

However, the 'hybrid warfare' concept as we know it today was heavily reinterpreted and popularized by NATO and the EU in 2014: Hoffman's focus on battlefield integration was marginalized, and NATO added a number of means and aspects to the definition, such as misinformation campaigns and cyber-attacks as well as attacks on 'NATO's role, legitimacy, credibility and conduct' (Supreme Allied Commander, Europe 2010, 4). The concept has since further evolved. In the NATO understanding, 'hybrid warfare' still refers to the mix of military and non-military means (which is of course a characteristic of any war and not a recent invention, cf. Murray & Mansoor, 2012). Many commentators have, however, used the concept to discuss primarily, and sometimes exclusively, the use of non-military means such as political interference, economic pressure, or disinformation, and argued that the approach enables actors to stay 'below the threshold of war or direct overt violence' (Bilal, 2021). This brought the concept closer to the concept of 'grey zone warfare/challenges' to the point that many commentators use these two terms synonymously or consider them as inherently intertwined (cf. Libiseller, 2023).

The 'gray zone' has been considered as 'neither fully war nor fully peace' (US Department of Defense 2010, 73), 'a landscape churning with political, economic, and security competitions that require constant attention' (Schadlow, 2014), or as competition 'primarily below the threshold of armed conflict' (Morris et al., 2019, iii). These insights have been drawn mainly from China's disputation of territorial borders and creation of artificial islands in the South China Sea, but the concept has since been extended to a quasi-theory of revisionist states (Mazarr, 2015).

According to Barno and Bensahel (2015), 'gray zone' conflicts 'involve some aggression or use of force, but in many ways their defining characteristic is ambiguity—about the ultimate objectives, the participants, whether international treaties and norms have been violated, and the role that military forces should play in response'. Similarly, a US think tank report (Hicks et al., 2019, 3) claimed that '[t]he strategies and operations present in the space between peace and war are intentionally ambiguous, meant to defy easy categorization and therefore also effective responses'. According to their reports, the use of 'gray zone strategies' is inherently connected to the aim of challenging the status quo of international order while avoiding escalation to war. Incrementalism and *faits accomplis* are considered important elements of such a strategy. It is this piecemeal approach that still accomplishes territorial change—an objective these reports consider inherently connected to war—which supposedly renders finding an appropriate and timely US response difficult.

In addition to being built on a conventional understanding of war, the concepts of 'hybrid warfare' and 'gray zone' challenges thus showcase the use of family resemblance in concept formation. 'Gray zone' challenges might not include the use of force, but they allow the achievement of political aims 'typically' associated with war. Such an approach to concept formation, however, inherently leads to conceptual stretching and thus confusion as the concept of war is linked to instances that lack its fundamental characteristics. In other words, these concepts unsettle the existing conceptual network. From NATO's perspective, associating Russia's non-military approaches with war might have political benefits (cf. Caliskan & Liégeois, 2021); but from an analytical perspective this only muddies the waters. As Freedman (2012) has argued: '[w]ithout the element of violence the study of war loses all focus'.

The problem of using conventional war as a prototype for war is that it is actually a *stereotype*: purely conventional wars have rarely, if ever, existed. Therefore, it is to be expected that every war will differ from this prototype, encouraging the endless formation of diminished subtypes. As these are based on *missing* characteristics, they are ill-suited to improve our understanding of war, however. Moreover, and somewhat paradoxically, diminished subtypes reproduce the notion of their core concept as ideal (cf. Schaffer, 2016, 20); in other words, concepts that are coined in opposition to conventional war in order to challenge it at the same time reproduce the idea of conventional war.

The Structure Bias

All of these concepts discussed, as well as many others, circumscribe the malleability of the described phenomena and so reflect a lack of awareness of agency, tending instead to be inherently fatalistic. We call this tendency the *structure bias*. Concepts often enshrine the structural character of a war (e.g., asymmetric, limited, protracted) or focus on means used (e.g., hybrid, cyber, or information) as if this was sufficient to understand the dynamics of a war. What is lost is an appreciation of how the agency of involved actors shapes the character of war. The character of a given war may change throughout its waging, but existing concepts generally enforce rigid conceptual structures which are difficult to adapt to shifting circumstances. They are similarly unable to understand future warfare. The real result is that the users of such concepts are, if not always, then certainly often surprised by the future history of war and warfare because it never fits into the fashionable concepts of the day—because of the flawed thinking which infuses those concepts.

The agency which is lost among these concepts is, ironically, that of both the adversary and ourselves, the latter instilling the fatalism which surrounds many of the concepts. The loss of sense of agency of the adversary features two particular characteristics. First, Western concepts tend to reflect a particular moral economy. Scholars highlighted the moral economies of asymmetric warfare during the counterinsurgency era, but the point is broadly applicable to most, if not all, other new concepts of war and warfare: 'the currency of the debates about asymmetric wars lies in its normative dimension: the idiom of asymmetry is not just a neutral descriptive military jargon; rather, it tends to moralize and depoliticize contemporary conflict constellations' (Winter, 2011, 490). Similarly, (Russian) hybrid warfare is understood as inherently iniquitous, as is (Chinese) gray zone activity. The political-moral asymmetry inherent in such concepts impedes actual engagement with the thinking and intentions of these actors by automatically delegitimizing it in favor of these already flawed Western interpretations. Such implicit moral foundations of a concept also lead to conceptual masking: hybrid warfare is arguably very similar to NATO's 'comprehensive approach' or the UK's 'integrated approach'—all three concepts refer to the idea that a war or defensive effort needs to include a variety of means beyond the military instrument. Yet, depending on whether NATO or Russia does it, a different label and different normative connotations are applied.

A second flaw of many of our concepts of war and warfare is the ethnocentric ignorance which often marks them as Western thinkers focus on the *Western* experience of warfare, even when the West is acting abroad. In making sense of the counterinsurgency and intervention era, the West typically characterized the resultant warfare as asymmetric. Asymmetry was simply assumed to be a characteristic of intrastate warfare in Africa. Yet scholars have noted that targeted African warlords, for example, only engaged Western armed forces asymmetrically. When warlords engage other warlords, they do so in essentially symmetrical ways, albeit certainly not at the level of professionalism and technological sophistication which the West expects in conventional warfare from conventional armed forces (Duyvesteyn, 2005, 75–76). As with the conceptual moral economies, the ethnocentrism inherent in Western concepts excludes real awareness of the adversary or, indeed, of any cultural other—especially once Western actors are directly involved.

The ultimate result of the political-moral economy and ethnocentrism embedded in Western concepts is that we assume they accurately describe not only what non-Western actors are doing but also how they are thinking, how they shape behavior and decide on intentions. This is often wrong, as particularly highlighted by how the Russians imported the concept of hybrid warfare from the West, which preferred to impose its own understanding of the Russians rather than listen to what the Russians were actually saying. One Western failing in this regard was, whereas Western thinking about hybrid warfare identified Russia as the aggressor, Russia has consistently painted the West as the aggressor as it sees the various liberal revolutions which occurred around Russia's periphery, in its old imperial territories, as Western-backed coups against legitimate, pro-Russian governments (Friedman, 2018). The West demonstrated a lack of awareness of Russia's moral self-perception and how it might affect Russian conduct. It is no surprise that the West is often surprised by the future, when it hardly pays genuine attention to the actors in favor of stereotypes and cookie-cutter templates of future conflicts.

Thus, this lack of Western intellectual attention extends in some ironic ways also to the West itself, particularly as specific concepts of war and warfare are forecast into the future. The concepts seem accurate in the present, if only because the intellectual flaws in developing those concepts have not been apparent to their authors, and so also provide a degree of intellectual security for understanding the future. Yet this intellectual security is not necessarily positive, as it encourages unfounded certainty.

There were a few years when urban warfare seemed like the future of warfare, a certainty with which every Western military would have to cope (Kilcullen, 2015). Yet this is a way of thinking in which the anticipated concept in practice is merely being inflicted upon a helpless West—*as if it's not Western political and strategic decisions which sends Western militaries into those cities*. This focus on structure does not enable us to enquire into the dynamics of war. It decontextualizes, depoliticizes, and thus 'destrategizes' war, meaning we focus on actors' means rather than intentions and (re)actions. The abundance of concepts focused on means is a testament to this.

From a practical perspective, the authors of the character of any war are those engaged in directing and waging it: policymakers, strategists, tacticians, soldiers, sometimes even civilians in their distinct capacity—on both sides, in interaction with each other, to varying degrees. Their aggregate input into decision-making and strategic, operational, and tactical performance shapes the character of any specific war (Milevski, 2016). Although such adversarial interaction in war often generates relational dynamics which are not necessarily controllable by either side, the war is not independent of those who wage it. To think in implicit terms of a particular form of warfare occurring to oneself is to abandon the opportunity to shape that future warfare to gain advantage. This can only result in poor policy, strategy, and tactics for and in war, ultimately leading to defeat. Thinking in terms of forms of war while underappreciating agency means that our concepts are often unfit for the future.

This is linked to the idea that the character of individual wars can be transferred across time and place. For example, in the 1990s, when scholars and practitioners were bound up in debates on the 'Revolution in Military Affairs', the assumption was that all wars in the future fought by the United States (or whichever state able to successfully 'exploit' the RMA) would mimic the 1991 Gulf War experience. One consequence was that when this approach to war failed to bring peace to Iraq and Afghanistan in the early 2000s, practitioners and scholars felt that that they have focused on 'the wrong kind of war' (cf. Nagl, 2007). This was corrected with the focus on another, seemingly more fitting, kind of war—counterinsurgency—but this change in focus did not solve the conventional war bias but merely temporarily shifted attention away from it, in a manner which still accepted it. This example clearly shows how focusing on one (any) kind of war limits our perspective and thus ability to understand individual wars as well as war as a general phenomenon.

A more recent strategic surprise to the West has been the return of major conventional warfare. The intense focus on 'hybrid war' and the 'gray zone' in academic and practitioners' debates on the contemporary and future character of war excluded any real consideration of any other potential development, usually on the back of a bare two cases—Crimea and the South China Sea, respectively. It limited perspectives to the extent that Western experts were first unwilling to read signs of Russian preparations to invade Ukraine as such and were then caught off guard when Russia finally launched its invasion in February 2022. As with the preceding surprises, this was not merely an intellectual failing, but one which has had real implications for defense as conventional capabilities had prior to 2022 been increasingly stripped away to free up budget for the capabilities deemed more pertinent to defense in a grey, hybrid-dominated world (Porter, 2023). This has left many Western countries barely able to help support Ukraine even when the West itself is at peace, never mind the non-zero possibility of actually needing to wage such a massive war itself in the future.

The structure bias, thus, privileges forms and means of war to the detriment of agency and intentions. Additionally, concepts formed this way often imply a moral economy that discourages deeper engagement with actors, usually those opposing Western states in one way or another. This leaves scholars and practitioners of war ill-prepared to understand both the present and the future of war.

Conclusion

When new concepts of war and warfare proliferate in response to pressing events or apparent practical demands, they do so in relation to conventional war rather than being systematically derived from a generic and foundational definition of war as such. The logical consequence is that the new concepts are necessarily diminished subtypes because of their immediate conceptual positioning in contrast to conventional war. As concepts, they do not represent war with added specificity but instead war in some way missing that desired conventionality. While the effort of bringing hitherto marginalized aspects into our understanding of war is laudable, this habit of proliferating diminished subtypes based on the prototype-relational model of concept formation does not improve our understanding of war. To the contrary, it further solidifies the conventional war bias.

Concepts are what enable effective communication. Without concepts or the terminology to describe them, humanity is irredeemably stuck in particulars without any hope of generalization. This is as true of communication between civilians and military practitioners regarding war as it is for any other branch of human experience. Yet the flawed habits of concept formation common to thinking about war as outlined above result in communication errors. First, the embedded assumptions and biases may not be equally shared among all involved communicators, resulting in mismatches between meanings sent and received. Second, the constant churn of new terminology and jargon for what are often older ideas, but also for new concepts, creates additional work simply to keep up with language use and increasingly isolates communicators in one academic field or professional context from others whose work may be relevant but—as a result of language use—no longer apparently current and for whom the effort and costs of trying to break into jargonistically and conceptually fast-moving environments is simply increasingly too high. Poorly formed concepts, generated at too high a pace, can easily cause poor communication.

If war is to be an effective concept and analytical category applicable across time and space, it needs to be defined based a) on empirical cases rather than ideal types; and b) on necessary and sufficient criteria. Only the latter prevent conceptual stretching and allow for accumulative conceptual innovation that does not fundamentally unsettle the existing conceptual network. Using the ladder of abstraction, this core concept can be made more specific to focus on subcategories of war or less specific to ensure fit across different subtypes. While we acknowledge the political function of labels, we warn that—if our purpose is to better understand war—we need to recognize that not every security challenge actually needs to be a sub-category of war. The metaphorical use of 'war' is appealing because of the urgency and relevance that comes with it; but this practice muddies our understanding of war.

References

Angstrom, J., & Widen, J. J. (2015). *Contemporary Military Theory*. Routledge.

Aron, R. (1969). The evolution of modern strategic thought. In A. Buchan (Ed.), *Problems of modern strategy: Part one, Adelphi Paper, 54* (pp. 1–17). International Institute of Strategic Studies.

Barno, D. & Bensahel, N. (2015, May 19). Fighting and winning in the "Gray Zone." *War on the Rocks*. https://warontherocks.com/2015/05/fighting-and-winning-in-the-gray-zone/.

Baylis, J., & Wirtz, J. J. (2016). Introduction: Strategy in the contemporary world—Strategy after 9/11. In J. Baylis, J. J. Wirtz, & C. S. Gray (Eds.), *Strategy in the contemporary world* (5th ed., pp. 1–14). Oxford University.

Bilal, A. (2021). Hybrid warfare—New threats, complexity, and 'trust' as the antidote. *NATO Review*. https://www.nato.int/docu/review/articles/2021/11/30/hybrid-warfare-new-threats-complexity-and-trust-as-the-antidote/index.html

Caliskan, M., & Liégeois, M. (2021). The concept of "hybrid warfare" undermines NATO's strategic thinking: Insights from interviews with NATO officials. *Small Wars & Insurgencies, 32*(2), 295–319.

Carstensen M. B., & Schmidt V. A. (2016). Power through, over and in ideas: Conceptualizing ideational power in discursive institutionalism. *Journal of European Public Policy, 23*(3), 318–337.

Collier, D., & Levitsky, S. (1997). Democracy with adjectives: Conceptual innovation in comparative research. *World Politics, 49*(3), 430–451.

Duyvesteyn, I. (2005). The concept of conventional war and armed conflict in collapsed states. In I. Duyvesteyn & J. Angstrom (Eds.), *Rethinking the Nature of War* (pp. 65–87). Frank Cass.

Endsley, M. & Jones, W.M. (1997). *Situation awareness information dominance & information warfare*. United States Air Force Armstrong Laboratory, https://apps.dtic.mil/sti/pdfs/ADA347166.pdf

Fabian, S. (2021). *Irregular versus conventional warfare: A dichotomous misconception*. Modern War Institute. https://mwi.westpoint.edu/irregular-versus-conventional-warfare-a-dichotomous-misconception/.

Freedman, L. (2012). Defining War. In J. Lindley-French & Y. Boyer (Eds.), *The Oxford handbook of war* (pp. 16–29). Oxford University Press.

Fridman, O. (2018). *Russian 'hybrid warfare': Resurgence and politicisation*. Hurst & Company.

Gerring, J. (1999). What makes a concept good? A criterial framework for understanding concept formation in the social sciences. *Polity, 31*(3), 357–393.

Goertz, G. (2006). *Social science concepts: A user's guide*. Princeton University Press.

Hanson, V. D. (1989). *The western way of war: Infantry battle in classical Greece*. Alfred A. Knopf.

Haug, K. E., & Maaø, O. J. (Eds.). (2012). *Conceptualizing modern war*. Hurst.

Heuser, B. (2021). *War: A genealogy of western ideas and practices*. Oxford University Press.

Hicks, K. H., A. Hunt Friend, Federici, J., Shah, H., Donahoe, M., Conklin, M., Akca, A., Matlaga, M., & Sheppard. L. (2019). *By other means: Part I:*

Campaigning in the gray Zone, a report of the CSIS International Security Program. Rowman & Littlefield 2019.

Hoffman, F. (2007). *Conflict in the 21st century: The rise of hybrid wars*. Potomac Institute for Policy Studies.

Hoffman, F. (2009). Hybrid warfare and challenges. *Joint Forces Quarterly, 52*(1), 34–39.

ICTY Appeals Chamber. (1995, October 2). *The Prosecutor* v. *Dusko Tadic*: *Decision on the defence motion for interlocutory appeal on jurisdiction*. Case No. IT-94-1-AR72.

Jackson, A. P., Zweibelson, B., & Simonds, W. (2018). Intellectual spring cleaning: It's time for a military "Do not Read" list; and some sources that should be on that list. *Defence Studies, 18*(2), 131–146.

Kilcullen, D. (2015). *Out of the mountains: The coming age of the Urban Guerrilla*. Hurst.

Lakoff, G. (1987). *Women, fire, and dangerous things: What categories reveal about the mind*. University of Chicago Press.

Libiseller, C. (2026, forthcoming). *Reconceptualising war: The rise and fall of fashionable concepts in strategic studies*. Oxford University Press.

Libiseller, C. (2023). "Hybrid warfare" as an academic fashion. *Journal of Strategic Studies, 46*(4), 858–880.

Mazarr, M. J. (2015). *Mastering the Gray zone: Understanding a changing era of conflict*. US Army War College Press.

Metz, S., & Johnson II, D.V. (2001). *Asymmetric and U.S. military strategy: Definition, background, and strategic concepts*. Strategic Studies Institute.

Milevski, L. (2014). Asymmetry is strategy, strategy is asymmetry. *Joint Force Quarterly, 75*, 77–83.

Milevski, L. (2016). The nature of strategy versus the character of war. *Comparative Strategy, 35*(5), 438–446.

Morris, L. J., Mazarr, M. J., Hornung, J. W., Pezard, S., Binnendijk, A., & Kepe, M. (2019). *Gaining competitive advantage in the Gray zone: Response options for coercive aggression below the threshold of major war*. RAND Corporation.

Murray, W., & Mansoor, P. (Eds.). (2012). *Hybrid warfare fighting complex opponents from the ancient world to the present*. Cambridge University Press

Nagl, J.A. (2007). Foreword to the University of Chicago Press Edition: The evolution and importance of army/Marine Corp field manual, counterin surgency. In *The U.S. Army/Marine Corps counterinsurgency field manual* (pp. 3–24). University of Chicago Press.

NATO. (2008). Assisting Afghanistan: The importance of a comprehensive approach, *Speech by NATO Deputy Secretary General Ambassador Claudio Bisogniero, at the GLOBSEC Conference*. https://www.nato.int/cps/en/natohq/opinions_7377.htm?selectedLocale=no

Porter, P. (2023). Out of the shadows: Ukraine and the shock of non-hybrid war. *Journal of Global Security Studies, 8*(3), 1–15.
Raska, M. (2020). The sixth RMA wave: Disruption in military affairs? *Journal of Strategic Studies, 44*(4), 456–479.
Rauta, V. (2021). A conceptual critique of remote warfare. *Defence Studies, 21*(4), 545–572.
Sartori, G. (1970). Concept misformation in comparative politics. *American Political Science Review, 64*(4), 1033–1053.
Schadlow, N. (2014, August 18). Peace and war: The space between. *War on the Rocks*. https://warontherocks.com/2014/08/peace-and-war-the-space-between/
Schaffer, F. C. (2005). Why don't political scientists coin more new terms? Committee on Concepts and Methods Working Paper Series.
Schaffer, F. C. (2016). *Elucidating social science concepts: An interpretivist guide*. Routledge.
Schedler, A. (2010). *Concept formation in political science* (CIDE Working Paper No. 219).
Smith, R. (2006). *The utility of force: The art of war in the modern world*. Penguin Books.
Strachan, H. (2013). Introductory Essay: The Changing Character of War. In K. E. Haug & O. J. Maaø (Eds.), *Conceptualising modern war* (pp. 1–25). Hurst & Company.
Strachan, H., & Scheipers, S. (2013). Introduction: The changing character of war. In H. Strachan & S. Scheipers (Eds.), *The changing character of war* (pp. 1–24). Oxford University Press.
Supreme Allied Commander, Europe, and Supreme Allied Commander, Transformation (2010, August). *Bi-SC Input to a New NATO Capstone Concept for the Military Contribution to Countering Hybrid Threats*.
Ucko, D. H., & Marks, T. A. (2018). Violence in context: Mapping the strategies and operational art of irregular warfare. *Contemporary Security Policy, 39*(2), 206–233.
UK Ministry of Defence. (2021). *Integrated operating concept*. UK Ministry of Defence. https://assets.publishing.service.gov.uk/media/612f91b28fa8f50328e2c8f5/Integrated_Operating_Concept_2025.pdf
United States Department of Defense. (2010). *Quadrennial Defense Review Report*. United States Department of Defense.
United States Department of Defense. (2024). *DoD dictionary of military and associated terms*. Department of Defense. https://www.hsdl.org/c/abstract/?docid=886178
Vacca, W. A., & Davidson, M. (2011). The regularity of irregular warfare. *Parameters, 41*(1), 18–28.

Whyte, C., Thrall, A. T., & Mazanec, B. M. (Eds.). (2021). *Information warfare in the age of cyber conflict*. Routledge.

Winter, Y. (2011). The asymmetric war discourse and its moral economies: A critique. *International Theory, 3*(3), 488–514.

Wittgenstein, L. (2016[1984]). Philosophische Untersuchungen. In L. Wittgenstein *Werkausgabe Band 1: Tractatus logico-philosophicus/Tagebücher 1914–1916/Philosophische Untersuchungen*. Suhrkamp.

CHAPTER 3

Pulling the Strings: Why Are Proxy Wars Back from the Margins?

Troels Burchall Henningsen

Introduction

The dynamics of the most consequential wars of the past 15 years, such as the civil war in Syria and Russia's war in Ukraine, cannot be understood without paying attention to the involvement of external sponsors. Battlefields in Syria and Ukraine have been shaped by the access to foreign-provided weapons, training, and intelligence, and major shifts in the fortune of war may be explained by interventions of new external sponsors or shifts in their level of support. In 2015, Iranian and Russian sponsorship allowed Bashar al-Assad to turn the tide in the Syrian civil war. Nine years later, reports indicate that Turkish support and direction made possible the sudden overthrow of the Assad regime (Shahbazov, 2024; Tol, 2024). After a substantial drop in proxy wars from 1991 to 2010, proxy wars are again moving to the middle of contemporary wars (Watts 2023, 7). Since 2010, new civil wars, such as Libya after 2013

T. B. Henningsen (✉)
Royal Danish Defence College, Institute for Strategy and War Studies, Washington, USA
e-mail: trhe@fak.dk

M. Robin et al. (eds.), *The Changing Fights and Fighters of Contemporary War*, https://doi.org/10.1007/978-3-032-05518-7_3

and Sudan after 2023, began as local conflicts but eventually expanded to proxy wars as the belligerents accepted external sponsorship. The most recent wars in Africa and the Middle East demonstrate similar proxy-sponsor dynamics. In the wake of Hamas' attack on Israel on October 7, 2023, the wars in Gaza, Lebanon, and the confrontation in the Red Sea all saw considerable involvement of external sponsors, especially Iran and the United States (Valbjørn et al., 2024, 13–14). In 2025, M23, a proxy insurgency group sponsored by Rwanda, renewed its offensive in the civil war in the Democratic Republic of Congo, which is already heavily influenced by external sponsors (Usher 2025). The importance of sponsor-proxy relationships in most wars after 2010 has led to renewed scholarly attention to proxy war and its implications for contemporary wars (for an overview see Moghadam et al., 2024).

This chapter aims to explain the prevalence of proxy wars today, i.e. how proxy wars have moved to the middle of contemporary wars and what consequences this move has for the practice of war. Existing literature that seeks to explain the recent rise in proxy war primarily identifies renewed great power competition as the key factor (Anderson, 2025; Byman, 2023; Hoffman & Orner, 2021; Noonan, 2021). Because the observed rise in the prevalence of proxy war corresponds with a period of heightened tension among the great powers, it is logical to connect the two developments. This literature points to how decreased trust among great powers causes zero-sum thinking and spurs ambitions of establishing zones of influence. As a result, great powers use proxy warfare as an instrument to defend allies, undermine competitors' influence, or establish control of disputed states, most typically by taking advantage of ongoing internal wars. However, as this chapter will argue, this is an important, but partial explanation of the movement of proxy war from the margins to the middle of modern war. Literature on specific proxy wars is often situated within area studies or takes on wider security studies issues, such as the impact of the commercialization of security, and does not offer overarching accounts of the rise of proxy wars. However, by carefully applying the concept of margins and middles in war, the chapter seeks to integrate these strands of literature to construct a comprehensive explanation. The chapter argues that the regional level offers additional explanations for the rise that identify regional margin-to-middle movements in contemporary wars. An analysis based on the thriving African and Middle East area studies both points to a rise in regional interventions and concerns about regional rivals, which has regional-specific causes not reducible to the global great power competition. Moreover, the chapter adds to the great power competition-explanation by examining how globalization and its associated move to the middle of communication technologies, commercialization of military services, and increasing importance of diasporas in war may contribute to the rise in proxy wars. Finally, the chapter argues that the move of proxy war from the margin to the middle of contemporary war changes the centers of gravity from the battlefield to the political relationship between sponsor and proxy. It might herald a move toward the integration of wars in the geographical margins into broader regional and global conflicts, which warrants further attention to external linkages in war.

Before I turn to the analysis, it is necessary to define proxy war. The differences in definitions tell a story about the development in the empirical manifestations of proxy war and the surrounding academic debate. In the wake of the terrorist attack on the United States in 2001, the United States engaged in several interventions in support of local governments in existing internal conflicts. In order to capture the political dynamic between the external sponsor and the local governments, scholars defined proxy war as a subset of military interventions, where at least one side was supported by an external sponsor. According to Tyrone Groh, proxy warfare is when external sponsors "direct the use of force by a politically motivated local actor to indirectly influence political affairs in the target state" (2019, 29). What sets proxy war apart from external support in general, is the external sponsor's attempted control of local events. To illustrate the definition, the war in Ukraine since 2014 is again helpful. Russia retained control of pro-Russian armed militias in Eastern Ukraine between 2015 and 2022 and directed their use of force against the government forces (Malyarenko & Wolff, 2018, 203). Conversely, it remains debatable to what extent the US-led Ukraine Defense Contact Group has directed the use of force by the Ukrainian government since 2022 (Marsh, 2023). The definition, thus, requires a qualitative assessment of the sponsor-beneficiary relationship in order to define a war as a proxy war

Proxy war may also be defined more narrowly as conflicts where both sides are supported by external sponsors, often great powers. During the Cold War this was the dominant understanding, defined by Karl Deutsch as "an international conflict between two foreign powers, fought out on the soil of a third country; disguised as conflict over an internal issue of that country" (1964, 102). This definition narrows the set of proxy wars, because only conflicts where the intentions of the external sponsor(s) go beyond the theater of war can be considered proxy wars. I understand proxy wars in this limited sense, except for the rather strict formulation that it should be "disguised as conflict over an internal issue." In most cases, the external sponsor will have a dual interest in the theater of war and in the wider conflict with the other sponsor(s). Moreover, it may cause methodological problems to identify the underlying, non-observable intentions. Confrontation among two or more external sponsors outside the immediate battlefield points to a potentially significant movement from the margins to the middle, namely that contemporary wars may increasingly be fought for interests lying outside the theater of war.

The method and approach of the chapter are based on a level-of-analysis approach that integrates explanations at the international level, with fine-grained and particular regional and local explanations to offer a comprehensive explanation. The first part analyzes the impact of great power competition on the rise in proxy wars, by examining the differences among the great powers in their use of proxy warfare. Specifically, I compare three great powers' use of proxy war, namely China, Russia, and the United States. They are selected because proxy war literature primarily pays attention to these three and because they have either been most actively involved in proxy wars or are deemed most likely to be so in the future. As a consequence, I have deselected powers such as the United Kingdom, a historically very active sponsor in proxy wars, but with declining relative power. Afterward, the chapter turns to the regional drivers and compares literature on proxy wars in the Middle East and Africa to gauge to what extent regional dynamics offer explanations of the move to the middle of proxy war that are independent from global ones. These two regions are selected because the main part of contemporary proxy wars has taken place here, albeit I analytically treat Africa as made up of separate regional security complexes. The third part examines the ways that non-state actors in civil wars may have become empowered to attract external interventions in a way that increases the likelihood of proxy wars. I do so by engaging the wider security studies literature on the effects of globalization, a literature often overshadowed by renewed attention to great power dynamics. The final section discusses the consequences of the movement to the middle of proxy war and examines both intrastate and interstate wars with sponsor-proxy relations.

Back to the Cold War?

Parsimonious and intuitive, the explanation that great power competition causes the rise in proxy wars has merits. After all, the Cold War was characterized by an increasing number of proxy wars in the 1970s and 1980s (Westad 2005). Cold War historian Odd Arne Westad argues that the turn to proxy war came as a consequence of the Soviet Union and the United States' narrow ideological interpretation of the decolonization processes in wars in the Global South, which led to them to a lavish approach to military aid and a categorical unwillingness to accept the principle of non-interference (2007). On the future of Sino-US competition, Dominic Tierncy proposes that the risk of nuclear escalation will prevent the great powers from taking steps toward a direct confrontation. Instead, indirect confrontations will again unfold in the Global South: "These great powers could manipulate internal conflicts to protect a sphere of influence, maintain access to strategic resources, or counter the perceived intervention of the rival" (2021, 68). An environment of mistrust causes competitors to see the military interventions meant to serve counterterrorism or to protect economic investments as an effort to change the balance of power, which in turn mandates a military response.

The indirect character of proxy wars offers great powers two additional advantages compared to other methods of statecraft, namely escalation control and economy of force. The intervention can either be altogether denied or, more likely, portrayed as a limited concern for theater-related security issues, with no intention to hurt the competitor. More surprisingly, Austin Carson finds that competitors often tolerate barely concealed interventions in order to avoid pressure from the domestic audience and reputational costs vis-à-vis allies that might otherwise force it to escalate the confrontation (2016, 113–114). As a result, a great power can choose to intervene as long as it sufficiently discreet to offer its competitors a fig leaf for avoiding escalation. The second strategic advantage that proxy warfare offers is an economy of force option. In a review of the use of proxy warfare, Stephen Watts (et.al.) find "considerable evidence that states turn to proxy warfare to lower the economic costs of their efforts to undermine their rivals" (2023, 129). For cash-strapped great powers, such as Russia, or great powers with many obligations this is an important quality in order to sustain a global engagement.

Given these arguments, it seems plausible that the current rise of proxy wars reflects an increased zero-sum logic in great power relations. The renewal of great power competition has been picking up speed since the Russian invasion of Georgia in 2008 and the US identification of China as a major threat in 2011, which means I should be able to make observations of the expected behavior among global powers. To do so, I briefly analyze the use of proxy war in that period by China, Russia, and the United States, the three great powers most often discussed in the proxy war literature. Has proxy war become a key method among the three powers, and to what extent is there variation in their behavior?

Russia

Russia is probably the easiest power to assess. The Russian intervention in Syria in 2015 marked a turning point because it was the first Russian intervention outside the territory of the former Soviet Union since 1991. Russia sought to control the strategy of the Syrian regime to secure basing rights and halt the spread of militant Islamism, which fit the one-sided definition of proxy war. In addition, it seems highly likely that Russia considered its intervention as part of a two-sided struggle to prevent a US intervention in Syria akin to Libya in 2011 and to broaden the confrontation with the West following the Russian invasion of Ukraine in 2014 (Kofman & Rojansky, 2018, 8–9). This follows the zero-sum logic associated with great power competition, and Russia's action was highly consequential for the next nine years of the Syrian civil war.

A covert Russian intervention in Afghanistan from 2015 to 2021 also supports the proposition that aims outside the theater of war guided Russian interventions abroad. In this period, Russian intelligence officers ran an operation to incentivize the Taliban economically to prioritize the killing of US military personnel over Afghans (Dobrokhotov et al., 2025). The purpose was to bleed the United States to accelerate its withdrawal from Afghanistan and, thereby, further Russian influence in Central Asia. In the Sahel region, Russian military interventions look different, because Russia sought a realignment of the local states away from security cooperation with principally France and the United States toward Russia (Ramani, 2023). Yet, it still fits the expected behavior of great power competition and the zero-sum logic of establishing exclusive spheres of influence. It has forced Western powers and international organizations to leave Burkina Faso, Chad, Mali, and Niger, thereby dramatically altering the shape of the conflicts in the Sahel. Russia is a state heavily involved in proxy wars in its near abroad, the Middle East, and Africa.

The United States

Without comparison, the United States has been involved in most military interventions since 2001. The Global War on Terror tied internal conflicts into a global pursuit to dismantle al Qaeda and later the Islamic State. Most US military interventions have been unrelated to competition with regional or global powers. For example, SOF-provided military assistance to counterterrorist forces in the Philippines may technically be considered proxy warfare due to the clear sponsor-proxy relationship and US influence on the strategic and operational choices of the Philippines (Robinson, 2016). However, it was not (initially) driven by concerns for strategic competitors. Only after the launch of the US "pivot to Asia" in 2011 did the threat from China become the primary motivation for the US engagement (Ross 2024, 5). In the largest theaters, Afghanistan and Iraq, counterterrorism drove the interventions, albeit the Iraq war relied on a theory of victory that foresaw an ensuing regional transformation to prevent the growth of radical Islamism (Lake, 2019, 246). That said, in both interventions, the United States had to deal with competing regional interveners (first and foremost Iran and Pakistan), who sought to maximize their influence at the cost of the United States. Even after great power competition had begun to unfold, the United States' primary concern for intervening in Syria in 2014 was the rise of the Islamic State, not interests related to regional or global powers (Arnold & Nagl, 2023, 5).

In contrast, the Russian full-scale invasion of Ukraine immediately forced the United States to consider its military aid to Ukraine in the light of a larger potential confrontation. Although US assistance may not altogether qualify as proxy warfare, US decision-makers face the dilemmas typical of proxy wars. They have to balance the need of their proxies on the battlefield with the need to avoid an unwanted escalation with their Russian competitor. The United States seems to have settled on an attrition strategy to strike the balance. According to Lloyd Austin, former Secretary of Defense, the United States "wants to see Russia weakened to the degree that it can't do the kinds of things that it has done in invading Ukraine" (Bertrand et al., 2022). Although the US interventions are difficult to compare, they seem to follow a trend toward increased awareness of the regional and global dimensions of US involvement, which points toward a greater US willingness to local wars as part of an indirect, great power confrontation.

China

China is much less inclined to use military power outside its region, so its actions within the last 15 years do not fit the mold of great power competition-fueled proxy warfare. In fact, since Deng Xiaoping took power in 1978, China has not conducted proxy warfare (Watts et al., 2023). Moreover, Chinese support for governments involved in intra- and interstate wars follows a distinct approach far from the definition of proxy war. Typically, Chinese economic and diplomatic engagements precede the initiation of the conflict and China's aim is to preserve its long-time engagement. It does so by offering diplomatic protection, e.g. in the United Nations Security Council in line with the principle of non-intervention and respect of sovereignty as well as continuing its long-term economic partnership during the conflict (Demirtaş, 2023). This was the case in both Sudan during the Darfur conflict and in Ethiopia during the Tigray war. Chinese experts contrast the benefit of staying the course of long-term modernization with other great powers' reliance on military means: "The great powers do not want to leave [the region] and, yet do not want to invest more resources in it, especially in large-scale military operations. So, the Europeans, the Americans, and the Russians are all trying different models of intervention with a light footprint, and low costs" (Chinese expert quoted in Ghiselli, 2024, 172). Clearly, the current Chinese approach does little to support the suggestion that increased US-China competition has caused the rise in proxy wars.

A common counterargument is that the main part of the competition is yet to come. Frank Hoffmann and Andrew Orner build on Andrew Mumford's argument that China will seek to alter the balance of power through indirect methods, for example through its many private military companies, due to the prohibitive cost of a direct confrontation (Hoffman & Orner, 2021; Mumford, 2013). It might even be argued that the discreet Chinese material and diplomatic support of Russia's war in Ukraine constitutes a first step toward a new assertive Chinese use of indirect confrontations, or even its first attempt at proxy war. However, the private Chinese Russian interactions make it difficult to discern Chinese influence on Russian strategy. If China chooses to resort more systematically to proxy warfare, it will still be but one aspect of Chinese handling of wars overseas. Its economy-driven and rather pragmatic foreign policy will also cause it to choose cooperation with the United States in many conflicts, where their interests overlap. Perhaps John Ikenberry gets the balance right in his estimate that "the United States and China will presumably continue to exercise hard power, but the specific qualities of their competitive relationship create incentives for both states to be seen as providers of stability and global goods" (2024, 136).

In sum, the behavior of the three great powers does not entirely support the argument that increased great power competition explains the rise in proxy wars for the last 15 years. Although Russia applied proxy warfare to enhance its global standing at the expense of Western powers, neither China nor the United States behaved in a way that unambiguously supported the global competition explanation. To get closer to understanding the proxy character of modern conflicts, we need to examine other analytical levels for potential explanations. The first stop is the regional level because the vast majority of proxy wars within the last 15 years took place in two regions: the greater Middle East and Africa.

Regional Drivers

One simple statistical fact points to regional or local explanations of the rise in the proxy wars. Between 1998 and 2017, the number of states providing external support in armed conflicts rose from 60 to 120 (Meier et al., 2023, 549). Current external support is carried out not just by great powers, but by coalitions and by regional powers, who have an interest in intervening and now possess a sufficient capacity to carry it out. Regional powers and even minor powers now engage in proxy warfare, which begs the question: why? Area studies literature shows that the answer is context dependent.

In the wake of the Arab Spring, internal uprisings in Libya, Syria, and Yemen turned into internationalized wars that involved the major states in the Middle East. Moreover, the region saw wars in Gaza, Iraq, Lebanon, and Sudan, in which external sponsors intervened. All these wars became part of a major power struggle among three blocs of more or less aligned states. The first bloc namely the Iran-led "resistance axis" consists of Iran and Syria (under President Assad) as well as militias, most notably Hezbollah, the Houthi movement, and Hamas. The second bloc is the informal alliance between Turkey and Qatar in support of the Muslim Brotherhood in various conflicts. The third is the status quo-oriented bloc of Arab Sunni states, such as Saudi Arabia and Egypt (Lynch, 2021). A debate within Middle Eastern studies concerns the motives behind the sponsorships of the three blocks in the proxy wars in the region. The Saudi-led bloc seems to have been driven primarily by concern for their own regime survival, especially after the Muslim Brotherhood took power in Egypt. Through proxy warfare, the status quo bloc sought to prevent Muslim Brotherhood-affiliated groups in Libya and Sudan from taking power, thereby reducing the movement's appeal and strength in their own countries (ibid). As a result, Turkey and Qatar supported regime change to empower parties affiliated with the Muslim Brotherhood and the first major success was the takeover of power in Syria in 2024. Iran's ambitions precede the Arab Spring. In 1981, the Revolutionary Guard established the Quds Force, a special unit for the conduct of proxy warfare in the Middle East. Observers disagree on the motivations behind Iran's extensive use of proxy warfare. One position is that Iran acts offensively and aims to spread the revolution to the rest of the Islamic world (Cohen & Shamci, 2022). The converse position is that Iran applies proxy warfare as a "forward defense" of the Iranian revolution (Akbarzadeh et al., 2023). Regardless of Iran's true motives, the Quds Force interventions have sparked security concerns among the other two blocs and have led to counter-proxy strategies.

In the Middle East, regional drivers of proxy warfare seem highly disconnected from the global great power competition. Even though concerns for regime survival may have been strengthened by the United States' unwillingness to protect incumbent regimes during the Arab Spring, they mostly reflected the Saudi-led status quo bloc's precarious domestic situations. Likewise, the ideological cleavages in the region have no resemblance to the political issues that divide China, Russia, and the United States. Nor do any of the three blocs fit neatly into any spheres of influence, although the "resistance axis" drifted toward a closer alignment with Russia. In the Middle East, the region most exposed to proxy wars, drivers specific to the region were behind the rise in proxy wars.

The trend among regional powers in the Middle East to use proxy warfare as part of their statecraft may also spring from historical and geostrategic circumstances. Stephen Watts (et al.) find that once states develop the institutional capacity to support proxies, they become much more likely to engage in proxy warfare (2023, 140–141). In the case of Iran, the agencies responsible for proxy warfare hold a prominent position within the foreign policy establishment, which increases their influence. Although less bureaucratically formalized, Turkey has gradually expanded its capacity to conduct proxy warfare. Its growing arms industry and the formation of a deployable proxy force of fighters from Syria allowed Turkey to intervene decisively in the conflict in Nagorno-Karabakh and reverse the tide of war in Libya. Also, a spiraling security dynamic of action-reaction may be at play, where Iran's early use of proxy warfare provoked responses from the competing blocs in the regions.

A quick glance into the regional dynamics of the major African wars adds a new layer to why the proxy dimension has become a prominent character of contemporary wars. Unlike the Middle East, Africa has witnessed few interstate wars since decolonization but comparatively many intrastate wars, several of which have a proxy war dimension (Williams, 2013, 94). A first set of explanations for the proxy character of African wars is the combination of a disproportionately high risk of coups and insurgencies combined with a low aggregate conventional military power, which makes ruling elites prone to intervene in a war in a neighboring state if they deem that the war will increase their own internal threats (Tamm & Duursma, 2023). This is not unlike the explanation of why the Saudi-led bloc chose to conduct proxy warfare in the Middle East, but the importance of transnational bonds is greater in Africa. The political significance of kinship, transnational trading, and religious networks means that bonds of political loyalty often cut across state borders, and political leaders may have more loyalty toward their kin in other states than their own population (Cooper, 2002, 159). In addition, the strength of political clientelism among conflict-ridden states and their neighbors in Africa provides clients with economic interests in proxy wars. Access to mines, logging, and other natural resources provides clients in the armed forces of, e.g. Uganda and Rwanda with material benefits deriving from their close support to proxies in, e.g. the Democratic Republic of Congo (Tamm, 2016, 158ff).

While this explanation provides clues to explaining the proxy aspect of devastating wars, such as the war in Congo, it offers little in terms of why proxy wars should be on the rise within the last 15 years. Alex de Waal proposes that transnational, regional ties in wars in East Africa have evolved in a way that makes it easier and more profitable for regional powers to act as sponsors in neighboring wars for the past decades. Specifically, the decline of ideologically motivated armed groups and their newfound eagerness to renegotiate the price of loyalty attracted new, regional sponsors (de Waal, 2015). In addition, sponsors may finance their troop deployments to the war zone by acting as regional peacekeepers, paid by Western donors through regional organizations such as the African Union and ECOWAS. De facto, they most often boost their proxies in the conflict. One example is AMISOM's support of the militias that make up the military forces of the Somali Federal Government (ibid, 125).

Regional-level explanations added several pieces to the puzzle. Context-specific developments in the Middle East and Africa meant that these two regions have witnessed a rise in proxy wars. Most notable were the political divides among the three blocs in the Middle East, which drove the initial dynamics of the region's proxy wars, a political landscape that the global powers navigated in and, only at times, tipped the scale on. In Africa, well-known facets of African proxy wars, such as the importance of transnational ties, clientelism, and the absence of conventional threats, became even more impactful drivers of proxy wars, as the commodified political marketplace developed and new extra-regional actors from the Middle East made their entry. Now I will turn to the last level of analysis, namely the local level. A final set of explanations may lie in the possibilities of local belligerents to attract external sponsors.

Attracting Support

Within the last five years, thoughts on the effects of globalization on war have decidedly taken a backseat, eclipsed by renewed attention to direct great-power confrontations. However, the flow of money, information, people, and goods associated with globalization keeps moving. In fact, within the last 15 years the volumes of, e.g. trade, refugees, and the number of people with internet access have all grown significantly.[1] In that light it seems reasonable to look for explanations for the rise in proxy wars that highlight the ability of local belligerents to utilize these global flows to attract sponsors.

Social media use and smartphones are ubiquitous in contemporary wars. Audiences outside the battlefield gain real-time information about

[1] Since 2000, the zenith of academic interest in globalization, global trade quadrupled, the number of refugees more than tripled, and the number of internet users has grown from 360 million to more than 5 billion in 2022.

the war, much of which serves the purpose of promoting specific interests. In the words of Andreas Krieg and Jean-Marc Rickli "War is situated within this cyberspace – not just the operations themselves but most importantly the narratives of war that shape global opinion" (2019, 51). The battle of the narrative is about swaying specific audiences, be it prospective sponsors or foreign fighters. In this battle, extremist organizations may hold an advantage, at least based on the ability of militant Islamist groups to attract outside support. This may be a potent tool to attract dissatisfied individuals as foreign fighters. For this chapter's purpose, however, the most interesting part may be the connection between extremist content and the ability to attract sponsors. In this regard a noteworthy development within the 15 years is the involvement of non-state sponsors, such as al-Qaeda, the Islamic State, and even Hezbollah. For them a proxy foremost serves the political purpose of increasing the support and legitimacy of the transnational movement, which makes social media propagation much more important to non-state sponsors than state sponsors (Moghadam & Wyss, 2022). As a result, contemporary armed groups have more ways to attract state or non-state sponsors through the well-directed use of information operations.

Commodification of security provision may also make it easier for local belligerents to attract state sponsors (Mumford, 2013, 42). Especially the rise of semi-private military companies, such as the Wagner group, creates hitherto unseen possibilities for both state sponsors and proxies. The state sponsor may publicly arrange the sale of weapons and diplomatic support, while unofficially endorsing the deployment of its semi-private military company. Not only are costs negligible, but eventual casualties may also be deferred as business matters, thereby lowering the political risk for state sponsors. For the proxy, the bargain provides material and political benefits, as well as control of armed personnel with few caveats, although they need to spend precious money.

However, it raises the difficult question of who may claim to be the sponsor and who the proxy. On the one hand, the external intervener appears as the sponsor, as the whole range of material, diplomatic, and delegated private military companies offers the external state considerable leverage over the local belligerent. On the other hand, the local belligerent pays for most of the services and, at least formally, exercises sponsorship of any private military company. It seems fair to suggest that for all the power of the external state, the local actor holds more cards under a semi-commercial arrangement. Not only can the local actor withhold payment and set up conditions for the proxy operations of the private military company, but it may also scan the market for competitors to potentially replace the external intervener. Turkey has advanced a state-controlled commercial model, which leaves the local belligerent with less political leverage, because Turkey bears the cost. The model consists of Turkey hiring ex-fighters from the Syrian civil war to support proxies affiliated with Turkey. These Syrian proxies have fought for the Government of National Accord in Libya since 2019 and for Azerbaijan in the war against Armenia in 2022 (Melcangi & Mezran, 2022). Although the Syrian fighters receive lucrative pay, the high number of volunteers may also be explained by the fact that Turkey has pressured its proxy group in Syria to send fighters. Prolonged civil wars in the Middle East have created the conditions for a grey zone market of private-state proxy warfare services. Undoubtedly, the commercialization and delegation of proxy warfare have made it easier to attract regional and global power in the past 15 years.

Finally, diasporas are growing due to migration and forced displacement. Resettled in a new host state, most people from conflict zones will have a strong interest in the fate of their co-ethnics in war zones. Individuals may even decide to return as volunteer fighters, which was an important recruitment base for the Islamic State. For some diasporas the interest translates into a more systematic economic or material support. Sara Daub argues that the relationship between diasporas and a party in a conflict could be described as a proxy relationship (Daub, 2024). A diaspora may work as a sponsor in a direct, transnational way and in an indirect way through their new host state. Directly, diasporas may provide financial and material aid that are organized through support organizations. Although diasporas in some cases act as mediators and push for a peaceful settlement, they more often become less compromising in their attitude toward the other side in the conflict (Daub, 2024). However, Tyrone Groh's definition of proxy war required that the sponsor exercise some level of control over the proxy's strategy. It might be difficult for a diaspora spread across states to achieve a level of coordination and exercise pressure on the proxy. Even if it seems questionable to label it a sponsor-proxy, the possibility of receiving aid from diaspora groups might still change the calculus of the recipient actor, which needs to cater to audiences outside the war zone through, e.g. the use of social media. Diasporas gain indirect influence by lobbying their new host state to sponsor co-ethnics in the war. However, Stephen Watts (et. al) find that diasporas hold—on average—little sway over their new host state's decisions on proxy warfare (2023, 129). If the rise in the number and sizes of diasporas continues, armed groups will become more likely to cater to its transnational audience to attract aid, even if the relationship hardly falls within the proxy war construct.

The ongoing processes of increased use of social media, commercialization, and growing diasporas provide potential proxies with new tools and opportunities to appeal for support from state and non-state sponsors. However, to what extent local actors' utilization of these processes has turned civil wars into proxy wars for the past 15 years is very difficult to establish. Nonetheless, a systematic analysis of particular instances of proxy war would benefit from studying how sponsor-client relations are established, including the agency of the incipient client. A holistic framework would study these processes in conjunction with political dynamics at the regional and global levels. I now turn to examine how the move to the middle of the proxy dimension of war impacts modern wars.

Consequences for Modern War

Modern wars are no islands. Regional and great powers routinely intervene in both intra- and interstate wars to influence the outcome. Proxy war is once again moving to the middle of contemporary war, after the end of the Cold War relegated it to the margin. The analysis demonstrates that, while proxy war seems to move to the mainstream, it does not necessarily follow the Cold War playbook. Instead, the analysis showed a marked difference in the behavior among the three global great powers, and that China so far has abstained from using proxy war as a foreign policy tool. Also, regional power dynamics cannot be reduced to an echo of global conflict lines but have permeated conflicts in their own right in both Africa and the Middle East. Arguably, societal and technological changes brought about by globalization have catalyzed proxy war's move to the middle by making belligerents more able to attract outside support. None of these three drivers of the current move to the middle seems to be going away within the next decades, which is why the proxy war dimension of modern war will highly likely remain in the middle.

Our analyses of contemporary wars would, therefore, benefit from a wider consideration of particular proxy war logics. In Clausewitzian terms, proxy war removes actual war further from absolute war. Absolute war is characterized by the belligerents' utmost energy in their use of force, picturized by the dueling wrestlers' need to match and surpass the energy of the opponent. Sponsors add to the political limitations of real war, where political considerations constrain warfare. Even though proxy war literature points out the relative autonomy of the proxy due to, e.g. information asymmetry (Ladwig III 2017, 290ff), their military actions are still bounded by the interests of their sponsors. Ultimately, the sponsor may withdraw its support or circumvent the proxy by intervening directly. Consequently, the proxy must take into account the political motives of the sponsor when choosing a course of action. Even though the proxy's military considerations point toward attacking the center of gravity of its enemy, it may be politically unviable due to the sponsor's wish to avoid an escalation of the war. When a sponsor delegates warfighting to a proxy, it is motivated by risk and cost reduction, as previously discussed. This may rule out actions that may generate decisive outcomes but also entail the risk of escalation and spread of the conflict. As a result, on average proxy wars are prolonged, bloody, and indecisive wars, which does not bode well for civilians caught in war (Anderson, 2025). To unpack how these dynamics unfold, it might be fruitful to distinguish between proxy intrastate wars and proxy interstate wars.

Intrastate wars are by far the most prevalent form of war, and regional actors (at least in Africa and the Middle East) are willing to integrate otherwise marginal intrastate wars into the regional security dynamics. Yemen provides a telling example. Between 2011 and 2015, Saudi Arabia supported the government against the Houthi movement, which in turn successfully vied for Iranian sponsorship. In 2015, the stalemate made the United Arab Emirates and Saudi Arabia launch a major intervention, which was blunted by an increase in Iranian support of the Houthi movement. As a consequence of Iran's sponsorship, Yemen was drawn into the recent war between Israel, Hamas, and Hezbollah. In only twelve years, the Houthi movement went from an isolated and regionally marginalized insurgency group to an actor able to wield advanced missile and drone technology in a regional war, due to the massive support of intelligence, advisories, and materiel from Iran.

As the example shows, the prominence of proxy warfare results in increasingly integrated regional security complexes, which is defined by the degree to which "a set of units whose major processes of securitization, desecuritization, or both are so interlinked that their security problems cannot reasonably be analyzed or resolved apart from one another" (Buzan & Wæver, 2003, 44). Whereas the Houthi movement's original security concerns were related to their conflict with the Yemenite government, the movement now securitizes its relations with actors in the geographical middle of the region, which in turn is securitized by regional and global actors acting in the region. In all likelihood, the spread of proxy warfare will lead to further integrated regional security complexes that make it more difficult to distinguish between geographical middles and margins. In the same vein, proxy warfare may gradually bind together separate regional security complexes, if belligerents successfully attract support from sponsors in neighboring regions or global powers. The involvement of extra-regional actors may eventually alter the boundaries and character of regional security complexes, and in extension, the character of wars fought in these regions.

Within war studies, Russia's second invasion of Ukraine brought renewed attention to interstate wars. The war between a global power and a European middle power certainly has involved more cost and risk than Russia's proxy involvements in Africa and the Middle East. This might also explain the double-sided character of Western support for Ukraine: On the one hand, the size and level of advanced weaponry delivered to Ukraine are very significant. On the other hand, in general, Western powers have been highly risk-averse and have sought to avoid crossing any real or imagined red lines, which have arguably delayed and deluded the impact of Western support. Western aid for Ukraine helped Ukraine sustain its war effort, and Iranian, Chinese, and North Korean civilian and military aid allowed Russia to keep up the intensity of its operations. The combined effect has been an extension of the war in Ukraine, which indicates how proxy-like dynamics are at play. Although Russia and Ukraine cannot be considered proxies, risk calculations in Beijing, Washington, or Paris have a strong influence on the scope of the war in Ukraine and speak to the monumental pressure to avoid escalating to nuclear war. This is visible in the circumvented ways that the Russian armed forces fight with the greatest (conventional) intensity in Eastern Ukraine and in the air war over Ukrainian cities, while at the same time only sparingly targeting Western logistics and facilities in Ukraine. Even if great power competition intensifies in the coming decades, interstate wars of the scale of the Ukraine war will be rare, but significant events that the global power can only fight infrequently. Still, it speaks to a move toward the middle of issues of global order and nuclear war. Decisions made during the war and in its transition toward peace may fundamentally alter the balance of power, international norms, and even issues of global order. Thereby, the move toward the middle of proxy warfare has brought back dimensions of war, which have been moved to the margins since possibly the world wars.

Conclusion

Proxy warfare has moved to the middle of contemporary warfare. This chapter highlighted three reasons behind the shift from margins to middle within the last 15 years. Increased great power competition initially led Russia to employ proxy warfare. The United States has also made use of proxy engagements, whereas China has so far abstained from its use. In the light of the sporadic usage of proxy warfare among great powers, the chapter argued that regional power dynamics are also important drivers. In the wake of the Arab Spring, the rise of three regional blocs turned civil wars in the Middle East into proxy wars and even drove proxy dynamics in North Africa. In East Africa and the Democratic Republic of Congo, regional powers intervened for different reasons but nonetheless added a proxy dimension to civil wars in the regions. Finally, the fade of attention to globalization as an empirical fact runs the risk of neglecting the increased power of belligerents to attract outside support. Participants in otherwise regionally marginalized conflicts may appeal to diasporas by broadcasting the war through social media and may turn to commercial arrangements with sponsors, which all make proxy engagements more likely.

None of these reasons sufficiently explains the rise in proxy wars by themselves, but conjoined they offer a comprehensive account. The fact that local, regional, and global dynamics are at play has important implications for the character of modern and future wars. Not only are proxy wars lengthier and bloodier than other wars, but they also change the center of gravity from the battlefields and the belligerent states to the maintenance of sponsor-proxy relationships and the political dynamics among greater powers. The move of proxy wars from the margin to the middle is part of the larger shifts in war portrayed in this anthology, and a highly consequential one.

References

Akbarzadeh, S., Gourlay, W., & Ehteshami, A. (2023). Iranian proxies in the Syrian conflict: Tehran's 'forward-defence' in action. *Journal of*

Strategic Studies, 46(3), 683–706. https://doi.org/10.1080/01402390.2021.2023014

Anderson, N. (2025). *Wars without end: Competitive intervention, escalation control, and protracted conflict*. Oxford University Press.

Arnold, B., & Nagl, J. (2023). A light footprint in Syria: Operational art in operation inherent resolve. *Small Wars and Insurgencies*. https://doi.org/10.1080/09592318.2023.2197671

Bertrand, N., Atwood, K., Liptak, K., & Marquardt, A. (2022, April 26). Austin's assertion that US wants to 'weaken' Russia underlines Biden strategy shift. *CNN*. https://edition.cnn.com/2022/04/25/politics/biden-administration-russia-strategy/index.html

Buzan, B., & Wæver, O. (2003). *Regions and Power: The Structure of International Security*. Cambridge University Press.

Byman, D. (2023). Are Proxy Wars Coming Back? *Washington Quarterly, 46*(3), 149–164. https://doi.org/10.1080/0163660X.2023.2259667

Carson, A. (2016). Facing off and saving face: Covert intervention and escalation management in the Korean War. *International Organization, 70*(1), 103–131. https://doi.org/10.1017/S0020818315000284

Cohen, R. A., & Shamci, G. P. (2022). The "Proxy Wars" strategy in Iranian regional foreign policy. *The Journal of the Middle East and Africa, 13*(4), 385–405. https://doi.org/10.1080/21520844.2022.2061789

Cooper, F. (2002). *Africa since 1940: The past of the present*. Cambridge University Press.

Daub, S. (2021). Diasporas and proxy wars. In A. Moghadam, V. Rauta, & M. Wyss (Eds.), *Routledge handbook of proxy wars* (pp. 204–216). Routledge. https://doi.org/10.4324/9781003174066-19

de Waal, A. (2015). *The real politics of the horn of Africa: Money, war and the business of power*. Polity Press.

Demirtaş, T. (2023). Conflict in the neo-colonial order in Africa. *Insight Turkey, 25*(2), 187–208. https://doi.org/10.2307/48732440

Deutsch, K. (1964). External involvement in internal war. In H. Eckstein (Ed.), *Internal war: Problems and approaches* (pp. 100–110). The Free Press of Glencoe.

Dobrokhotov, R., Grozev, C., & Weiss, M. (2025, January 8). Afgantsy redux: How Russian military intelligence used the Taliban to bleed U.S. forces at the end of America's longest war. *The Insider*. https://theins.ru/en/politics/277723

Ghiselli, A. (2024). An opportunistic Russia in the Middle East, a view from China. *Cambridge Review of International Affairs, 37*(2), 163–181. https://doi.org/10.1080/09557571.2023.2207814

Groh, T. L. (2019). *Proxy war: The least bad option*. Stanford University Press.

Hoffman, F., & Orner, A. (2021, September 2). The Return of Great-Power Proxy Wars. *War on the Rocks*. https://warontherocks.com/2021/09/the-return-of-great-power-proxy-wars/

Ikenberry, G. J. (2024). Three worlds: The west, east and south and the competition to shape global order. *International Affairs, 100*(1), 121–138. https://doi.org/10.1093/ia/iiad284

Kofman, M., & Rojansky, M. (2018). What Kind of Victory for Russia in Syria? *Military Review*, March-April, pp. 6–23.

Krieg, A., & Rickli, J. (2019). *Surrogate warfare: The transformation of war in the twenty-first century*. Georgetown University Press.

Ladwig, W. C., III. (2017). *The forgotten front: Patron-client relationships in counter insurgency*. Cambridge University Press.

Lake, D. A. (2019). Iraq, 2003–2011. In E. Berman & D. A. Lake (Eds.), *Proxy wars: Suppressing violence through local agents* (pp. 238–263). Cornell University Press.

Lynch, M. (2021). Proxy war and the new structure of middle east regional politics. In J. L. Gelvin (Ed.), *The contemporary middle east in an age of upheaval* (pp. 238–252). Stanford University Press. https://doi.org/10.1515/9781503627703-016.

Malyarenko, T., & Wolff, S. (2018). The logic of competitive influence-seeking: Russia, Ukraine, and the conflict in Donbas. *Post-Soviet Affairs, 34*(4), 191–212. https://doi.org/10.1080/1060586X.2018.1425083

Marsh, N. (2023). Responding to needs: Military aid to Ukraine during the first year after the 2022 invasion. *Defense & Security Analysis, 39*(3), 329–352. https://doi.org/10.1080/14751798.2023.2235121

Meier, V., Karlén, N., Pettersson, T., & Croicu, M. (2023). External support in armed conflicts: Introducing the UCDP external support dataset (ESD), 1975–2017. *Journal of Peace Research, 60*(3), 545–554. https://doi.org/10.1177/00223433221079864

Melcangi, A., & Mezran, K. (2022). Truly a proxy war? Militias, institutions and external actors in libya between limited statehood and Rentier State. *The International Spectator, 57*(4), 121–138. https://doi.org/10.1080/03932729.2022.2061225

Moghadam, A., Rauta, V., & Wyss, M. (2024). *Routledge handbook of proxy wars*. Routledge. https://doi.org/10.4324/9781003174066

Moghadam, A., & Wyss, M. (2022). The political power of proxies: Why nonstate actors use local surrogates. *International Security, 44*(4), 119–157.

Mumford, A. (2013). Proxy warfare and the future of conflict. *The RUSI Journal, 158*(2), 40–46. https://doi.org/10.1080/03071847.2013.787733

Noonan, M. P. (2021). *Irregular soldiers and rebellious states: Small-scale U.S. interventions abroad*. Lanham: Rowman & Littlefield Publishers.

Ramani, S. (2023). *Russia in Africa resurgent great power or bellicose pretender?* Hurst Publisher.
Robinson, L. (2016). The SOF Experience in the Philippines and the Implications for Future Defense Strategy. *Prism: A Journal of the Center for Complex Operations, 6*(3), 150–167.
Shahbazov, F. (2024, December 5). What Turkey Hopes to Gain From the HTS Offensive in Syria. *Stimson Commentary*. https://www.stimson.org/2024/what-turkey-hopes-to-gain-from-the-hts-offensive-in-syria/
Tamm, H. (2016). The origins of transnational alliances: Rulers, rebels, and political survival in the Congo Wars. *International Security, 41*(1), 147–181. https://doi.org/10.1162/ISEC_a_00252
Tamm, H., & Duursma, A. (2023). Combat, commitment, and the termination of Africa's mutual interventions. *European Journal of International Relations, 29*(1), 3–28. https://doi.org/10.1177/13540661221112612
Tierney, D. (2021). The future of sino-U.S. proxy war. *Texas National Security Review*, 4(2), pp. 49–73. https://tnsr.org/2021/03/the-future-of-sino-u-s-proxy-war/
Tol, G. (2024, December 11). How Turkey won the Syrian civil war. *Foreign Affairs*. https://www.foreignaffairs.com/turkey/how-turkey-won-syrian-civil-war
Usher, B. P. (2025, February 8). Who's pulling the strings in the DR Congo crisis? *BBC*, downloaded from https://www.bbc.com/news/articles/cp8qp6p39e9o.
Valbjørn, M., Bank, A., & Darwich, M. (2024). Forward to the past? Regional repercussions of the Gaza war. *Middle East Policy, 31*(3), 3–17. https://doi.org/10.1111/mepo.12758
Watts, S., Frederick, B. A., Chandler, N., Toukan, M., Curriden, C., Mueller, E. E., Geist, E., Tabatabai, A., Plana, S., Corbin, B., & Martini, J. (2023). *Proxy warfare in strategic competition: state motivations and future trends.* RAND Corporation. https://www.rand.org/pubs/research_reports/RRA307-2.html
Williams, P. D. (2018). *War and conflict in Africa*. Wiley

CHAPTER 4

From Lines to Layers: Redrawing the Middle and Margins of the Battlefield

Amelie Theussen

Introduction

> [W]here were the markers of war, such as artillery and trenches? (Jefferis, 2012, 47)

From the earliest depictions of armed conflict to the frontlines in Ukraine today, battlefields—the "piece[s] of ground on which a battle is fought" (Oxford English Dictionary, n.d.)—have been the location of war. Often depicted as literal fields occupied by two opposing forces clashing in violent struggle (e.g. Brooks, 2004, 730), the image of the battlefield is characterized by a large number of infantry forces, chariots, or cavalry forces, and later on artillery, trenches, poison gas, tanks, ships, and planes. The changing face of war also changed the battlefield, which expanded to include the maritime and air domain. Nevertheless, battlefields are generally seen as bounded by geography and time.

A. Theussen (✉)
Royal Danish Defence College, Copenhagen, Denmark
e-mail: amth@fak.dk

M. Robin et al. (eds.), *The Changing Fights and Fighters of Contemporary War*, https://doi.org/10.1007/978-3-032-05518-7_4

Over the course of the last twenty-five years, however, new technologies and actors with global reach have arguably expanded the battlefield both geographically and temporally. In this chapter I argue that these changes in actors' reach and means and methods of warfare have created what I call a "layered battlefield," that includes globalized, geographically unbounded aspects, where spaces often considered peaceful become potential battlefields of equal importance to the physical clash of armed forces on a frontline.

This "layered battlefield," I argue, complicates the criteria of space and time which traditionally defined how we understand the battlefield. Historically, indeed, the concept of the battlefield denotes a geographical space in time, where the opposing forces clash with armed force. As such it "has a core and a periphery" (Megret, 2011, 133); or in the words of this book, the battlefield has a middle and it has margins. While it does not have sharply drawn, pre-defined borders, the battlefield exists because it is possible to distinguish between what occurs within it and what is beyond it. For the geographical space to have any meaning, there must be an understanding of its purpose and its rules. As McRandle puts it, the battlefield is an "imaginary arena" (McRandle, 1994, 39); it is as much an idea—a conceptual understanding—as it is a geographical space (Megret, 2011).

The idea of the geographically and temporally limited battlefield provides war with its limitations. It dictates logistical and psychological constraints (Khan, 2006), as well as the confines for the normative framework of the laws of war, which allow lethal force to be used against an enemy. Where peacetime is the normal state of affairs, war—and its geographical space, the battlefield—is the exception (Theussen & Jakobsen, 2021). In the words of Megret, "[t]he battlefield thus stands for this peculiar ideal that, whilst war may and will rage, what distinguishes it from random violence is the fact that it unfolds in discreet spaces insulated from the rest of society, confining military violence to a confrontation between specialized forces whose operation should minimally disrupt surrounding life" (Megret, 2011, 135). In this understanding, the location where the specialized militaries engaged in armed struggle against each other makes up the middle of the battlefield, while the rest of society goes about their lives at its margins (cf. the use of the term "arrière" in French to describe those not fighting in the trenches during World War 1). This chapter, however, shows how both actors and technologies expand the margins of the battlefield across space and time.

In doing so, they shift the traditional center—specialized armed forces—toward the margins, while bringing what was once peripheral—society itself—into the center of conflict. It is worth noting that these movements of expansion and substitution are not necessarily new, but rather the accumulation of technological developments that have been ongoing for decades or even centuries.

The chapter proceeds in three parts: it starts with the question of why defining the battlefield and its margins and middle matters. This is followed by an investigation into how technological developments push the core elements of the battlefield—its geography and temporality—outward by expanding the reach of actors and enabling new means and methods of warfare. A case study of the Russia-Ukraine war since 2022 follows to illustrate how these changes together with a more traditional frontline create a multi-layered battlefield where each layer has its own middle and margins. Russia's war against Ukraine is chosen for two reasons: first, it is a prominent ongoing armed conflict and the largest conventional armed conflict in Europe since World War 2; and second, it represents a traditional armed conflict in the sense that it is characterized by the existence of frontlines and a battlefield in the traditional understanding outlined above. Yet, it has also triggered significant debate regarding the role of new technology and new domains for the battlefield and what can be learned from the Ukrainian experience. The chapter then ends with a conclusion on the margins, middle, and boundaries of contemporary battlefields and what that implies for armed conflict in the years to come.

A few words on method and limitations: this chapter builds entirely on open sources and analyzes an ongoing conflict. While sources and information were verified to the author's best ability consistent with common academic research practices and standards, the analysis in this chapter can only provide a snapshot in time of the war and its underlying dynamics. It is thus possible—likely even—that the battlefield in Ukraine will change when underlying dynamics change. The middle/margin lens employed in this chapter should, however, prove equally useful for any future analyses of the battlefield in this and other wars.

Why Does Defining the Battlefield Matter?

The battlefield is, of course, of utmost military significance. Wars are won—and lost—on the battlefield. But more than just performance on the battlefield, it is about defining and shaping the battlefield to one's advantage. From identifying advantageous positions for own forces to forcing the enemy into disadvantageous positions, already Sun Tzu cautions that the side that better understands and makes uses of the battlefield is more likely to win (Sun Tzŭ, 1910).

In international law, the battlefield is the defining space for where it is legal to kill combatants. The boundaries of the battlefield determine two central legal issues: first, where the parties to an armed conflict have the right to conduct military operations; and second, whether the law of armed conflict applies to a given situation or another set of rules. Generally, the territory of states that are not parties to the armed conflict falls outside the boundaries of the (potential) battlefield; no military operations may be conducted on these states' territories.[1] Inversely, the territories of the states who are party to the conflict, including the maritime and air domain, exclusive economic zones (EEZs), the high seas, and international airspace, are part of the area of war in which military operations may take place. There are those who argue that there are geographical limits even within the area of war, that military operations are only permitted in proximity to already ongoing fighting (see, e.g. O'Connell, 2010). Yet, others argue that there is no support for this in state practice, with history full of examples of states striking other states far from the frontlines, as "[s]uccess in warfare at any level, from single combat to global military strategy, is based upon the ability to strike your opponent in places where he is vulnerable and in ways he does not expect" (Lewis, 2012, 303).

Also in non-international armed conflicts—fought between non-state actors or between a non-state actor and a state—the battlefield was initially confined to the territory of the state where the conflict is occurring. However, the rise of transnational terrorism has led many

[1] The law of neutrality sets the geographical limits of the battlefield. It is beyond the scope of this chapter to examine neutrality law; and for the purpose of this chapter, it is sufficient to mention that if a neutral state permits one side to conduct operations on its territory, or use its territory as a sanctuary, the status of neutrality is lost. A case that illustrates the application of neutrality law and the use of armed force far from the frontlines is the *Graf Spee* incident (see Lewis, 2012).

commentators to argue that an extension of the battlefield beyond the boundaries of that state is necessary. As one scholar argues, the application of criteria from the Tadic case determines the boundaries of the battlefield; but the deciding factor is not so much the intensity of violence in one particular, limited, geographical location, but rather the intensity of violence between the actors across all the geographical areas where such violence takes place (Lewis, 2012). The chapter returns to this debate in the subsequent section.

Even on the battlefield, however, there are legal limitations on what may be the target of military operations: according to the principle of distinction, only military objectives may legally be targeted; protected zones can be established within the theater of operations; and some buildings, such as those of historical or architectural interest, are given special protection under the law (unless they constitute military objectives) (Martin, 2015). The same also counts for the natural environment, which may not be destroyed "unless required by imperative military necessity" (Henckaerts et al., 2009, Rule 43). Thus, these areas are legally off limits and generally fall outside the legal scope of the "battlefield," understood here as the marker of where military operations can be conducted lawfully, while geographically being located within it.

Defining the battlefield and its boundaries thus matters greatly for international law. Because of the idea of the battlefield, a distinction between the battlefield and civilian areas is at least theoretically possible, and identifiable battlefields allow an identification and calculation of military objectives and necessity (see e.g. Geiß, 2006). The concept of the battlefield thus embodies the limitations of war, but also its status as exception to the (peaceful) normality: "the laws of war do not merely seek to regulate the battlefield. They are also part of its symbolic maintenance and even construction as a particular space defined by the norms that apply to it" (Megret, 2011, 135). In international law, military objectives and military necessity are constructed as the middle of the battlefield, while civilian areas and states not party to the armed conflict are its margins.

This means that defining the battlefield plays at least two crucial roles in constructing an understanding of war: on the one hand, defining the battlefield also defines what constitutes legitimate forms of the use of armed force. The construction of the battlefield defines and shapes the understanding of the conflict one is engaged in, and allows to garner support for the use of force, or other political decisions. On the other hand, attempting to push the boundaries of the battlefield, doing away with some of its constraints, can give an advantage over the adversary. This is highly visible in so-called guerrilla or asymmetric warfare; but also applies to contemporary instances of grey zone or hybrid threats, where the military might of the West is negated by keeping the activities—and thus conflict—below the threshold of armed conflict (Theussen & Jakobsen, 2021). As Birch notes, "[t]hroughout history there have always been strategic motivations to muddy those boundaries, and corresponding attempts to define them in the hope that this will mitigate the worst effects of conflict. In the present day new technologies, the global reach of some actors and the corresponding response, and a dramatically unequal and unstable battlefield means that these boundaries are in danger of disappearing completely" (Birch, 2016, 10).

The Middle and the Margins of the Battlefield: A Focus on Geography and Time

It is thus no surprise that its existence in space—geography—and its existence in time are the defining features of the battlefield. Already Sun Tzu gave advice on which geography makes favorable battlefields through considerations about "the field," "earth," including distances and topographical features, and "terrain," such as advising to occupy high and sunny spots (Sun Tzŭ, 1910). Clausewitz similarly describes the battlefield in terms of a hill, or a bridge, and other geographical and topographical features (Von Clausewitz, 1976). The battlefield's geographic characteristics might make it more suitable for offense or defense, or give advantage to certain battlefield tactics and maneuvers over others. That the geographical features of the battlefield are a defining factor cannot only be seen in the division of military forces into the three traditional branches, dealing with warfare on land, in the air, and on (and under) water; but also in the fact that further specializations emerged, such as the German "Gebirgsjäger."[2] McRandle argues that the geographical aspect is reinforced by "the soldiers themselves [who] regard the battlefield as limited, a tangible area for which they can fight and of which they can take possession" (1994, 140).

[2] Light infantry trained in mountain warfare, currently part of the armed forces in Germany, Austria, and Switzerland.

When Everywhere Becomes the Battlefield

Over time, improvements to the range of weapons have pushed the geographical margins of the battlefield outward. An early example is the invention of gunpowder, which gradually came to replace muscle-powered weapons with increasingly effective and long-ranging small and large firearms, artillery, and bombs. Additionally, developments in modes of transportation allowed troops and military equipment to move swiftly from one theater to the next, expanding the size of the (potential) battlefield significantly from the second half of the nineteenth century onward (Heuser, 2012).

A significant change came with the invention of the airplane, making substantial portions of the adversary's territory accessible to be targeted by air—the battlefield grew behind enemy lines. This not only impacted the extent of the battlefield, but also its middle and margins. Where previously the middle of the battlefield was found at the frontline, suddenly population centers became another center of gravity. Civilians, who previously often had been able to flee from the frontline, now had nowhere to go where airplanes could not reach. The development of long-range missile technology further exacerbated this development (Gasser, 1993).

The Second World War marks the zenith of this evolution, where countries' entire infrastructure and population became targets of firebombing, such as during the London Blitz, battle of Stalingrad, or bombing of Dresden. Because of their core role for the state's war machine, major industrial and population centers became (part of) the core of the war effort, and thus the middle of the battlefield. This is not to say that there were no frontlines anymore, but the battlefield certainly was no longer confined to the immediate vicinity of the frontlines. Shaw argues that this change in the military significance of society is due to industrialization. National economies and societies became not only the physical infrastructure of the enemy's military power, "but also its social, political and mental basis" (Shaw, 2003, 131). Bombing them did not just target capabilities, but also morale. Additionally, due to the interconnectedness of the Empires and their colonies, the battlefield expanded around the globe. In his address after the Japanese attack on Pearl Harbor, US President Roosevelt noted: "all the continents of the world, and all the oceans, are now considered by the Axis strategists as one gigantic battlefield" (Roosevelt, 1941).

The advent of nuclear weapons did not only end the Second World War, their use on Hiroshima and Nagasaki marked the culmination of firebombing population centers—at least in the context of direct war between nuclear powers. Weapons so powerful they can eradicate entire population centers meant that war between nuclear powers became unthinkable because of the resulting mutually assured destruction. The thought of these weapons' destruction on the imagined battlefield—that now encompassed the entire nation and its territory with a focus on population centers—was and still is so shocking that "[t]he probability of major war among states having nuclear weapons approaches zero" (Waltz, 1990, 740). As Shaw describes: "The very environment of life on earth was at risk. [...] The battlefield was everywhere; everywhere was the battlefield" (Shaw, 2003, 134). Because of the deterrent effect of nuclear weapons' imagined battlefield, Waltz argues, the nuclear armed powers step away from the brink "every time that events even remotely threatened to get out of hand at the center of international politics" (Waltz, 1990, 735). The invention of nuclear weapons did not end all war, but war has "more and more become the privilege of poor and weak states" (Waltz, 1990, 744). Either nuclear armed big powers are only more or less indirectly involved in some form of proxy war (see Henningsen's chapter in this volume), or they are engaged against a non-nuclear opponent.

Another method of warfare that makes society the battlefield is insurgent or guerrilla warfare. The premise of these is to avoid direct battle with a militarily superior foe on the battlefield. Thus, insurgents hiding among civilians and the opponents' struggle for the population's hearts and minds puts society at the very center of the battlefield. Terrorism works similarly: the majority of terrorist attacks target civilians in spaces of everyday life, with the intent to shock, terrorize, and put immense political pressure on (primarily, but not exclusively, democratic) states (e.g. Megret, 2011; Shaw, 2003). Developments in communications technology enabled terrorist networks to operate worldwide and gave them a global audience, magnifying the effect of violence. Decentralized access to information and social media and their alternative communications channels allow terrorists to recruit and spread their message much more widely internationally. So much so that Megret argues that global terrorism "loses any territorial connection so that it becomes as much a fight against a certain vision of society, making the idea of the battlefield even less relevant. Terrorism is perhaps the ultimate refusal of the battlefield, a commitment to bring violence when and where one pleases, unbound by any requirement that it unfold in a particular space and be constrained by particular norms" (Megret, 2011, 149).

But also the counterterrorism methods employed to fight these global terrorist networks expand the margins of the battlefield. The development of drone technology allows the counterterrorist to target terrorists wherever they are hiding, with (almost) no risk to their soldiers' lives (but see Karyoti's chapter in this volume). The effect of these technological developments meant that those parts of the so-called "War on Terror" that are not fought on the battlefields of Afghanistan or Iraq are fought on a globalized battlefield, taking the form of a "everywhere war" (Gregory, 2011). Here, the geographically bounded nature of the battlefield has been lost.

When All the Time Becomes Wartime

At the same time, the War on Terror gave rise to questions regarding its temporal limits as well, leading scholars to describe it as "endless war" (Keen, 2010) or "the forever war" (Filkins, 2009). With no clearly defined end point and an enemy that hardly can be wholly defeated, the War on Terror turned into perpetual war. This does not work well with the temporal boundedness of war. Looking at the UN Charter, the resort to armed force—a situation of war—is the exception to otherwise peaceful relations between states. In the Western understanding of war, wars have a beginning and an end; and while they might last many years, they are limited in time (Dudziak, 2012; Theussen & Jakobsen, 2021). This, unsurprisingly, also applies to the battlefields on which these wars are fought. No military engagement or operation lasts forever—or at least that used to be the expectation. But scholars highlight the element of persistence in the New Wars of the twenty-first century, where political and/or economic gain for the warring parties stems from the continuation of the armed violence, rather than from winning the war (Chinkin & Kaldor, 2017; Kaldor, 2012, 2013; Münkler, 2005).

The dimension of time works in two ways: firstly, in relation to the military operation that makes the geographic location in question a battlefield. A hill, waterway, or other geographical location only becomes a battlefield because a clash of armed force took place. This clash can be just starting, ongoing, or have ended a long time ago, but it has a temporal dimension including some form of beginning and end. This is important, inter alia, for the application of the laws of war. They only apply when there is a resort to armed force, when the war has started. And once the violence ends, so does the applicability of the laws of war. Secondly, this geographic location maintains the status of battlefield throughout time to come, adding a historical dimension. Prominent battlefields turn into sites for tourism, such as the beaches of Normandy or Gettysburg (Chylińska, 2020).

The Dissolution of the Battlefield in Space and Time

The emergence of the cyber domain as a (part of the) battlefield alongside the traditional domains of land, maritime, air, and space due to further developments in information and communication technology contributes to the dissolution of the battlefield by fully removing its geographical and temporal limits. The 2010 Stuxnet virus became the first cyber-attack that damaged a physical target, Iranian nuclear centrifuges. Highly targeted and sophisticated, a variety of sources pointed to state involvement (Halliday, 2010; Markoff, 2010); most likely, though unconfirmed, a cooperation between the US and Israel (Sanger, 2012). Stuxnet was described as "the new face of 21st-century warfare: invisible, anonymous, and devastating" (Gross, 2011). Cyber war was born and with it came a global, digital battlefield (see Laudrain's chapter in this volume).

While the cyber domain is listed alongside the more traditional domains of warfare, two things are noteworthy about the cyber battlefield: first, its "geography" is entirely artificial, a man-made dimension, with properties fully under human control. This stands in contrast to the other domains, which at least to a certain extent are subject to the laws of nature (Siroli, 2018). As for the temporal aspect of the battlefield, the speed of operations is very high, with operations in the cyber domain allowing "instant and simultaneous attacks world wide," while the preparations of such attack can take many months or even years (Theussen & Jakobsen, 2021, 173). This gives new vectors of attack through disinformation, espionage, and sabotage, without the need for physical armed forces at the location of the attack.

Second, the other domains are rapidly becoming digitalized, with cyber elements being integrated into the other domains of warfare. Thus, the domains at least partially overlap and interact. As Siroli describes "[c]yber is becoming a sort of glue, a framework underlying the military infrastructures that integrate the modern battlefield and coordinate inter-domain operations" (2018, 112). The concept of Multi-Domain Operations incorporates this thinking. Defined by NATO as "the orchestration of military activities, across all domains and environments, synchronized with non-military activities, to enable the Alliance to create converging effects at the speed of relevance" (NATO, 2023, 1), MDO brings in the space and cyber domains to achieve integration and synergy effects between warfighting domains. Originally devised by the US Army in the context of increasing attention on competitor states and the possibility of interstate warfare between major powers (US Army TRADOC, 2018), the US version of the concept has interesting differences to the NATO version. It does not focus on the integration with non-military activities to the same extent as NATO, but it includes operations across the continuum of conflict, from competition below the threshold of armed conflict, over crisis, to armed conflict (*Field Manual 3-0 Operations*, 2025). Where previously "geographic and time boundaries were primarily determined by the ranges and speed of their [weapons] formations. Today, weapons systems are so fast, so lethal, have so much range—and, in some cases, have effects that transcend geographic relevance (cyber)—that 'formation size' and 'weapons caliber' are insufficient metrics for determining [the battlefield]" (Wesley & Simpson, 2020, 4).

This focus on activities below the threshold of armed conflict bares resemblance to the concepts of hybrid threats and grey zone warfare. When set in the grey zone between peace and war, below the threshold of armed conflict, hybrid activities are employed to achieve strategic political objectives without triggering a military response from a superior adversary (the US and/or NATO). These concepts emphasize a broad array of non-military means and domains, for example economy, diplomacy, information, law, culture, and so on. This contributes to a blurring of the distinction between war and peace (see Libiseller and Milevski's chapter in this volume). In grey zone warfare, "[t]he key to winning is no longer the ability to use force successfully to defeat opponents on the battlefield, but the ability to coordinate and synchronize an ever-increasing number of nonmilitary instruments and actors in order to undermine the target's capability and willingness to resist the demands of the attacker" (Theussen & Jakobsen, 2021, 164). The battlefield has moved: its middle is no longer characterized by fielding and fighting military capabilities but instead made up of an actor's ability to integrate a variety of nonmilitary (and possibly some military) means, actors, and tactics to achieve the strategic goal. Military means are relegated to the margins; the use of force and conventional capabilities have become supplementary, where the use of armed force often is seen as the last step and not the first (Theussen & Jakobsen, 2021). The usefulness of concepts such as hybrid warfare or grey zone conflict is highly disputed (see Libiseller and Milevski in this volume), and the idea to use other means to pursue war is not new. As Shaw notes, "war is often pursued by other means. … [T]he West has moved to increasing use of economic and political sanctions as a complement to military force … [which] can constitute indirect killing fields" through poverty, diseases, and strategic exploitation of sanctions by regimes and other powerful actors (Shaw, 2003, 138–139). Nevertheless, Western military supremacy and technological advancements in information and communications technology have expanded the reliance on and effect of such combinations of non-military means to the extent that their (perceived) use has given rise to the concepts of hybrid and grey zone warfare.

What then does this mean for the middle and margins of the battlefield today? While the fight against non-state terrorist groups continues, the last years have seen a reorientation toward the (possible) fight against peer-competitor states. With technological advances regarding the range and destructive potential of weapons, unmanned means of delivery and an ever-increasing integration of dual use information and communications technologies giving rise to a new importance of private companies, the battlefield of today is global, digital, and potentially encompasses the whole of society. Its geographical and temporal boundaries have shifted to a point where the battlefield in its traditional meaning has vanished (Megret, 2011). Yet, as the following analysis of the war between Russia and Ukraine illustrates, more traditional frontlines also remain. In combination with the previously outlined developments, this creates a multi-layered battlefield, where each layer has its own middle and margins.

The Russia-Ukraine War and the Margins and Middle of Its Battlefield

The full-scale invasion of Ukraine by Russia in 2022 has led to the return of the image of traditional battlefields, while also highlighting the impact of the technological developments identified in the previous section. The novelty of the war and battlefield in Ukraine is the subject of major debate: on the one side, there are those who are seeing "a genuine military revolution" (T. X. Hammes quoted in Biddle, 2023), a "pivotal moment in military history" (Johnson, 2022) and consider heavy conventional weaponry, such as the tank, as "pushed into obsolescence" (O'Brien, 2022) and "doomed" (Gardener, 2022). These observers of the war emphasize the use of advanced technologies in the war, from drones over space-based surveillance, precision weapons, artificial intelligence, to hypersonic missiles and handheld jammers, to name just the most prominent ones; and these technologies' abilities to fundamentally impact and alter the battlefield. On the other side of the debate, there are those who argue for the similarity of this war to conventional warfare of earlier times, such as World War 1 and 2. These observers highlight the trenches, minefields, role of artillery, and the importance of production capabilities for ammunition and other military equipment (Biddle, 2023; Kofman, 2024). To come back to the quote in the very beginning of the chapter: in Ukraine, the markers of war—and the battlefield—in form of artillery and trenches are very much present.

In any case, in the war between Russia and Ukraine, technological innovation reshapes (parts of) the battlefield, while more traditional observations still remain relevant. This all observers agree upon, even though they disagree as to how fundamental the impact of the (technological) changes is. As the largest conventional armed conflict in Europe since the Second World War, the Russo-Ukrainian war is thus an ideally suited case study to investigate the changing dynamics of the battlefield and its shifting middle and margins.

The Frontline: The First Layer of the Battlefield

At the time of writing in spring 2025, there are at least three layers to the Russo-Ukrainian battlefield, each with their own middle/margin dynamic, displaying a widening of the battlefield in various ways on the different levels.[3] Starting out narrow in sense of geography, the first layer of the battlefield is the frontline and its vicinity. Despite being the geographically smallest layer of the battlefield in the Russo-Ukrainian war, the frontline is over 1,000 kilometers long. Here, the battlefield is characterized by extended periods of static engagements, alternating offensives and counteroffensives, urban sieges, phases of intense attrition, as well as operations to break through fortified defensive positions. According

[3] This chapter does not aim to give a comprehensive overview over the course of the Russo-Ukrainian war. For an overview over the development of military operations through the different phases of the war, see, e.g. Kofman (2024).

to Kofman, these battlefield conditions are created by the fact that both Russia and Ukraine struggle to generate mass and employ forces at scale, as well as suffer from a lack of firepower and inability to attain a fires advantage, though at different points in time. While new technologies are important, "they operated alongside established systems rather than rendering them obsolete, as both sides engaged in cycles of adaptation and iterative learning from each other" (Kofman, 2024, 100). Biddle argues similarly that the war displays a "mix of successful offense and successful defense, not a pattern of consistent offensive frustration. And all this—both the breakthroughs and the stalemates—has occurred in the face of new weapons and equipment. Conversely, older legacy systems such as tanks played prominent roles in both the offensive successes and failures" (Biddle, 2023).

Yet, for other observers, the ubiquitous use of small, cheap, commercial drones that emerged over the course of the war causes new challenges on the frontline, or even a "cheap-drone revolution" (Perrett, 2024). There can be no doubt about their tactical impact. Ukrainian officials estimate that one-way attack drones cause 70% of casualties on the frontline (Horowitz et al., 2025). Boyer and Becker argue that the proliferation of such drones has created a transparent battlefield, where (almost) complete and continuous surveillance compels forces to disperse, making it difficult to concentrate forces for offensive action and maneuver warfare and inhibiting the achievement of operational surprise (Boyer & Becker, 2024). Since early 2024, Russia only managed to capture around 5000 km^2 of Ukrainian territory along the entire frontline. Compared to much larger territory being traded on both sides during the war's first year, this can be attributed to the difficulties of breaking through prepared defensive lines and the challenges of mustering "large-scale offensive operations in today's battlefield environment" (Jones & McCabe, 2025, 9). Despite the highly surveilled "transparent" battlefield, Ukraine's Kursk offensive in the summer of 2024 shows that surprises are still possible (Boyer & Becker, 2024). The purpose and usefulness of this incursion into Russian territory is disputed and has (mostly) come to an end after a Russian offensive including North Korean soldiers regained control with the region (Terajima, 2025).

As also Kofman and Biddle agree, the impact of technological development depends on learning and adaptation to use the technology. This is visible in the types of drones employed. After guided antiaircraft missiles were used to defend against more expensive and sophisticated drones earlier on in the war, a larger number of cheaper, less sophisticated drones was put in use. These in turn are countered by equipping vehicles and soldiers with electronic warfare devices capable of jamming the drones' signals. Vehicles were also outfitted with additional protective coverings to shield against drone attacks. One way to avoid electronic warfare counter-drone measures is to have the drone rely on artificial intelligence (AI) guidance once the connection to the pilot is lost. This capability is improving quickly in Ukraine, with the reach of the best guidance systems expanding from 500 meters to 2 km in the span of one year, while also decreasing necessary training times for human operators and increasing performance. Currently, "perhaps one in ten drones is AI guided. But this is the lowest it will ever be" notes Joshi (2025, 118). The latest innovation to counter electronic interference such as signal jamming is the use of fiber optic cable-guided drones. These drones also have drawbacks—their reach is smaller, the cable can get stuck in trees or other obstacles, and they are slower—but their widespread use makes changing positions near the frontline deadly for soldiers. Thus, movement near the frontline is highly restricted, soldiers are staying at their positions for longer, waiting for cloud cover or high winds before moving, and offensive maneuvers are usually carried out by small groups, often on highly mobile vehicles such as motorcycles or the like (Limaye, 2025; Nabukhotny, 2025). The development and use of drones in Russia's war against Ukraine are not limited to the aerial domain, however. Ukraine has very successfully employed drone boats and loitering torpedoes against the Russian Black Sea Fleet, and recently both Russia and Ukraine have started to make use of (fiber optic) ground drones as well, among other purposes for resupplying troops at the frontline and casualty evacuation, but also lethal force (Horbatenko, 2025; Kunertova, 2024).

For the frontline level of the battlefield, it is thus possible to identify a dynamic where drone technology moved from the margins to the middle of the battlefield, significantly impacting how the war is being fought. While previous difficulties of mass and firepower already had caused the Russo-Ukrainian war to stagnate and become entrenched, drone technology exacerbated these developments, causing further challenges to potentially decisive large-scale offensive operations. First studies show that control of the aerial domain through drone operations is essential for achieving success in ground combat by linking effective drone use to higher combat vehicle losses, indicating the central role of drone operations on future battlefields (Mittal & Goetz, 2025). As Kunertova points out "[p]rior to Russia's war in Ukraine, drones were thought to be most useful in conflicts where one side maintains air superiority, that is, to replace boots on the ground. In Ukraine, however, drones have boots" (Kunertova, 2024, 7). The point here is that drone technology has moved from marginal conflicts, those where putting boots on the ground was seen as too costly or unnecessary, to the core of the modern battlefield, where it is employed by soldiers on the frontlines. The technology has also changed: where previously small numbers of large, military drones with long ranges and flight times at high altitudes were the norm, these drones have disappeared almost completely from the battlefield in the war between Russia and Ukraine (Kunertova, 2024). Instead, masses of smaller, cheaper, faster to produce drones are changing warfare. This is not to say that conventional weapons systems are no longer relevant on the modern battlefield; but as Crombe and Nagle note "[t]ools and tactics that were viewed as niche capabilities in previous conflicts are becoming primary weapons systems that require education and training to understand, exploit, and counter" (Crombe & Nagl, 2023, 24). The analytical lens of movements from the margins to the middle helps in making these changes visible without getting lost in them.

The National Level: The Second Layer of the Battlefield

Geographically wider, the second layer of the battlefield in Russia's war against Ukraine is made up of the national territory of the warring parties. In line with the developments identified above that expanded the margins of the battlefield, in the Russo-Ukrainian war cities far from the frontline are also the targets of attacks. While it seems that Russia avoided civilian casualties in the early stages of the war, probably with the hope that the Ukrainian population would accept a Russian occupation (or Russian-controlled government), as the war progressed Russia gradually accepted more civilian casualties. It even began to deliberately strike civilian targets to instill fear and attempt to undermine morale and support for the Ukrainian government, for example by attacking energy infrastructure in winter, or residential neighborhoods (Rakov & Fainberg, 2023). Jones and McCabe point out that "Russia has utilized stand-off strikes from ground, air, and naval platforms to terrorize Ukrainian civilians through a punishment strategy" effectively disconnected from the frontline and maneuvers there (2025, 3). Ukraine has also hit targets in Russia, seemingly attempting to make the war visible to the Russian population and affect their morale, as well as degrade Russia's fighting power. This is visible in repeated attacks on Moscow, long-distance attacks (for example against Olenya airbase near Murmansk, almost 2000 km away from Ukraine), as well as the recent Operation Spiderweb that used drones and explosives that had been smuggled into Russia to target four major Russian airbases and degrade Russian air superiority. For this purpose, and connecting to the third layer of the battlefield analyzed below, Ukraine developed its own long-range one-way attack drones. These drones do not only fill a significant capability gap against Russia's long-range drone and missile attacks on cities throughout Ukraine, "[t]hey also circumvent the restrictions on the use of long-range missiles donated by supportive Western governments" (Kunertova, 2024, 10).

The Ukrainian national drone industry is booming. Observers estimate that there are around 200 companies in Ukraine that produce aerial drones, and still others that are producing ground based and maritime drones. Other countries are learning from Ukraine how to use—and produce—drones and AI tools for the battlefield. As Ling observes "[e]ntrepreneurship and innovation is scaling up a sizable drone industry in the country, and it's making new technological leaps that would make the Pentagon envious" (Ling, 2024). It is nothing new that economy matters in war. But Ukrainian drone manufacturers are allowed to charge a profit of up to 25% even though wartime economies usually discourage profiteering, and are supported by Bravel, a government-run incubator and technology agency that was set up in 2023. Ukraine's government also makes use of crowd-funding with its platform United24 and Army of Drones project (Ling, 2024).

But the role of civilians on the wider, national battlefield goes beyond being a target for attack to affect morale and political decision-making or national manufacturing power. The Russo-Ukrainian war shows that "civilians in modern warfare constitute a sub-system within the broader ecosystem of the conflict, thereby transcending their traditional roles" (Rakov & Fainberg, 2023, 3). By using personal smartphones and digital solutions in cyber space, and taking on a wide range of roles from intelligence gathering over early warning to documentation of attacks and suspected war crimes, civilians "have weaponized the digital space, influencing the dynamics of the battlefield and states' ability to achieve their strategic objectives" (Rakov & Fainberg, 2023, 3). The role of social media became visible in the Arab Spring and Syrian civil war, decentralizing news sources and enabling the organization of large numbers of individuals in spontaneous bottom-up processes. And digitalization processes have only picked up speed. It is thus not surprising that the battle in the information and cyber space has become more important, as well as digital strategic communication and leadership (see also Robin's chapter in this volume for the construction of terrorist propagandists as fighters). Ukrainian President Zelensky's "mastery of the digital front" (as Rakov and Fainberg 2023, 4 call it) has sparked detailed analyses of his social media communication strategy, the "Zelensky method," heralded as blueprint for others (Carey, 2022), "that conceives social networks as one more part of the battlefield" (Plazas-Olmedo & López-Rabadán, 2023, 188). This underscores social media's importance for the contemporary battlefield.

At the national level of the battlefield, the importance of citizen support and the key role of the industrial base reflect earlier expansions of the battlefield to include cities and industrial centers as core targets in armed conflict. The importance of Ukraine's drone industry, much of it comprised of small and highly innovative start-up has, however, expanded the understanding of which industry sectors are important for the war-time economy and how these can be incentivized. Meanwhile, social media has increased the variety of roles that civilians play in war and opened up a "digital front" on which successful communication strategies are crucial for maintaining morale and citizens' support. Similar to the frontline level, the middle, or core, of the national layer of the battlefield in the Russo-Ukrainian war—morale, mobilization, and industrial capacity—has not changed; but it has widened to include industrial sectors that were previously at the margins (drones, AI) and the digital domain as targets, as well as foundations for battlefield success.

International Support: The Third Layer of the Battlefield

In its war effort, Ukraine largely depends on Western support in the form of financial and military donations. Russia also is dependent on support and weapons from state actors such as China, North Korea, and Iran. International companies and private citizens also play a large role on this war's battlefield. This section thus looks at the third layer of the battlefield, the one that goes beyond the national borders of Russia and Ukraine.

While Russia has greatly increased national military production, it also relies on foreign supplies from China, Iran, and North Korea. This includes personnel: as mentioned earlier, soldiers from North Korea helped defeat the Ukrainian incursion into Russia's Kursk region. In a war of attrition, the side that more readily can replace lost soldiers and equipment, including the enormous amounts of ammunition used, and is willing to accept large numbers of losses, generally has the upper hand. When population mass and the strength and production capacity of the defense industrial base are the decisive factors, Russia has the advantage over Ukraine. Ukraine is thus dependent on Western military and financial support in order not to lose the war to Russia. An end of U.S. assistance to Ukraine, without other countries stepping in to fill the void, "would likely tip the balance in favor of Russia" (Jones & McCabe, 2025, 11). Russia thus hopes to win on the battlefield, if the US can be convinced to end its assistance.

As a consequence of the importance of international support, both sides are trying to end the assistance given to the opponent. Western governments have imposed sanctions on individuals and companies in third states that help Russia circumvent the sanctions implemented against it. They have also imposed sanctions on Belarus, Iran, and North Korea for supplying Russia with military equipment (Mills, 2025). At the time of writing, there is increasing support for a bipartisan bill in the U.S. that would impose harsh sanctions on countries that purchase Russian oil (Jimison, 2025). Russia has imposed retaliatory sanctions, but also targeted international support for Ukraine with wide-ranging hybrid activities that range from assassination attempts (for example against the CEO of Rheinmetall, a leading European arms manufacturer) over sabotage (such as cyber-attacks on critical infrastructure and damaging submarine cables) to disinformation and fake news campaigns (Plesner & Oien, 2025). While these activities are designed to remain below the threshold of armed conflict to avoid triggering a conventional war between Russia and NATO, many of the actions involve physical damage and destruction and some even (planned) death; and many of the targets are directly linked to support for Ukraine. The level of activities has led observers to call it "shadow war" (Jones, 2025), with former German foreign minister Annalena Baerbock noting that "Russia is waging a hybrid war of aggression" (Mahnke, 2024). While the impact of the individual actions is limited, this is a clear attempt by Russia to diminish Western support for Ukraine as well as increase the discord between Western allies with the aim to weaken cohesion within NATO and the EU. This might not be conventional war, but is part of the battlefield in the war between Russia and Ukraine.

Some of the targets of these activities have been international private companies, which play a significant role on the battlefield, not just through delivering crucial military technology such as weapons systems, ammunitions, and drones, but also through battlefield communication, intelligence processing, or targeting assistance. In the early days of the war, a large-scale Russian cyber-attack hit Viasat's KA-SAT satellite network in an attempt to disrupt Ukraine's military command and control. This caused widespread communication outages in Europe affecting over 30,000 terminals across various sectors (Reuters, 2022). Nevertheless, the feared large-scale cyber war on Ukraine did not materialize. Not because the cyber domain did not play a role as part of the battlefield, but rather because Ukraine's cyber defenses were effective in defending against Russian cyber operations and Ukraine has a significant amount of international support in the cyber realm. US Cyber Command and NATO allies have been providing support to Ukraine to strengthen the country's cyber capabilities, and big international IT companies, such as Amazon and Microsoft also assisted with comprehensive support. Moreover, SpaceX's Starlink satellite internet service has played a major role in strengthening Ukraine's cyber resilience and military command and control (Kurosaki, 2023). Yet, the reliance on other states and private companies poses a significant vulnerability for Ukraine. President Trump has on several occasions halted or threatened to halt military aid to Ukraine to pressure the country in negotiations; and during the negotiations for a deal on critical minerals between the US and Ukraine negotiators allegedly threatened the possibility of curtailing Ukraine's access to the vital Starlink system (Shalal & Roulette, 2025).

Just like "the digital front" was important on the national level, it also has an international dimension that goes beyond more traditional diaspora support and a global audience. Aside from foreign volunteers that join the frontline fight in Ukraine (see Carlson in this volume regarding the phenomenon of foreign fighters), Ukraine is supported by another army of international volunteers: the "IT Army of Ukraine," a global digital community that conducts a wide range of cyber operations against Russian targets and in defense of Ukrainian cyber infrastructure. The members of this army remain physically in their home countries, but receive instructions from Ukraine through social networks, i.e. Telegram. Kurosaki calls this a "notable form of belligerency, owing to cyberspace, without geographical or temporal limits" (Kurosaki, 2023, 341). The cyber domain is part of the battlefield in Ukraine, and the war is fought globally through individuals, companies, and third states. Additionally, international individuals have also contributed in other digitally enabled ways, for example through private donations, fundraising, or crowdsourcing of drone technology for Ukraine (Kunertova, 2024).

Also for the international layer of the battlefield the same pattern emerges: more traditional core aspects of the battlefield in attrition warfare, such as the ability to replenish ranks and equipment through international support, continue to play a key role. However, information and communications technology expands the battlefield beyond the national borders of the warring parties through the involvement of private companies, individuals, and a diverse range of hybrid activities to undermine other states' critical support.

The three layers of the battlefield identified here are interconnected in their middle and margins. While the war can be lost on any layer—through defeat on the frontline, loss of morale and/or industrial capacity on the national level, or through the loss of international support—it needs to be won on all three layers simultaneously. An analysis of the middle and margins of the battlefield helps to uncover and understand these dynamics of interaction between the layers.

Conclusion: The Changing Margins and Middle of the Battlefield and the Battlefields of the Future

This chapter has analyzed the development of the margins and middle of the battlefield. As Megret notes, "the idea of the battlefield captures more of what constitutes war as an activity than many other indictors" (Megret, 2011, 132). Zooming in on the movement of actors, technologies, and capabilities from the margins to the middle and vice versa of the battlefield deepens our understanding of the armed conflict in question and its dynamics. As the case study of the Russia-Ukraine war shows, the margins and middle lens enables the identification of a battlefield that exists on several layers, each with their own margins and middle. It also helps with the identification of the interactions between the layers of the battlefield and leads to a realization that, while the war can be lost on any of the layers, it will need to be won on all three. To the astute observer of the war, this conclusion might not come as a surprise. But uncovering the margin/middle movements of actors, technology, and other aspects of war, as well as the interaction between the margins and middle, allows us to identify blind spots in understandings of what the battlefield looks like.

Developments in weapons and communication technology and resulting changes to means and methods of warfare have caused the battlefield to become more detached from its geographical limits. At least in certain aspects it has become globalized. Also the temporal aspect has shifted, allowing for never-ending operations against illusive enemies. While the battlefield in the war against Ukraine includes a very real, geographically bounded frontline, it also includes global cyber space and a campaign of hybrid activity that brings the battlefield to its vanishing point, making it increasingly difficult to determine its boundaries.

Boundless battlefields, however, no longer provide war with limitations. When the battlefield is everywhere at all times, the rules for the protection of civilians risk losing their meaning; and so does the understanding that the use of armed force in international relations is the exception, and not the normal state of affairs. This chapter has shown that opponents attempt to shape the battlefield to their advantage. Insurgents, for example, hide among the population to avoid open conventional military confrontation; and to avoid Western conventional military superiority, competitors employ hybrid activities below the threshold of armed conflict. There is a risk, however, that "every deconstruction of the battlefield by one party is accompanied by a similar move to further deconstruct the battlefield by the other party" (Megret, 2011, 141). This threatens not only the international rules-based order by undermining its fundamental principle of peaceful relations between states; it also risks substantially weakening liberal values, fundamental freedoms, and democratic processes in liberal democracies. Uncovering how the idea of the battlefield and what constitutes its margins and middle changes over time is the first step toward securing not only the ability to fight—and win—the next war, but also to preserve important values and freedoms in the process.

References

Biddle, S. (2023). Back in the trenches: Why new technology hasn't revolutionized warfare in Ukraine. *Foreign Affairs, 102*(5), 153–164.

Birch, M. (2016). What's in a battlefield? Disappearing boundaries and the selective use of sanctioned killing. *Medicine, Conflict and Survival, 32*(1), 4–13.

Boyer, D., & Becker, R. K. (2024). *How Ukraine overcame the transparent battlefield to achieve operational surprise in Kursk* (Red Diamond). U.S. Army Training and Doctrine Command, G-2. https://g2webcontent.z2.web.core.usgovcloudapi.net/OEE/Red%20Diamond/TRADOC_19AUG2024_UKR_Battlefield_Operational_SUrprise_Kursk_Boyer_Becker.pdf

Brooks, R. E. (2004). War everywhere: Rights, national security law, and the law of armed conflict in the age of terror. *University of Pennsylvania Law Review, 153*(2), 675–761.

Carey, J. (2022). The Zelensky method: How to win hearts, minds and algorithms. *Influence, Q4*. https://influenceonline.co.uk/The-Zelensky-method-How-to-win-hearts,-minds,-and-algorithms

Chinkin, C., & Kaldor, M. (2017). *International law and new wars*. Cambridge University Press.

Chylińska, D. (2020). "Nameless landscapes"—What can be seen and understood on a battlefield? *Tourism Geographies, 22*(4–5), 787–812.

Crombe, K., & Nagl, J. A. (2023). A call to action: Lessons from Ukraine for the future force. *The US Army War College Quarterly: Parameters, 53*(3).

Dudziak, M. L. (2012). *War time*. Oxford University Press.

Field Manual 3-0 Operations. (2025). Department of the Army, United States.

Filkins, D. (2009). *The forever war*. Vintage.

Gardener, F. (2022, July 7). *Ukraine war: Is the tank doomed?* BBC. https://www.bbc.com/news/uk-61967180

Gasser, H.-P. (1993). *International humanitarian law: An introduction*. Paul Haupt Publishers. https://icrcndresourcecentre.org/wp-content/uploads/2016/03/EnglishTotal.pdf

Geiß, R. (2006). Asymmetric conflict structures. *International Review of the Red Cross, 88*(864), 757–777.

Gregory, D. (2011). The everywhere war. *The Geographical Journal, 177*(3), 238–250.

Gross, M. J. (2011, March 2). A declaration of cyber war. *Vanity Fair*. https://www.vanityfair.com/news/2011/03/stuxnet-201104

Halliday, J. (2010, September 24). Stuxnet worm is the "work of a national government agency." *The Guardian*. https://www.theguardian.com/technology/2010/sep/24/stuxnet-worm-national-agency

Henckaerts, J.-M., Doswald-Beck, L., & Alvermann, C. (Eds.). (2009). *Customary international humanitarian law. Vol. 1: Rules* (Reprint, with corr). Cambridge University Press.

Heuser, B. (2012) Denial of change: The military revolution as seen by contemporaries. *International Bibliography of Military History, 32*(1), 3–27.

Horbatenko, S. (2025, May 15). Fibre-optic drones replace drivers to deliver critical supplies to Ukraine's frontlines. *Radio Free Europe/Radio Liberty*. https://www.rferl.org/a/ukraine-war-fiber-optic-ground-drones-supplies/33415190.html

Horowitz, M. C., Kahn, L. A., & Schwartz, J. A. (2025, July 4). What drones can—And cannot—Do on the battlefield. *Foreign Affairs*. https://www.foreignaffairs.com/united-states/what-drones-can-and-cannot-do-battlefield

Jefferis, D. C. (2012). Battlefield borders, threat rhetoric, and the militarization of state and local law enforcement. *National Security Law Brief, 3*(1), 37–73.

Jimison, R. (2025, July 9). Thune says Russia sanctions vote could come as soon as this month. *The New York Times*. https://www.nytimes.com/2025/07/09/us/politics/russia-sanctions-senate-thune-trump.html

Johnson, D. (2022, August 25). Ending the ideology of the offense, Part II. *War on the Rocks*. https://warontherocks.com/2022/08/ending-the-ideology-of-the-offense-part-ii/

Jones, S. G. (2025). *Russia's shadow war against the west* (CSIS Briefs). Center for Strategic and International Studies. https://csis-website-prod.s3.amazonaws.com/s3fs-public/2025-03/250318_Jones_Russia_Shadow.pdf?VersionId=LHamL2L7HJwLgZ7a_wq6xkTIwMh3TFpk

Jones, S. G., & McCabe, R. (2025). *Russia's Battlefield Woes in Ukraine* (CSIS Briefs). Center for Strategic and International Studies. https://www.jstor.org/stable/resrep70744

Joshi, S. (2025). AI on the battlefield: A Fait Accompli? *Survival, 67*(2), 115–122.

Kaldor, M. (2012). *New and old wars: Organised violence in a global era* (3rd ed.). Polity Press.

Kaldor, M. (2013). In defence of new wars. *Stability: International Journal of Security and Development, 2*(1), 1–16.

Keen, D. (2010). *Endless war? Hidden functions of the "war on terror."* Pluto Press.

Khan, L. A. (2006). *A theory of international terrorism: Understanding Islamic militancy*. Martinus Nijhoff Publishers.

Kofman, M. (2024). 6. The Russia-Ukraine War: Military operations and battlefield dynamics. In H. Brands (Ed.), *War in Ukraine: Conflict, strategy, and the return of a fractured world* (pp. 99–120). Johns Hopkins University Press. https://muse.jhu.edu/pub/1/oa_edited_volume/chapter/3881920

Kunertova, D. (2024). *Learning from the Ukrainian battlefield: Tomorrow's drone warfare, today's innovation challenge*. Center for Security Studies, ETH Zurich.

Kurosaki, M. (2023). Unprivileged belligerency in a deterritorialized cyber battlefield? Some lessons learned from the Russia-Ukraine conflict. In S. Furuya,

H. Takemura, & K. Ozaki (Eds.). *Global impact of the Ukraine conflict* (pp. 339–357). Springer Nature Singapore.

Lewis, M. W. (2012). Drones and the boundaries of the battlefield. *Texas International Law Journal, 47*(2), 293–314.

Limaye, Y. L. (2025, May 28). *Fibre optic drones: The terrifying new weapon changing the war in Ukraine*. BBC News. https://www.bbc.com/news/articles/ckgn47e5qyno

Ling, J. (2024, March 2). Inside Ukraine's killer-drone startup industry. *Wired*. https://www.wired.com/story/ukraine-drone-startups-russia/

Mahnke, L. (2024, July 12). „Mit dem Schlimmsten rechnen“: Entsetzen über Putins Attentatsplan auf Rheinmetall-Chef Pappberger. *Merkur.de*. https://www.merkur.de/politik/entsetzen-reaktion-attentat-plan-rheinmetall-armin-pappberger-ukraine-krieg-russland-nato-gipfel-zr-93183397.html

Markoff, J. (2010, September 27). A silent attack, but not a subtle one. *The New York Times*. https://www.nytimes.com/2010/09/27/technology/27virus.html

Martin, J.-C. (2015). Theatre of operations. In M. Weller (Ed.), *The Oxford handbook of the use of force in international law* (pp. 752–772). Oxford University Press.

McRandle, J. H. (1994). *The antique drums of war*. Texas A&M University Press.

Megret, F. (2011). War and the vanishing battlefield. *Loyola University Chicago International Law Review, 9*(1), 131–155.

Mills, C. (2025). *Sanctions against countries supporting Russia's invasion of Ukraine*. House of Commons Library. https://commonslibrary.parliament.uk/research-briefings/cbp-10048/

Mittal, V., & Goetz, J. (2025). A quantitative analysis of the effects of drone and counter-drone systems on the Russia-Ukraine battlefield. *Defense & Security Analysis*, 1–14.

Münkler, H. (2005). *The new wars*. Polity Press.

Nabukhotny, V. (2025, June 10). *Ukrainian innovations are redefining the role of drones in modern war*. Atlantic Council. https://www.atlanticcouncil.org/blogs/ukrainealert/ukrainian-innovations-are-redefining-the-role-of-drones-in-modern-war/

NATO. (2023). *Alliance concept for Multi-Domain Operations (MDO)*.

O'Brien, P. P. (2022, May 26). War will never be this bulky again. *The Atlantic*. https://www.theatlantic.com/ideas/archive/2022/05/ukraine-russia-putin-war/638423/

O'Connell, M. E. (2010). The choice of law against terrorism. *Journal of National Security Law & Policy, 4*, 343–368.

Oxford English Dictionary. (n.d.). Battlefield. Retrieved August 1, 2024, from https://www.oed.com/search/dictionary/?scope=Entries&q=battlefield&tl=true

Perrett, B. (2024, January 22). Small, cheap and numerous: A military revolution is upon us. *The Strategist*. https://www.aspistrategist.org.au/small-cheap-and-numerous-a-military-revolution-is-upon-us/

Plazas-Olmedo, M., & López-Rabadán, P. (2023). Selfies and speeches of a president at war: Volodymyr Zelensky's strategy of spectacularization on Instagram. *Media and Communication, 11*(2), 188–202.

Plesner, F., & Oien, M. (2025, January 14). Kæmpe kortlægning viser Ruslands hybride angreb på Europa—TV 2. *nyheder.tv2.dk*. https://nyheder.tv2.dk/udland/2025-01-14-kaempe-kortlaegning-viser-ruslands-hybride-angreb-paa-europa

Rakov, D., & Fainberg, S. (2023). *The growing impact of the civilian population on the modern battlefield* (No. 0123E). Elrom Center for Air and Space Studies, Tel Aviv University; European Leadership Network.

Reuters. (2022, February 28). Satellite outage knocks out thousands of Enercon's wind turbines. *Reuters*. https://www.reuters.com/business/energy/satellite-outage-knocks-out-control-enercon-wind-turbines-2022-02-28/

Roosevelt, F. D. (1941, December 9). *On the war with Japan | Miller Center* (Vol. 19). National Archives. https://millercenter.org/the-presidency/presidential-speeches/december-9-1941-fireside-chat-19-war-japan

Sanger, D. E. (2012, June 1). Obama ordered wave of cyberattacks against Iran. *The New York Times*. https://web.archive.org/web/20170225103053/https://www.nytimes.com/2012/06/01/world/middleeast/obama-ordered-wave-of-cyberattacks-against-iran.html

Shalal, A., & Roulette, J. (2025, February 23). Exclusive: US could cut Ukraine's access to Starlink internet services over minerals, say sources. *Reuters*. https://www.reuters.com/business/us-could-cut-ukraines-access-starlink-internet-services-over-minerals-say-2025-02-22/

Shaw, M. (2003). *War and genocide: Organised killing in modern society*. Polity.

Siroli, G. P. (2018). Considerations on the cyber domain as the new worldwide battlefield. *The International Spectator, 53*(2), 111–123.

Sun Tzŭ. (1910). *Sun Tzŭ on the art of war: The oldest military treatise in the world* (L. Giles, Trans.). Luzac & Co. https://www.gutenberg.org/cache/epub/66706/pg66706-images.html

Terajima, A. (2025, April 1). *The rise and fall of Ukraine's Kursk gambit*. The Kyiv Independent. https://kyivindependent.com/the-rise-and-fall-of-ukraines-kursk-gambit/

Theussen, A., & Jakobsen, P. V. (2021). In the shadows: The challenge of Russian and Chinese gray zone conflict for the West. In S. Rynning, O.

Schmitt, & A. Theussen (Eds.), *War time: Temporality and the decline of western military power* (pp. 161–183). Brookings and Chatham House.

US Army TRADOC. (2018). *TRADOC Pamphlet 525-3-1.* https://adminpubs.tradoc.army.mil/pamphlets/TP525-3-1.pdf

Von Clausewitz, C. (1976). *On war* (M. Howard, Ed.). Princeton University Press.

Waltz, K. N. (1990). Nuclear myths and political realities. *The American Political Science Review, 84*(3), 731–745.

Wesley, E. J., & Simpson, R. H. (2020). *Expanding the battlefield an important fundamental of multi-domain operations* (No. 131; Land Warfare Paper). The Association of the United States Army. https://www.ausa.org/sites/default/files/publications/LWP-131-Expanding-the-Battlefield-An-Important-Fundamental-of-Multi-Domain-Operations.pdf

CHAPTER 5

The Middle-Ground Amidst Great (Cyber) Power Competition: From Pawns to Kingmakers?

Arthur P. B. Laudrain

Introduction

As Great Powers intensify their geopolitical rivalries, a new domain of confrontation has emerged over the past two decades. Cyberspace has infused into the practice of contemporary conflict, creating opportunities for states to project influence, disrupt adversaries, and ensure their sovereignty without resorting to traditional kinetic warfare. For middle-ground states, those that navigate between alignment with dominant blocs and the pursuit of strategic autonomy, cyber capabilities represent both a challenge and a transformative opportunity.

The concept of "middle-ground states" encompasses nations that neither fully align with Western-led liberal democracies nor authoritarian powers of the like of China and Russia. Instead, these states occupy

A. P. B. Laudrain (✉)
Center for Security Studies (CSS), ETH Zürich, Zürich, Switzerland
e-mail: arthur.laudrain@sipo.gess.ethz.ch

M. Robin et al. (eds.), *The Changing Fights and Fighters of Contemporary War*, https://doi.org/10.1007/978-3-032-05518-7_5

a distinct position in global politics. They balance complex relationships with competing powers while advancing their own regional and global interests. While India represents a typical middle-ground state with its foreign-policy roots in the non-aligned movement (Raghavan, 2017), Israel and North Korea deviate from the archetypal definition of middle-ground actors—particularly in terms of their broader geopolitical alignments. Israel and North Korea share commonalities in that sense. They are both supported by a Great Power (the United States and China, respectively) and have developed nuclear capabilities outside of the Non-Proliferation Treaty (NPT) for regime survival purposes. Although their interests often align with those of their Great Power patron, they have their own political agenda and autonomy, leading to occasional bilateral tensions.[1] However, their inclusion challenges and enriches the conceptual boundaries of what constitutes a middle-ground state, and their strategic behavior in the cyber domain reveals dimensions of middle-ground activity that are worth exploring. Indeed, despite their diversity in power, political direction, and strategic priorities, these three states share a commonality: their ability to leverage cyber tools to overcome conventional military and economic disparities, shaping contemporary conflict in ways that challenge traditional power hierarchies (Nye, 2009).

In this chapter's context, cyber capabilities refer to the tools, systems, and operations that enable states to exploit, defend, or operate within cyberspace, in its physical, logical, social, and information layers (Choucri & Clark, 2019). The use of the "cyber moniker" brings the risk of conceptual dilution, and warrants some precision if we are to use it (Futter, 2018). For the purpose of this study, cyber capabilities encompass offensive and defensive dimensions, influence operations, espionage, and cyber-electronic warfare integration.

Cyber capabilities are indeed tools, but they act as a transformative enabler that redefines power dynamics, strategies, and the operational capabilities of middle-ground states. It shifts the battlefield from geographic and kinetic arenas to a digital domain where states can project

[1] Despite North Korea's dependence on China as an economic lifeline, their alliance is fraught with mutual distrust and often diverging interests. Pyongyang behaves more like an independent, opportunistic actor than a client state. Indeed, North Korea is sometimes seen as more of a liability than a reliable ally for Beijing. This independent streak justifies treating North Korea as a middle-ground player for the purposes of this study, as it exploits Great Power tensions while resisting full alignment with any patron.

influence, disrupt adversaries, and assert sovereignty with great flexibility and precision if they so wish. It offers unique advantages to middle-ground states, enabling them to act as asymmetric players in the global arena. Unlike kinetic warfare, cyber operations are relatively low-cost, scalable, and provide some level of deniability (Clarke & Knake, 2010; Kello, 2017). This allows states with the political will, as well as technical and human resources, to conduct espionage, sabotage, and influence operations without risking direct confrontation and exposing its leadership to audience cost (Baum, 2004; Carson, 2018). At the same time, cyber operations expand the spectrum of conflict, blurring the lines between war and peace by enabling constant engagement below the threshold of traditional military escalation (Kello, 2017), and beyond the effects special operations can provide.

This chapter examines how cyber capabilities reshape the battlefield for middle-ground states, with Israel, India, and North Korea as case studies. While these states differ geopolitically, they all face complex relationships with major powers without fully aligning with any one bloc. India balances between the United States and China, Israel pursues regional autonomy while maintaining ties with the United States, and North Korea, despite its ties to China, hedges through engagement with Russia and diplomatic maneuvers. Together, these cases illustrate the diverse ways in which cyberspace and technologies shape conflict dynamics. The three cases represent distinct yet complementary cyber power models: Israel as an advanced cyber-military power, India as an emerging cyber power balancing regional threats, and North Korea as a disruptive cyber actor engaging in financial cybercrime and asymmetric operations. Despite different motivations and strategies, all three countries use cyber capabilities to influence regional and global security dynamics in ways that defy traditional military constraints.

Contemporary warfare is undergoing a transformation where traditional centers of power are dissolving into the margins, and marginal capabilities such as cyber operations are emerging as central determinants of conflict. The digital domain has not only provided a new arena for conflict but has also fundamentally altered the strategic calculus of states, even as they face challenges in managing resource constraints and ethical issues. Cyber, therefore, is not just a new tool. It is a transformative force that reshapes the very geography of power in international relations. In essence, this analysis situates itself within the broader discourse on asymmetric power projection in international relations, demonstrating how digital tools enable smaller or mid-tier states to challenge stronger actors while avoiding full-scale confrontation. In doing so, the chapter contributes to the wider discussion of cyber strategy and geopolitics by highlighting how the diffusion of cyber capabilities is reshaping state behavior, leveling aspects of the playing field, and providing middle-ground states with new avenues to assert their autonomy and influence.

The Cyber Domain as an Enabler

The proliferation of cyber capabilities has redefined the parameters of conflict, creating a battlefield that is less confined by physical geography or constrained by traditional notions of war. Unlike conventional domains, where force projection requires significant resources and physical presence, the cyber domain offers low-cost, high-impact tools that allow states of varying capabilities to compete asymmetrically. There are some controversies and limits to these characterizations, however. Cyberspace still very much relies on physical infrastructure (undersea cables, exchange points, server farms, etc.), but remains highly decentralized and mostly under private actors control. Similarly, there is increasing consensus that humanitarian law—and generally speaking international law—applies to the cyber domain (Schmitt & NATO Cooperative Cyber Defence Centre of Excellence, 2017). But, as a domain that facilitates covert operations due to difficulties in attribution and the multiplicity of state, state-aligned, and non-state actors, enforcing such principles are even more challenging than in traditional domains of warfare. In addition, there are limits to what can be achieved by offensive cyber operations. While some can get close to a kinetic effect, they bring trade-offs (resources and planning requirements, risks of detection and attribution, of collateral damages, etc.) and hardened targets might require traditional weaponry (Maschmeyer, 2021; Nye, 2017). Still, for middle-ground states, this transformation is particularly significant, as it enables them to counter more powerful adversaries, assert influence, and achieve strategic objectives in ways previously unattainable or only possible at prohibitive costs.

Key Attributes of the Cyber Domain

Cyberspace possesses several attributes that distinguish it from traditional theaters of conflict. These include its non-physical nature, inherent asymmetry, uncertainty in attribution, and the tendency toward continuous engagement.

First, cyberspace's partial non-physical nature means it transcends national borders, enabling actors to launch operations or conduct espionage from virtually anywhere. This challenges traditional notions of sovereignty and national security, as threats emanate from geographically diffuse sources (Boos, 2017). For instance, a ransomware attack launched from North Korea, such as the widely reported WannaCry incident attributed to the Lazarus Group, can cripple critical infrastructure in a distant country, bypassing traditional security mechanisms entirely (Ghafur et al., 2019). A massive ransomware attack that emerged in May 2017, WannaCry rapidly infected over 200,000 computers in 150 countries by exploiting a vulnerability in Microsoft Windows. The malware encrypted users' files and demanded a Bitcoin ransom in exchange for the decryption keys. Such attacks erode the utility of traditional border protection and force states to adopt new strategies of deterrence and constant vigilance, as we will see below. However, it also triggers a backlash in that it incentivizes states to reinforce traditional views of sovereign borders on the digital (Balzacq & Cavelty, 2016).

Second, cyberspace allows for greater asymmetry. Cyber operations are cost-effective compared to conventional military action, allowing states with limited resources to achieve outsized effects. Even advanced exploits require modest investments relative to a state budget (Kello, 2017). But they can yield significant financial, political, or strategic gains. For example, Iran's cyber capabilities were most likely developed at a fraction of the cost of its military budget, yet allowed it to target Saudi Aramco in 2012, disrupting 30,000 computers in a symbolic blow to its regional rival (Bronk & Tikk-Ringas, 2013). Cyber operations can also be outsourced to private proxies, whether for offensive, defensive, espionage, or influence purposes (Egloff, 2022). For middle-ground states, this levels the playing field, enabling them to challenge larger powers.

Third, the domain brings with it great uncertainty. Cyber operations are notoriously difficult to attribute, allowing states to act with plausible deniability. This ambiguity provides cover for aggressive actions while complicating retaliation or legal accountability. The difficulty of pinpointing the perpetrator is compounded by the use of proxy actors, which further obfuscates responsibility and allows for false-flags techniques. For instance, the TV5Monde attack first seemed to have been claimed by the Islamic State (*Daesh*), but strong suspicions quickly emerged that a Russian threat actor was behind it (Limonier, 2023).

Finally, unlike traditional conflict which tends to be episodic, cyber operations are constantly ongoing. States remain in constant engagement, conducting espionage, preparing infrastructure for future attacks, or spreading information manipulation, in what has been described as a state of unpeace (Kello, 2017). Practitioners and scholars alike have recognized that cumulative cyber activities can collectively yield significant strategic effects (Harknett & Smeets, 2022; Healey, 2019). By moving beyond traditional coercive tactics, the US doctrine of persistent engagement seeks to maintain the initiative through proactive operations, effectively transcending the conventional offensive-defensive dichotomy. This concept of "grey zone" operations, where coercive activities occur below the threshold of armed conflict, has been widely observed in Great Power cyber interactions (with mutual pre-positioning of implants on critical infrastructures between Russia, China, and the United States, for instance), and increasingly among middle-ground states (Mazarr, 2015). The use of cyber capabilities in the grey zone is not an anomaly but a deliberate strategy. It allows middle-ground states to shift power dynamics, shape adversaries' behavior, and secure strategic advantages with a lesser risk of triggering conventional military escalations. This approach also has implications for the development of cyber norms, as it encourages an environment of tacit bargaining and agreed competition, where states establish mutual understandings of acceptable behavior through repeated interactions, rather than relying solely on explicit agreements (Harknett & Fischerkeller, 2018).

Amplifying Asymmetry for Middle-Ground States

The inherent asymmetry of cyber capabilities offers middle-ground states tools to compensate for limitations in conventional military or economic power. These tools allow them to challenge stronger adversaries and protect their interests with fewer resources.

The first domain of activity is espionage and intelligence gathering. Cyber tools allow states to infiltrate adversary systems, gather sensitive information, and monitor activities continuously. While stronger adversaries might also invest in sophisticated intelligence capabilities, middle-ground states benefit from cyber espionage in two key ways. First, the decentralized and often poorly defended nature of networks means that even well-resourced adversaries can be penetrated using relatively inexpensive methods. Second, cyber intrusions are notoriously hard to detect and defend against, allowing middle-ground actors to harvest critical intelligence without the need for expensive traditional surveillance assets. A prime example is Israel's use of Pegasus spyware to gather intelligence on adversaries and counter threats at home (Antoniuk, 2023). This operational edge can level the playing field when facing adversaries with larger conventional intelligence apparatuses.

Looking at offensive operations, sabotage and preemptive strikes allow states to disable adversarial capabilities before conflicts escalate. Attacks on critical infrastructure, communications systems, or military assets can deter aggression or weaken an opponent's capacity without kinetic engagement. In situations like the Galwan Valley standoff, Indian cyber units have allegedly conducted operations to disrupt Chinese communications and command networks, thus degrading the enemy's operational readiness. Because these actions occur below the threshold, they allow India to deter aggression while maintaining plausible deniability and avoiding a kinetic response (Singh, 2024).

Cyber campaigns also extend the battlefield into the informational domain, where states can manipulate narratives, destabilize societies, and erode trust in institutions. These tactics are particularly valuable for middle-ground states seeking to influence their regional equilibrium without direct confrontation. North Korea, for instance, has been implicated in disinformation campaigns targeting its southern neighbor, designed to exploit social divisions and undermine public confidence in government institutions (Haggard & Noland, 2017).

Another key dimension of the cyber domain is its integration with electronic warfare (EW). Cyber tools complement EW by enabling precision targeting, disrupting enemy communications, and amplifying the effects of kinetic operations. By disrupting enemy communications or blinding radar systems, cyber operations can pave the way for more effective kinetic actions. This is particularly valuable for middle ground states, which might lack the sheer firepower or mass of their adversaries but can nonetheless create a significant operational advantage.

Cyber Capabilities as a (Relative) Force Multiplier for Middle-Ground States

Ultimately, this synergy allows middle-ground states to enhance their limited conventional assets with covert cyber interventions, effectively creating a force multiplier. However, this integration is effective only if the state also maintains a credible level of conventional military capability. In other words, while cyber-kinetic or cyber-EW integrations can disrupt adversary networks and degrade their command-and-control systems, the middle-ground state must still possess sufficient air, land, and naval power to respond to or deter further escalation by a stronger enemy. Without a robust conventional military backbone and/or a credible nuclear deterrent, cyber risks being countered by adversaries with overwhelming force. Thus, successful hybrid operations depend on a balanced portfolio: agile cyber capabilities to strike at vulnerabilities combined with credible conventional defenses to ensure overall deterrence and survivability in a contested environment. This also raises the stakes, as adversaries increasingly adopt countermeasures and escalate their own cyber capabilities in response.

Finally, the strategic value of cyber operations remains a disputed topic (Harknett & Smeets, 2022; Maschmeyer, 2021). There is an increasing consensus that cyber operations are insufficient on their own to shape the battlefield—least against a more powerful adversary (Kostyuk & Zhukov, 2019), in particular in an all-out conflict (Pedersen & Jacobsen, 2024). Yet, as we will see in the case studies below, cyber capabilities are most potent for the middle-ground when leveraged against peer or greater-than-peer adversaries, whether they are powerful state-sponsored proxies, paramilitary groups, or neighbors.

Case Studies: Reconfiguring Asymmetric Power and Conflict

The role of cyber capabilities in reshaping the battlefield for middle-ground states is best understood through specific examples. Israel, India, and North Korea represent three diverse cases of how middle-ground actors leverage cyber capabilities to project power, enhance strategic autonomy, and influence regional and global conflicts. These states employ cyber tools to complement their existing strengths or offset conventional weaknesses, using tactics ranging from sabotage and espionage to financial theft and influence operations.

Israel: A Cyber Power by Necessity

Israel's status as a cyber power is closely tied to its broader national security strategy, which emphasizes deterrence, preemption, and adaptability (Freilich, 2018). Cyber capabilities amplify these goals, enabling Israel to extend its reach beyond its geographic limitations, neutralize adversaries without resorting to conventional military engagements, and maintain a strategic edge in a volatile region. As a middle-ground state, Israel uses cyber tools not only to manage asymmetric threats from non-state actors like Hezbollah and Hamas but also for diplomacy and influence. Its capabilities span offensive cyber operations, electronic warfare integration, and global cybersecurity leadership.

Espionage and Preemptive Sabotage

One of Israel's most notable operations is the Stuxnet attack on Iran's nuclear facilities, executed in collaboration with the United States. Stuxnet, a sophisticated malware discovered in 2010 but suspected of having been deployed years beforehand, targeted the centrifuges at Iran's Natanz facility, causing them to suffer early failures while presenting false operational readings to Iranian engineers (Zetter, 2015). The operation delayed Iran's nuclear ambitions significantly, buying time for international diplomacy and thus avoiding kinetic strikes from Israel (Lindsay, 2013).

This covert operation allowed Israel (in collaboration with other actors) to neutralize a potential regional threat while avoiding the political, diplomatic, and collateral damage risks that would have come with an airstrike. Stuxnet was not just a technical breakthrough. It fundamentally reshaped the logic of warfare by proving that highly targeted, covert cyber operations can achieve strategic objectives traditionally reserved for kinetic strikes.

This challenges traditional notions of warfare, where kinetic operations were once seen as the only credible means of altering a state's strategic posture.

Beyond sabotage, Israel has excelled in cyber espionage. The Pegasus spyware, developed by NSO Group, has been used to infiltrate communications networks and gather intelligence on adversaries and private citizens alike across a dozen countries. While officially marketed as a tool for counterterrorism, reports suggest its use in a range of geopolitical contexts, including monitoring high-level adversaries and ensuring preemptive security measures. Such incidents have drawn criticism from human rights organizations and strained Israel's diplomatic relations with some allies (Dumbrava, 2023). Domestically, Israel faces debates over the balance between security and privacy. Critics argue that unchecked cyber surveillance could erode democratic norms, particularly if used against political dissenters or minority groups. These concerns highlight the need for clear oversight mechanisms to prevent the misuse of cyber tools.

Pegasus, and other similar spywares, function as a potent cyber intelligence tool. They grant real-time access to devices, allowing operators to monitor conversations, track movements, and remotely activate cameras and microphones. This level of surveillance enables Israel to gather critical information about potential adversaries, which can inform preemptive measures and strategic decision-making. Such capabilities blur the traditional line between espionage and cyber warfare, making covert intelligence gathering an integral part of deterrence and power projection.

More broadly, the deployment of Pegasus and other spywares signals that contemporary warfare is increasingly about information dominance. Instead of relying solely on kinetic forces or overt military actions, states now use digital surveillance to shape the battlefield before a conflict even begins. By monitoring high-level officials, Israel can anticipate troop movements, disrupt potential threats, and exert a form of asymmetric power that can compensate, to an extent, for conventional military shortcomings. This approach reflects a broader trend in warfare where non-kinetic operations such as cyber surveillance, disinformation, and psychological operations are becoming decisive components of traditional military engagements.

Cyber-Electronic Warfare Integration

While EW primarily manipulates the electromagnetic spectrum to jam or deceive enemy sensors and communications, cyber operations exploit vulnerabilities to achieve similar or complementary effects.

Operation Orchard, which took place in 2007, provides a compelling example of this synergy. In this covert strike, Israeli jets destroyed a suspected Syrian nuclear reactor near Deir ez-Zor. Before the airstrike, Israel deployed cyber capabilities to neutralize Syria's Russian-supplied anti-access/area denial (A2/AD) systems, including radar and air defense networks. Reports suggest Israeli cyber forces compromised Syrian radar systems, effectively "blinding" them by injecting false signals or shutting them down entirely (Couretas, 2024). This cyber-enabled disruption allowed Israeli aircraft to penetrate heavily defended airspace undetected, ensuring the success of the mission without prolonging the engagement.

More recently, the Lebanon Pager Attack (2024), marked a groundbreaking combination of supply chain interception, cyber-physical implants, and kinetic action. Hezbollah, concerned about the pervasive Israeli espionage capabilities, as we demonstrated with Pegasus, abandoned cell phones in favor of pagers and walkie-talkies. This move was intended to shield their communications from digital surveillance. Unbeknownst to them, Mossad had compromised the supply chain, modifying their firmware and embedding explosives in these devices and distributing them through a front company (Berg, 2024).

In two separate waves, Israel sent a fake message to the devices purporting to be from Hezbollah leadership, and shortly after remotely detonated thousands of compromised pagers and walkie-talkies across Lebanon and Syria. The attack eliminated 1500 Hezbollah fighters and injured over 2750 people, including Iran's ambassador to Lebanon. As a secondary effect, it severely disrupted command-and-control structures and put into question the trust operatives had into their own equipment.

At first glance, the act of physically embedding explosives in communication devices might seem "old school," reminiscent of traditional sabotage, and not a *prima facie* cyberattack (Lin, 2024). However, this operation was the product of sophisticated tactics aimed at hijacking a supply chain and manipulating device firmware. Rather than using traditional EW jamming or cyber-intrusions, Israel weaponized Hezbollah's own communication devices, turning them into targeted explosives. This approach represents a new form of kinetic warfare, where software and hardware sabotage lead directly to casualties.

Conclusion

Israel's documented use of cyber weapons and tools shows well how middle-ground states can leverage these capabilities to amplify their influence and address security challenges. By integrating cyber capabilities with traditional military ones, Israel achieves precision and reach that exceed its geographic or economic limitations. In particular, its focus on countering asymmetric threats ensures its relevance in a region marked by instability. At the same time, Israel's dominance in and beyond the cyber domain raises questions about the ethical and political dimensions of its capabilities and use by the private sector against civil society targets.

India: Sovereignty and Regional Leadership

India's approach to cyber capabilities reflects its dual priorities: safeguarding sovereignty in a volatile neighborhood and asserting regional leadership in the Indo-Pacific. As a quintessential middle-ground state with non-aligned roots, India seeks to leverage cyber power not only as a defensive necessity but as a proactive instrument of statecraft. While India is often portrayed as hedging between major global powers, in the regional context it is primarily countering Chinese assertiveness and Pakistani destabilization. By building both offensive and defensive cyber capabilities, fostering technological self-reliance, and engaging in cyber diplomacy, India positions itself as a key actor in regional and global cyber governance. These efforts demonstrate India's intent to reshape conflict dynamics on its own terms, using cyberspace to deter aggression and project influence without escalating to full-scale warfare. Whether these efforts will materialize into enough capabilities remain to be seen.

Part of the Arsenal Against Regional Threats

India's geographic position and persistent border tensions shape its cyber strategy in a uniquely proactive way. Facing conventional threats from both China and Pakistan, India has not simply adopted cyber tools to plug defensive gaps. It has sought to transform its digital infrastructure into a strategic asset. The establishment of the Defence Cyber Agency (DCA) in 2019—an integrated military cyber command—and the inclusion of cyberspace in the 2017 Joint Armed Forces Doctrine signaled India's intent to develop offensive cyber capabilities (Basu, 2022). High-level officials have stressed the need to "build suitable response measures including the capability to conduct cyber operations" if required (Basu, 2022). Such statements from figures like Deputy National Security Advisor Arvind Gupta reinforced the push for a credible offensive option to hedge against external cyber threats, complementing India's traditional military deterrent. Notably, the DCA's formation was explicitly aimed at combating threats from "foreign hackers" from China and Pakistan (Singh, 2019), a recognition that India's primary security challenges in cyberspace emanate from these two fronts.

Importantly, India's cyber statecraft is integrated into its wider national strategy and foreign policy agenda (Devanny & Laudrain, 2025). Unlike other middle powers that may incorporate cyber capabilities solely for defense, India is leveraging its robust IT sector and digital economy to assert leadership. This proactive posture is evident in its alleged cyber operations during the Galwan Valley clash between Indian and Chinese troops (Temple-Raston, 2021). In late 2020, during the border standoff, a China-linked cyber campaign dubbed "Red Echo" injected malware into Indian power control systems. This led to a massive power outage in Mumbai, which Indian officials later attributed to a coordinated Chinese cyber-attack (Sanger & Schmall, 2021). The incident, causing trains to halt and hospitals to lose power, vividly demonstrated the potential of cyber operations to inflict disruption as a form of coercive signaling. In response, India ramped up its defenses around critical infrastructure and heightened its cyber vigilance. Reports also suggest Indian cyber units have been conducting reconnaissance on Chinese infrastructure, preparing for potential countermeasures, and signaling that India could answer cyber aggression in kind. Indeed, analysts observed an "acceleration in cyberspace" activity from India as well after the Galwan clash (Temple-Raston, 2021), indicating that India is willing to take preemptive or retaliatory cyber actions despite the asymmetry in capabilities.

India has long accused Pakistan of abetting cross-border terrorism and orchestrating cyber espionage and disinformation campaigns as part of its hybrid warfare toolkit. In turn, Indian cyber teams have reportedly targeted Pakistan's military and terrorist networks, seeking to disrupt communications, finance, and propaganda channels. For example, in 2019 Indian cyber units helped expose a network of Pakistan-linked social media pages that were spreading disinformation to fuel unrest in Kashmir. Investigations revealed that this coordinated manipulation network—which included Facebook pages masquerading as Kashmiri and Pakistani interest groups—was run by Pakistani military's public relations wing (ISPR) and was subsequently taken down (Gleicher, 2019). In neutralizing these networks, India blunted Pakistan's efforts to internationalize the Kashmir issue. Indian operatives have also worked to "disrupt adversary operations" by penetrating militant communications and infrastructure. On several occasions, unofficial Indian hacker groups retaliated against Pakistan-based actors, for instance following major terror attacks in 2016 and 2019, by defacing Pakistani government websites or claiming access to critical systems (Baezner, 2018). While often kept deniable or unattributed, these offensive measures serve a deterrent purpose. They signal to Pakistan that its cyber hostilities and proxy operations will face in-kind reprisals, thus reshaping the cost calculus of such conflicts.

India's current cyber capabilities and posture appear adequate for regional deterrence against Pakistan yet still lag behind China's capabilities. This raises questions about its long-term strategic effectiveness amid escalating bilateral tensions. In this way, India employs cyber capability as a tool of both deterrence and preemptive action against its regional adversaries, filling the gap between mere diplomatic protest and a potentially escalatory military response.

Technological Sovereignty and Domestic Cyber Policy

A cornerstone of India's cyber strategy is its pursuit of technological sovereignty. Recognizing the risks of dependency on foreign technology, the country has launched ambitious initiatives like Digital India to promote domestic innovation and build resilient digital infrastructure. Launched in 2015, it aims to transform the country into a digitally empowered society and knowledge economy. The program includes expanding internet access, improving digital literacy, and securing critical infrastructure. Measures such as nationwide cybersecurity training and the strengthening of CERT-In (India's Computer Emergency Response Team) have set the stage for a coordinated defense and incident response capability across government and industry.

The government has been pushing for data localization and indigenous platforms, in the hope of better controlling its information domain. The proposed Personal Data Protection Bill (and its successor legislation) mandate that sensitive personal data be stored on local servers, reducing reliance on foreign tech giants and guarding against unauthorized data access by foreign agencies. This focus on data sovereignty has been sharpened by rising cybersecurity concerns, including the misuse of popular foreign apps for espionage or influence operations. In a landmark move amid the 2020 border crisis, India banned 59 Chinese mobile apps including TikTok and WeChat, citing threats to national security and sovereignty (*The Economic Times*, 2020). The ban not only removed platforms deemed prone to Chinese surveillance but also signaled India's willingness to exercise its digital economic power as leverage in geopolitical disputes. By developing indigenous alternatives and asserting tighter control over its cyberspace, Delhi reduces vulnerabilities to foreign coercion. These efforts, coupled with international cyber cooperation initiatives (such as the Quad Cybersecurity Partnership in the Indo-Pacific), enhance India's capacity to shape regional cyber norms and assist smaller states, bolstering its image as an emerging "techno-security" leader.

Challenges and Ethical Concerns
Despite significant progress, India faces formidable challenges in fully realizing its cyber strategy. Resource constraints and capacity gaps remain impediments to building a truly robust cyber defense across all sectors. India's critical infrastructure, including energy grids, transportation networks, health services, and banking systems, remains vulnerable to sophisticated cyberattacks. For instance, in 2022 a ransomware attack attributed to a China-linked group crippled the AIIMS hospital in Delhi for days, exposing weaknesses in healthcare IT security and the risks to critical data. While institutions like CERT-In have improved incident response, the sheer scale of threats and vulnerabilities often outpaces the government's ability to address them. A shortage of skilled cybersecurity professionals further limits India's ability to reach its ambitions, as the demand for talent far exceeds supply in both the public and private sectors. While India appears to be taking the necessary steps to reinforce its posture and stature as a regional cyber power, it still contends with vulnerabilities in critical infrastructure and challenges in executing structural reforms and developing capabilities consistently. On the offensive side, debate remains as to what extent its declaratory stance is backed up by actual capabilities development, or if it will remain performative signaling (Devanny & Laudrain, 2025). Nonetheless, the overall trajectory indicates that India is striving to punch above its weight, using cyber capabilities as a force multiplier to complement its conventional deterrence.

India's cyber policies also spark domestic debates over privacy and civil liberties. Some government measures have been criticized for overreach. For example, authorities have repeatedly imposed internet shutdowns in the Kashmir Valley during periods of unrest, steps justified as security necessities to curb militant communications and misinformation, but which civil society groups argue undermine freedom of expression and access to information.

Conclusion

India's integration of cyber tools into its national security strategy is emblematic of a broader shift in the contemporary battlefield, where cyber operations are not just defensive necessities but strategic assets that can redefine power dynamics.

By employing offensive cyber capabilities against regional adversaries, India adds a layer of deterrence and first-strike option that can impede an opponent's plans without crossing the threshold of conventional war. In parallel, its efforts to achieve technological sovereignty enable India to assert greater influence in the Indo-Pacific. However, India's experience also illustrates the delicate balance middle powers must strike: leveraging innovation to enhance security and strategic autonomy, while coping with resource limitations and upholding the democratic principles that can be tested by the imperatives of *raison d'État* in an imperfect democracy.

North Korea: A Pillar of Its Regime Survival Strategy

North Korea's leadership has publicly declared cyber warfare as an "all-purpose sword"[2] alongside nuclear weapons and missiles, reflecting its centrality in the regime's survival strategy (Ji-Young et al., 2019).

North Korea's use of cyber capabilities highlights its reliance on asymmetric strategies to maintain regime stability, project influence, and challenge its adversaries despite significant economic and military constraints. With its conventional military capabilities limited by outdated technology and international sanctions, Pyongyang has turned to cyber tools as a low-cost, high-impact alternative to achieve strategic goals. Through financial cybercrime, espionage, and disruptive operations, North Korea has elevated itself to a significant actor in the cyber domain, demonstrating how even an isolated state can leverage cyberspace for outsized geopolitical impact.

Economic Cyber Operations: A Lifeline for the Regime

One of North Korea's primary uses of cyber capabilities is to generate revenue, circumvent international sanctions, and sustain its regime. North Korea's cyber program, led by units such as Bureau 121 under the

[2] "Cyberwarfare is an all-purpose sword that guarantees the North Korean People's Armed Forces ruthless striking capability, along with nuclear weapons and missiles."

Reconnaissance General Bureau, has executed some of the world's most lucrative financial cybercrimes.

In one of the most high-profile examples of state-sponsored cyber theft, North Korean hackers infiltrated in 2016 the SWIFT banking system to steal $81 million from the Bangladeshi central bank. Exploiting vulnerabilities in the bank's IT infrastructure, the attackers used sophisticated malware to initiate fraudulent transactions and mask their activity (Corkery & Goldstein, 2017). Although the operation was partially thwarted, it shows North Korea's ability to execute complex, global financial heists with significant economic and geopolitical implications.

In recent years, North Korea has expanded its focus to cryptocurrency theft, which offers anonymity and easier laundering compared to traditional financial systems. Reports estimate that North Korea stole over $400 million in cryptocurrency in 2021 alone (Chainalysis, 2022). These funds are believed to support the regime's nuclear weapons program, allowing Pyongyang to sustain its strategic ambitions despite crippling economic sanctions (Department of Justice, 2018).

Espionage

North Korea's cyber operations also serve as tools for espionage, targeting both governmental and private sector organizations to gather intelligence on adversaries and support strategic planning. North Korea has persistently targeted South Korea's government, media, and critical infrastructure.

Cyber units such as Lazarus Group have conducted espionage campaigns to infiltrate defense ministries, energy grids, and technology firms (Kim, 2024). These operations provide North Korea with valuable intelligence on South Korean military capabilities and economic vulnerabilities, reinforcing its ability to counterbalance its neighbor. North Korea's espionage efforts extend beyond the Korean Peninsula. The regime has targeted defense contractors, international financial institutions, and global human rights organizations to gather strategic information and disrupt adversarial operations (White et al., 2019).

Disruption and Coercion

In addition to financial and espionage focused operations, North Korea employs cyber tools to disrupt adversarial systems and coerce political concessions. In addition to creating leverage in international negotiations, these disruptive campaigns reinforce the regime's image as a formidable actor.

The Sony Pictures hack remains one of the most infamous examples of cyber coercion, although directed at a private actor. In response to the release of *The Interview*, a satirical film about an assassination plot against Kim Jong-un, North Korean hackers launched in 2014 a devastating cyberattack on Sony's networks. The attackers not only leaked sensitive corporate data such as unreleased films and plans, they also destroyed internal systems and issued threats of further harm (FBI National Press Office, 2014), leading Sony to cancel the release. The operation highlighted North Korea's willingness to use its offensive cyber capabilities to project influence globally and to retaliate against perceived slights to its leadership.

North Korea has repeatedly targeted South Korea's critical infrastructure, including power grids, transportation systems, and financial networks. These attacks aim to destabilize South Korean society, sow distrust in its government, and create opportunities for political leverage. For example, in 2013, a large-scale cyberattack attributed to North Korea disrupted South Korean banks and media organizations, causing widespread operational paralysis and public concern (Zetter, 2016). The scale and tempo of such operations is not expected to decrease. In 2025, the same Lazarus Group allegedly stole 1.5bn$ in crypto assets from ByBit (Tidy, 2025), and Kim Jong-Un has reportedly ordered the establishment of a new cyber unit, Research Centre 227, dedicated to both leveraging and exploiting AI tools (Joo, 2025).

Conclusion

This case study shows how the contemporary battlefield has transformed. North Korean cyber operations are not a supplement to conventional force but have become the very domain in which it wages war. Lacking the economic and military heft to project power on traditional battlefields, the regime has shifted its strategic focus to cyberspace, in conjunction to the development of its nuclear arsenal. In this new dimension of the battlefield, low-cost covert operations can deliver outsized geopolitical effects and have successfully coerced a large corporation. In parallel, state-sponsored cybercrime and digital espionage serve as North Korea's primary means of sustaining its regime and undermining adversaries. This reordering of the battlefield, from kinetic to digital, highlights that what was once relegated to the margins can, under the right conditions, assume a central destabilizing role.

Section Conclusion

The cases of Israel, India, and North Korea illustrate the diverse ways in which middle-ground states leverage cyber capabilities to achieve strategic objectives and reshape conflict dynamics. These states demonstrate the asymmetric potential of cyberspace, where limited resources and unconventional strategies can yield outsized impacts.

Israel shows how cyber tools can complement and enhance existing military power. By integrating cyber with kinetic and electronic warfare, Israel has neutralized advanced defenses, conducted precision strikes, and positioned itself as a global leader in cybersecurity. Its offensive operations, such as Stuxnet, and its targeted hacks on A2/AD systems showcase how cyber enables preemptive actions with minimal collateral damage.

India's approach reflects a dual focus on regional security and technological sovereignty. Faced with persistent threats from China and Pakistan, India employs cyber tools to safeguard its sovereignty and assert regional leadership. Its initiatives in data localization, indigenous technology development, and cyber capacity-building also underline its ambition to shape the Indo-Pacific's digital domain and counterbalance rival powers

North Korea's reliance on cyber capabilities highlights their potential role as a substitute for conventional strength. Through financial theft, espionage, and disruptive operations, North Korea sustains its regime, funds its weapons programs, and challenges adversaries like South Korea and the United States. Its actions, from the Bangladesh Bank Heist to the Sony hack, are good examples of the destabilizing or coercive potential of state-sponsored cybercrime.

Together, these cases illustrate how cyber capabilities transform middle-ground states into agile and influential actors, capable of altering power relations in contemporary conflicts. Despite their varied motivations and methods, these states collectively highlight the strategic value of cyberspace in the pursuit of national interests.

Conclusion

This study demonstrates that cyber capabilities have become a cornerstone of middle-ground states' strategic behavior amid Great Power competition. States that once had to between rival blocs now exploit cyberspace as a means to enhance their autonomy and influence without aligning fully with any side. The low-cost, scalable, and deniable nature of cyber operations makes this domain an ideal arena for such states to project power, hedge against stronger adversaries, and protect their sovereignty. As a result, countries like Israel, India, and North Korea are mobilizing cyber tools to transcend some of their traditional limitations, using these capabilities to secure their independence and shape outcomes in regional conflicts.

Each of the three case studies shows a distinct model of cyber power deployment, while sharing an underlying motive of leveraging asymmetry. Israel has embraced a sophisticated model that complements its conventional military strength. By integrating offensive cyber operations with electronic and kinetic warfare, it extends its strategic reach beyond what its small geography might suggest. India, similarly, sees cyber capabilities as vital for safeguarding sovereignty and bolstering its regional leadership. It has invested in both defensive and offensive tools, from establishing a dedicated cyber command to promoting indigenous technological development, reflecting a hedging strategy that balances threats from China and Pakistan. North Korea stands apart as an outlier. Lacking advanced conventional forces, it relies on cyber as a primary instrument of statecraft, using financial crime, espionage, and disruptive hacks to sustain the regime and challenge its adversaries. Thus, while Israel and India incorporate cyber as an enhancer of their existing power, North Korea adopts it as a substitute for it.

For all three states, cyberspace has become a major theater for geopolitical competition, allowing them to punch above their weight. Cyber operations enable these middle powers to counterbalance stronger adversaries and deter threats in ways that were previously out of reach. Israel, for instance, can hold regional foes like Iran at risk through covert strikes, while India can blunt pressures from China or Pakistan by threatening retaliation and disruption instead of risking open war. North Korea's heists and coercive operations put far more powerful nations than it on notice, showing that even a sanctioned, economically weak state can project influence internationally through cyberspace. In essence, cyber capabilities function as a strategic equalizer. They allow middle-ground states to impose costs on superior opponents and to extend their influence regionally and globally without the need for traditional force projection. This demonstrates how the cyber domain adds a new dimension to balance-of-power politics, providing these states with leverage disproportionate to their size or resources.

Finally, the rise of cyber conflict is fundamentally reshaping these states' strategic calculus. The ability to engage adversaries in the "grey zone" blurs the line between peace and conflict and allows continuous contestation without triggering traditional military responses. This, combined with the integration of the cyber dimension into conventional military plans, has expanded the spectrum of strategies available to middle-ground states. They can now calibrate their actions more finely, choosing when to provoke, disrupt, or remain covert, thereby managing risks in unprecedented ways. In effect, cyberspace has altered the cost-benefit equation. Actions that once might have been too escalatory or costly are increasingly viable options.

These case studies challenge the established dichotomy between center and margins, suggesting that the boundaries are now fluid and contested. In contemporary warfare, the margins can be as decisive as the center, and *vice versa*. They confirm that a state which masterfully wields cyber capabilities can shift from being a peripheral player to an influential force in international politics. Rather than remaining pawns in a Great Power game, middle-ground states with mature and directed cyber capabilities are increasingly able to shape outcomes and assert their agency—emerging, if not as true kingmakers, then certainly as far more consequential actors in the international plane.

References

Antoniuk, D. (2023, September 29). Israel allows police to use Pegasus spyware to probe killings of Palestinian citizens. *The Record*. https://therecord.media/israel-allows-police-pegasus-palestinians

Baezner, M. (2018). *Hotspot analysis: Regional rivalry between India-Pakistan. Tit-for-tat in cyberspace* (CSS cyber defense project). Center for Security Studies (CSS), ETH Zürich. https://css.ethz.ch/content/dam/ethz/special-interest/gess/cis/center-for-securities-studies/pdfs/Cyber-Reports-2018-01.pdf#:~:text=23,The%20Indian%20individual%20arrested%20in

Balzacq, T., & Cavelty, M. D. (2016). A theory of actor-network for cyber-security. *European Journal of International Security, 1*(2), 176–198.

Basu, A. (2022). *India's international cyber operations: Tracing national doctrine and capabilities* (No. 5; International cyber operations research paper series). UNIDIR. https://unidir.org/files/2022-12/UNIDIR_India_International_Cyber_Operations.pdf

Baum, M. A. (2004). Going private: Public opinion, Presidential Rhetoric, and the domestic politics of audience costs in U.S. Foreign Policy Crises. *The Journal of Conflict Resolution, 48*(5), pp. 603–631.

Berg, R. (2024, December 23). *Ex-Israeli agents reveal how Hezbollah pager attacks were carried out*. BBC News. https://www.bbc.com/news/articles/cwy3l02wxqdo

Boos, T. (2017). Geographies of cyberspace: Internet, community, space, and place. In T. Boos (Ed.), *Inhabiting cyberspace and emerging cyberplaces: The case of Siena, Italy* (pp. 13–38). Springer.

Bronk, C., & Tikk-Ringas, E. (2013). The cyber attack on Saudi Aramco. *Survival, 55*(2), 81–96.

Carson, A. (2018). *Secret wars: Covert conflict in international politics*. Princeton University Press.

Chainalysis. (2022). *North Korean hackers have prolific year as their unlaundered cryptocurrency holdings reach all-time high.* https://www.chainalysis.com/blog/north-korean-hackers-have-prolific-year-as-their-total-unlaundered-cryptocurrency-holdings-reach-all-time-high/

Choucri, N., & Clark, D. D. (2019). Cyberspace: Layers and Interconnections. In N. Choucri & D. D. Clark (Eds.), *International relations in the cyber age: The co-evolution Dilemma* (pp. 33–65). The MIT Press.

Clarke, R. A., & Knake, R. K. (2010). *Cyber war: The next threat to national security and what to do about it*. Harper Collins.

Corkery, M., & Goldstein, M. (2017, March 22). North Korea said to be target of inquiry over $81 million cyberheist. *The New York Times*. https://www.nytimes.com/2017/03/22/business/dealbook/north-korea-said-to-be-target-of-inquiry-over-81-million-cyberheist.html

Couretas, J. M. (2024). Tactical cyber effects. In [author] *Cyber operations: A case study approach* (195–204). Wiley.

Department of Justice. (2018, September 6). *North Korean regime-backed programmer charged with conspiracy to conduct multiple cyber attacks and intrusions* [Press Release]. Office of Public Affairs. https://www.justice.gov/opa/pr/north-korean-regime-backed-programmer-charged-conspiracy-conduct-multiple-cyber-attacks-and

Devanny, J., & Laudrain, A. P. B. (2025). *Interpreting India's cyber statecraft* (Research Paper). Carnegie Endowment for International Peace.

Dumbrava, C. (2023). *Investigation of the use of Pegasus and equivalent surveillance spyware (No. PE 747.923)*. European Parliamentary Research Service. https://www.europarl.europa.eu/RegData/etudes/ATAG/2023/747923/EPRS_ATA(2023)747923_EN.pdf

Egloff, F. J. (2022). *Semi-state actors in cybersecurity*. Oxford University Press.

FBI National Press Office. (2014, December 19). *Update on Sony investigation* (Press release). https://www.fbi.gov/news/pressrel/press-releases/update-on-sony-investigation

Freilich, C. D. (2018). Introduction. In C. D. Freilich (Ed.), *Israeli National security: A new strategy for an era of change* (pp. 3–13). Oxford University Press.

Futter, A. (2018). 'Cyber' semantics: Why we should retire the latest buzzword in security studies. *Journal of Cyber Policy, 3*(2), 201–216.

Ghafur, S., Kristensen, S., Honeyford, K., Martin, G., Darzi, A., & Aylin, P. (2019). A retrospective impact analysis of the WannaCry cyberattack on the NHS. *NPJ Digital Medicine, 2*(1), 1–7.

Gleicher, N. (2019, April 1). *Removing coordinated inauthentic behavior and spam from India and Pakistan*. Meta. https://about.fb.com/news/2019/04/cib-and-spam-from-india-pakistan/

Haggard, S., & Noland, M. (2017). *Hard target: Sanctions, inducements, and the case of North Korea*. Stanford University Press.

Harknett, R. J., & Fischerkeller, M. P. (2018, November 9). *Persistent engagement and Tacit bargaining: A path toward constructing norms in cyberspace*. Lawfare. https://www.lawfaremedia.org/article/persistent-engagement-and-tacit-bargaining-path-toward-constructing-norms-cyberspace

Harknett, R. J., & Smeets, M. (2022). Cyber campaigns and strategic outcomes. *Journal of Strategic Studies, 45*(4), 534–567.

Healey, J. (2019). The implications of persistent (and permanent) engagement in cyberspace. *Journal of Cybersecurity, 5*(1), 1–15.

Ji-Young, K., Jong In, L., & Kyoung Gon, K. (2019). *The all-purpose sword: North Korea's cyber operations and strategies*. 2019 11th International Conference on Cyber Conflict (CyCon), 900, pp. 1–20. https://doi.org/10.23919/CYCON.2019.8756954

Joo, J. T. (2025, March 12). N. Korea ramps up cyber offensive: New research center to focus on AI-powered hacking. *Daily NK English*. https://www.dailynk.com/english/n-korea-ramps-up-cyber-offensive-new-research-center-to-focus-on-ai-powered-hacking/

Kello, L. (2017). *The Virtual weapon and International order*. Yale University Press.

Kim, J. (2024, April 23). *North Korea hacking teams hack South Korea defence contractors—Police*. Reuters. https://www.reuters.com/technology/cybersecurity/north-korea-hacking-teams-hack-south-korea-defence-contractors-police-2024-04-23/

Kostyuk, N., & Zhukov, Y. M. (2019). Invisible digital front: Can cyber attacks shape battlefield events? *Journal of Conflict Resolution, 63*(2), 317–347.

Limonier, K. (2023). Chapitre 6. Le cyberespace, nouveau lieu de conflictualités géopolitiques. In [author]. *Introduction à la géopolitique* (2e éd. pp. 245–277). Armand Colin.

Lin, H. (2024, February 10). *Reflections on the Lebanon Pager Attack*. Lawfare. https://www.lawfaremedia.org/article/reflections-on-the-lebanon-pager-attack

Lindsay, J. R. (2013). Stuxnet and the limits of cyber warfare. *Security Studies, 22*(3), 365–404.

Maschmeyer, L. (2021). The subversive Trilemma: Why cyber operations fall short of expectations. *International Security, 46*(2), 51–90.

Mazarr, M. (2015). *Mastering the Gray Zone: Understanding a changing era of conflict*. U.S. Army War College Press. https://press.armywarcollege.edu/monographs/428

Nye, J. S. (2009). Get smart: Combining hard and soft power. *Foreign Affairs, 88*(4), 160–163.

Nye, J. S., Jr. (2017). Deterrence and dissuasion in cyberspace. *International Security, 41*(3), 44–71.

Pedersen, F. A. H., & Jacobsen, J. T. (2024). Narrow windows of opportunity: The limited utility of cyber operations in war. *Journal of Cybersecurity, 10*(1), 1–18.

Raghavan, P. S. (2017). The making of India's foreign policy: From non-alignment to multi-alignment. *Indian Foreign Affairs Journal, 12*(4), 326–341.

Sanger, D. E., & Schmall, E. (2021, February 28). China appears to warn India: Push too hard and the lights could go out. *The New York Times*. https://www.nytimes.com/2021/02/28/us/politics/china-india-hacking-electricity.html

Schmitt, M. N., & NATO Cooperative Cyber Defence Centre of Excellence (Eds.). (2017). *Tallinn manual 2.0 on the international law applicable to cyber operations* (2nd ed.). Cambridge University Press.

Singh, N. (2019, May 15). *India's new defence cyber agency*. MEDIANAMA. https://www.medianama.com/2019/05/223-indias-new-defence-cyber-agency-nidhi-singh-ccg-nlud/

Singh, T. K. (2024). *India's cybersecurity policy: Evolution and trend analyses* (1st ed.). Routledge.

Temple-Raston, D. (2021, September 21). Report: China-linked hackers take aim at Times of India and a biometric bonanza. *The Record*. https://therecord.media/report-china-linked-hackers-take-aim-at-times-of-india-and-a-biometric-bonanza

The Economic Times. (2020, July 29). India bans 59 Chinese apps including TikTok, WeChat, Helo. *The Economic Times*. https://economictimes.indiatimes.com/tech/software/india-bans-59-chinese-apps-including-tiktok-helo-wechat/articleshow/76694814.cms?from=mdr

Tidy, J. (2025, March 10). *North Korean hackers cash out hundreds of millions from $1.5bn ByBit hack*. BBC News. https://www.bbc.com/news/articles/c2kgndwwd7lo

White, E., Jung-a, S., & Findlay, S. (2019, November 7). Suspected North Korea hackers targeted Indian space agency. *Financial Times*. https://www.ft.com/content/ac6a8782-ffad-11e9-b7bc-f3fa4e77dd47.

Zetter, K. (2015). *Countdown to zero day: Stuxnet and the launch of the world's first digital weapon* (Reprint edition). Crown.

Zetter, K. (2016, February 24). The Sony hackers were causing Mayhem years before they hit the company. *Wired*. https://www.wired.com/2016/02/sony-hackers-causing-mayhem-years-hit-company/

CHAPTER 6

Peacemaking from the Peripheries: Lessons from the Women of Sudan on Informal Pathways to Peace

Jacqueline G. Burns

Introduction

One hot day in Abyei—a disputed territory nestled between Sudan and South Sudan—in the middle of 2013, I sat on a plastic chair under an Acacia tree surrounded by local Ngok Dinka women sitting on the ground or in a smattering of other plastic chairs. At the time, I was a U.S. diplomat seeking answers on how to create community-level drivers of peace amidst destabilizing pressures from Khartoum and Juba, both of which had laid claim to the region. The women told me of the hardships caused by continued conflict between their pastoralist communities, the migratory Misseriya herders from Sudan, a multitude of armed militias, and the Sudanese Armed Forces. Where communities had once coexisted, different pressures—political, environmental, economic—had led to devastating raids and armed conflict variably between communal groups,

J. G. Burns (✉)
University of California, Irvine, CA, USA
e-mail: jgburns@uci.edu

M. Robin et al. (eds.), *The Changing Fights and Fighters of Contemporary War*, https://doi.org/10.1007/978-3-032-05518-7_6

militias, and armed forces of the two states, which in turn resulted in the destruction of villages, markets, and livelihoods along with forced migration. Before traveling to Abyei, I was told this was a highly political and ethnically charged conflict; that the Ngok Dinka were fully aligned with the political institutions in South Sudan, and the Misseriya with Sudan. That there was no trust between the communities or their politically aligned capitals and that there was little hope for progress. As I sat there listening to these women speak passionately about the need for reconciliation, their desire to convene with the Misseriya women and find a way toward peace—beginning with reopening their markets in which Ngok Dinka and Misseriya bought and sold goods to each other—I heard a very different narrative. Their efforts underscored a critical but often overlooked reality: I argue that in conflicts where formal political institutions are weak or absent, informal institutions and networks—often led or occupied by women—become central to both war and peace.

Women have often been historically marginalized from formal institutions and markets, particularly in former colonies of the Global South. This has led women to occupy an outsized role in informal markets and institutions (Duncanson, 2016). As war has entered increasingly informal spaces (Kaldor, 2012), this chapter explores both how women's marginalization and their role in such informal spaces impact modern conflicts and peace outcomes. I argue that the movement of wars from formal to informal spaces has made women's roles throughout the conflict lifecycle—from the fomentation of conflict to the waging of war, to its resolution and the consolidation of peace—increasingly prominent. This chapter is focused primarily on women's activities toward achieving peace outcomes in conflict-affected areas. It will also touch upon the common interactions between women's marginalization and the changing nature of conflict that also impacts women's participation in the enactment of war. I begin with an overview of the increasingly informal nature of war and women's roles in informal spaces. I then provide an overview of the different ways in which the peace and conflict literature has shown women to engage in peace activities, as well as in war, as I underscore the theoretical argument that these activities are increasingly prominent in new wars. Following, I provide evidence of these activities and their impact in the case of Sudan, concluding the chapter with thoughts on future research and why these dynamics are important for the study of peace and conflict.

Women on the Peripheries and the Changing Nature of War

While debates within international relations and conflict scholarship may not agree on the degree to which war has truly changed in nature, there is a relative consensus that contemporary wars—or new wars, as Kaldor (2012) describes them—are heavily occupied by informal or non-state actors and fought in informal spaces. Formal institutions are typically defined by "officially sanctioned rules that structure human behavior and expectations around a particular activity" (Brinks et al., 2019, 7). I refer to formal actors, activities, and spaces as those explicitly sanctioned within formal institutions. With regards to formal actors, this would include formal state militaries, ministries, heads of state, legislatures, central banks, and so on. Formal activities include those actions governed and sanctioned by formal institutions, such as the writing of constitutions and national-level legal codes, state-sanctioned welfare programs, the waging of conventional war in line with national and international legal codes and norms, and trade and investments carried out within national and international legal codes and norms. Formal spaces would include officially sanctioned geographic and temporal boundaries in which certain activities are to take place—such as national elections being determined by legal codes to happen at certain times and locations, or war being determined to take place only once officially declared within legal and normative constraints of justification and proportionality, and between easily identifiable combatants. As Kaldor (2012) details, however, new wars increasingly involve informal, non-state actors—including non-state militias, terrorist organizations, and criminal networks; include informal activities—such as illicit financing through smuggling, drug trafficking, and kidnapping; and take place in informal spaces that blur the lines between combatant and noncombatant and battlefield and civilian spaces. This includes raids and attacks on civilian populations to force displacements, terrorist attacks in civilian areas, cyber warfare, and so on.

I argue that the blurring between the formal and informal during conflict is particularly acute in states that lack strong institutions. This is true in many former colonies in the Global South, as their economies and formal political institutions were developed as commodity producers which created long-term relations of domination and subordination, keeping political institutions weak and state economies dependent (Kohli, 2020). As Marriage (2013) has argued, when many African states became independent, the social contracts between states and their populations that are the backbone of formal institutions and state security in the Global North were never established, with personalized systems of rule and international interventions that perpetuated systems of dependency becoming the norm. These personalized systems of rule—such as in the Democratic Republic of Congo, as noted by Marriage, and in Sudan, as discussed in this chapter—often operate in an intentional state of informality, relying on informal militias and economies to achieve goals, which tend to be focused on the security of the regime rather than the security of the population or state institutions.

The prominence of informal institutions, economies, and markets in many former colonies of the Global South has created a space in which women and other groups that have been historically marginalized from formal institutions and markets can sustain their livelihoods and exercise their agency. Within this dynamic, marginalized groups, and particularly women, tend to be overrepresented in informal sectors. These informal sectors include care, reproductive, and subsistence labor overwhelmingly carried out by women, particularly in informal economies where income-generating labor is scarce and often available only to men when available at all (Cohn & Duncanson, 2020; Consortium on Gender, Security and Human Rights 2017; UN Women, 2015). It is important to note that the informality of these sectors does not mean they have less impact on political or economic systems and realities within a given state. Informal sectors have significant influence, particularly in states that lack strong formal institutions, and have been shown to have significant influence in conflict-affected states in the Global South (see Cohn & Duncanson, 2020; Duncanson, 2016; Holland, 2017). Not only are these informal sectors the backbone of formal economic activities and responsible for the livelihoods of vast swaths of the populations in the Global South, but non-state actors have shown their ability to leverage resources through informal markets and institutions and deliver goals not in control of the state or formal institutions. In the case of new wars, as we have seen, this can be through privatized violence or illicit activities, or in support of peace outcomes as will be discussed in the next sections of this chapter.

This chapter argues that in an era of informal warfare, women's outsized role in informal markets and institutions—particularly in former colonies of the Global South where the majority of contemporary wars are being fought—has become increasingly important for conflict and peace outcomes. This has moved women—once seen at the margins of conventional warfare as they were often excluded from state militaries and formal political institutions—to a more prominent role in conflicts. This echoes a flurry of recent research into the importance of women in peacemaking and peacebuilding activities, where women's substantive participation and inclusion have been shown to improve the sustainability of peace (Adjei, 2019; Cohn, 2013; Ellerby, 2016; Krause et al., 2019). It should also be noted that women may be incentivized to participate in conflict—whether through armed or peaceful means—due to their structural marginalization. Research into women's activities in both combat and peacebuilding activities has highlighted that the reasons often given by individual women are a desire to improve their and their families' living conditions through renegotiated norms of women's place in society. In the case of Boko Haram, the extreme marginalization of women in the modern Nigerian state has led many women to turn to the elevated place given to women under Boko Haram's interpretation of Sharia law as a means of emancipation (Matfess, 2017). During conflicts in Rwanda and Botswana, women were able to take—at least temporarily—advantage of their increased roles and responsibilities in the informal sectors for grassroots networking and political mobilizing for greater economic and political equality (Berry, 2018). I argue that these opportunities for women to take advantage of conflict to improve their livelihoods and situation are more abundant in informal war, as women, as noted previously, were often excluded from or marginalized within the formal institutions involved in conventional, state-based warfare.

Women as Agents for Peace

This section provides an overview of the different ways in which the peace and conflict literature has shown women to engage in peace activities. This chapter is focused on women's informal pathways to achieving peace outcomes, as I argue that women's overrepresentation in informal sectors and institutions leads them to be particularly important actors in modern, informal wars. As noted above, the marginalization that has led to women's overrepresentation in informal sectors has been shown to incentivize women to take advantage of the opportunities presented around conflict and political instability to improve their political and economic situations. At the same time, women's pre-existing roles in informal sectors and institutions—which may be amplified even further during conflict if male family and community members are away fighting or killed in conflict (Berry, 2018; Cohn, 2013)—gives them critical access and influence to the very informal spaces in which wars are increasingly being fought.

Much scholarship has been dedicated to showing the ways in which women's marginalization has led to their victimization during conflict, and how women have overwhelmingly carried the burdens and suffering of war. Cohn (2013, 28–29) lays out the different ways in which gendered structural violence has made women particularly vulnerable in war, centered around the naturalization of gendered divisions of labor and patriarchal social structures. The naturalization of gendered division of labor, of which primarily women's labor is excluded from the formal economy, has been shown to make women particularly vulnerable during war. This includes the gathering of firewood and carrying water, which leaves women in rural areas vulnerable to attack. This also includes care labor, as women are unable to flee quickly during attacks when they are responsible for the children, the elderly, and the sick.

On the other hand, patriarchal social structures view women both as men's property and as the reproducers of collective—ethnic, national, and religious—identities. These structures leave women vulnerable to rape as a way of attacking the honor of men and their communities and committing ethnic cleansing. Rape as a weapon of war also becomes more likely under these patriarchal social structures, in which masculinity and the projection of militarized strength are emphasized. These structures also leave women more vulnerable after an attack, as they are often outcast as no longer honorable or valuable, while these same patriarchal structures also dictate that women cannot own property or receive inheritance leaving them without economic freedom or safety nets. While this chapter argues that women nonetheless find agency within marginalized and informal spaces that have made them increasingly important actors in peace and conflict outcomes, it would be disingenuous to not acknowledge the vulnerabilities created by that marginalization.

That said, while women are invariably made structurally vulnerable under gendered, patriarchal power structures and institutions, scholarship has historically ignored the critical ways in which they exert agency and influence during conflict. Feminist scholars have worked to correct that record, focusing on the ways in which women have utilized both formal and informal pathways to not only survive their vulnerabilities but improve the economic and political situation for themselves, their families, and their communities (Berry, 2018; Cheldelin & Eliatamby, 2011;

Cohn, 2013; Duncanson, 2016; Matfess, 2017). Building on this scholarship, I argue that the systemic and structural marginalization of women interacts with the increasingly informal nature of war in such a way that has led women to occupy more prominent roles in both conflict and peacemaking and peacebuilding activities.

While this chapter is focused primarily on women's role in resolving conflict or building peace, the ways in which women have actively engaged in waging conflict and how that interacts with the changing nature of war is worth noting—in part because they share similar trends. As noted, women's structural marginalization is both a key reason that women are overrepresented in the informal sector, as well as a key reason given by many women who have participated in conflict—whether through protests, armed combat, acts of terrorism, or in support roles to non-state armed groups—as they seek to improve their economic and/or political situations. The migration of conflict from formal to informal spaces has provided new opportunities for women to participate in wars, where they were once marginalized from much of the formal institutions that conducted war.

In the informal spaces of new wars, women have increasingly served as combatants in non-state as well as state militias, as suicide bombers, and in a variety of support roles to non-state armed actors. In 2005, Bouta et al. found that women were active participants in 55 different conflicts. In countries such as Eritrea, Nepal, and Sri Lanka, women have accounted for more than 30% of the fighting forces across the sides of the conflicts—between state and non-state actors. In these cases, women saw themselves with few economic or political alternatives, and violent action as a path to emancipation (Cheldelin & Eliatamby, 2011). Women suicide bombers have also been well documented in the cases of the Chechen Black Widows, the Black Tigresses of Death in Sri Lanka, Palestine, and Boko Haram in Nigeria (Cheldelin & Eliatamby, 2011; Matfess, 2017). Evidence points to many of these women joining due to limited alternatives, while some took on suicide missions out of retaliation. Women and girl soldiers in West Africa—whether through abduction or voluntary enlistment have served in various, often rotating, support roles as wives, cooks, looters, porters, sex slaves, and fighters (Cheldelin & Eliatamby, 2011; Matfess, 2017).

Turning to women's increasing prominence in peacebuilding and peacemaking activities, I argue that by focusing almost exclusively on women's participation within formal institutions, much of the peace and conflict scholarship both extends patriarchal power structures while also overlooking key ways in which women exert their agency and influence. To interrogate the different ways—both informal and formal—in which women work to influence peace outcomes, I have first identified three broad pathways supported within the literature in which women may exert their power: informal social movements, informal social networks, and formal power. The first two pathways are directly related to women's roles and participation in informal institutions and networks and draw on a growing body of scholarship looking at bottom-up peace formation efforts. As for the latter pathway, I contend that women's power in formal institutions is both the most studied and most narrow view of women's participation in peace efforts. However, I also argue that women's formal power may manifest as an extension of the first two pathways, as women's informal power is often highly intertwined with their ability to access formal power. Defining these different pathways provides a framework through which to identify and analyze how women have increasingly utilized their informal power to affect peace outcomes during conflict.

While critical and feminist scholarship has played an important role in identifying myriad ways in which women and other marginalized communities have drawn on informal power to affect broader social or political changes, the literature has yet to fully explore the interaction between women's outsized role in informal spaces and how that power is being exercised during increasingly informal conflicts. Further, most conflict and peace scholarship continues to treat informal peacebuilding and peacemaking efforts as "track two," tertiary, or subordinate to formal processes. This analysis seeks to flip that paradigm, arguing that informal conflicts often require informal pathways to resolution.

In the following section, I first provide an overview of women's access to informal and formal power building on existing literature, followed by a deeper description of the three identified pathways I have identified within it. The proceeding section will then draw upon specific examples of women's participation in peace activities in Sudan to assess the applicability of the different pathways during a contemporary conflict.

Pathways to Achieve Peace Outcomes

Formal peacemaking efforts are imbued with top-down and colonialist norms that replicate the very patriarchal and dependency-based power structures that are often responsible for contemporary conflicts in the first place (McLeod & O'Reilly, 2019; Richmond, 2014). Their patriarchal power structures make formal peacemaking processes difficult for women and other marginalized groups to access (Lynch, 2013; McLeod & O'Reilly, 2019; Smith & Verdeja, 2013). This has led recent critical and feminist security studies to shift focus to bottom-up peace formation efforts and how women access informal power that is fluid and multidirectional to achieve peace outcomes (Bayat, 2010). This work builds on Foucault's (1980) assertion that power is decentered and can exist in regional and local institutions working through individual citizen-subjects. The theoretical argument behind this informal and decentralized power is that "every day" and "local" activities are capable of creating systemic changes over time, which can in turn lead to greater equality and more representative forms of governance—whether formal or informal (Richmond, 2014). Some examples of this research provide direct insights into how women have utilized decentralized and informal power to create broad impact, influencing formal institutions and norms in post-conflict contexts (Berry, 2018).

Some formal peacemaking interventions have attempted to incorporate local, bottom-up approaches by increasing civil society participation; however, civil society, including women and other historically marginalized groups, are typically relegated to tertiary or "Track Two" status in processes that are predefined by political elite and third-party interveners. This has reinforced patriarchal structures in which even when women get a seat at the table, their objectives and interests are so far removed from the priorities of the predetermined process that they are unable to have any real influence (Cohn, 2017; Ellerby, 2016). For example, if women are concerned about structural gender inequalities that lead to political instability and women's vulnerability during war, but the agenda of the peace negotiations is limited to the splitting of land and resources between the warring parties and demobilization efforts, there is little space for women to have the interests addressed.

In exploring how women may use their informal power to change these dynamics, some scholars have focused on the women's position in informal economic sectors and markets (Duncanson, 2016), while others have focused on the efforts of direct political mobilization, such as through local peace councils and the formation of social movements (Chenoweth, 2021; Richmond, 2014). Drawing on these examples of women's use of informal and formal power, I detail three broad pathways in which women may use their agency toward peace outcomes below. I argue that defining these different pathways provides a framework through which we can more clearly identify and analyze how women utilize their informal power to affect peace outcomes during contemporary conflicts that are occurring in increasingly informal spaces. This framework can then be applied to assess the applicability, prevalence, and impact of different pathways in specific case studies, as I show in the following section with examples from Sudan. While the scope of the empirical analysis in this chapter is limited to specific cases, I argue that this framework can be applied more broadly in future research and can help identify generalizable trends in women's informal power in both peace and conflict.

Informal Social Networks: Women on the peripheries may exercise informal power to achieve peace outcomes through existing informal social networks and influence within informal markets. This pathway is based on scholarship that examines how informal markets and social networks have been utilized to affect formal decision-making processes (Duncanson, 2016; Richmond, 2014). This pathway has been well documented in Liberia, where women were able to use pre-existing networks of informal power—embedded within the patriarchal societal structures—to create their own systems of economic entitlements and informal methods of income generation. Despite not being allowed to hold any formal political roles, and despite women often being married at very young ages to much older husbands, women in central and northwestern Liberia had developed a secret society—*Sande*—that operated in parallel to the men's secret society, *Poro*—comprised of powerful elder chiefs. In southeastern Liberia, this manifested as a separate "women's chief" with their own council of elders. In both versions of these informal women's leadership networks, Liberian women have been documented to exert significant influence over local political and economic decisions, either by using a front man, through informal veto powers, or through collective demonstrations (Fuest, 2008; Moran, 2006). Women in Liberia also engaged in trade in informal markets to improve their economic well-being as most formal, wage-paying jobs remained off limits to them. While traditionally most of their market activities were confined close to home, during the Liberian civil war, women were able to utilize and build upon their pre-existing networks with these informal markets to expand their informal economic reach—sharing information and traveling across territories in which men from opposing sides of the conflict could not traverse and establishing economic gains that improved women's livelihoods long after the conflict ended. These networks also helped fund and drive women's peace activism and community-based organizing that included mass protests, peaceful sit-ins, and even the threat of a sex strike, which achieved at least some voice in formal peacemaking processes including gender equity provisions in the 2003 Liberian Peace Agreement (Fuest, 2008; Moran, 2012).

Another example of informal social networks can be drawn from marginalized communities in Latin America, where some poor communities have succeeded in utilizing informal power to achieve social welfare outcomes—and in particular, the government's decision to allow their communities to continue illegal street vending and squatting. As Holland (2018) documents in the cases of Santiago, Chile, Bogota, Colombia, and Lima, Peru, during the 1990s and 2000s communities were able to use their informal social networks—such as street-vending associations, informal mining cooperatives, and squatter associations—built through their roles in informal markets, to politically mobilize and achieve social welfare outcomes by influencing the behavior of formal institutions. This mobilization took a variety of forms, to include public protests and the mobilization of voters for or against political candidates.

Informal Social Movements: Women on the peripheries may exercise informal power to achieve peace outcomes through the intentional building of informal social movements or networks that can influence local or national discourses, either putting pressure on the parties within formal peace processes and/or generating localized peace outcomes. This pathway draws on social movement literature that examines marginalized women's organizing efforts outside of formal political spaces (Berry, 2018; Chenoweth, 2021; Stephen, 1997,). Some examples are drawn from Stephen's research in Latin America (1997), in which she highlights six instances of women's grassroots movements and networks in Latin America changing economic and political policies in the 1980s and 1990s. One example from her work was on the CO-MADRES (Committee of Mothers and Relatives of the Political Prisoners, Disappeared, and Assassinated of El Salvador). During the thirteen-year civil war in El Salvador, this grassroots network of women formed initially to demand information on the whereabouts of lost loved ones but soon expanded their mission to confront a range of human rights abuses and gender equity—to include rape, gendered and unpaid labor roles, women's political marginalization, and women's control over their bodies and reproductive health. They held public demonstrations, occupied churches, and lobbied for international attention and pressure. A similar example from Sri Lanka highlights how the Association of Parents of Servicemen Missing in Action (PSMIA) and the Association for War-Affected Women (AWAW) were founded in the late 1990s in response to the war between the government and the Liberation Tigers of Tamil Eelam (LTTE), growing to over 12,000 women from both sides of the conflict. The group has been attributed with fostering communication and understanding between and among communities and armed groups (Eliatamby, 2011). Similar stories also emerged from Bosnia (Hunt, 2011), Women of Zimbabwe Arise (WOZA) (Mutsi, 2011), and many other conflict-affected regions.

Formal Power: Alternatively, within the peace process literature, the most studied pathway for women's engagement is their direct participation in formal institutions. Women on the peripheries may seek access to formal power to achieve peace outcomes by entering the formal economy, obtaining formal education, getting elected to formal political office, and building formal civil society networks that lobby for funding or training, to name some common examples. This pathway is based on scholarship that examines women's entrance into formal roles during peace and transitional processes (Berry, 2018), as well as a large body of literature on capacity-building programs for women and other marginalized groups. In the case of post-conflict Rwanda, Berry (2018) details how some local grassroots women's organizations began transforming into formal civil society organizations that eventually applied for funding from INGOs, began training women to enter the formal economy, and successfully lobbied for an amended legal code that allowed women to inherit land, among other rights for women. The National Women's Council also formed within the formal political space to funnel women's concerns from communities to party officials, while Pro Femmes ran trainings for women to run for political office. In another example, in Burundi, women's civil society organizations lobbied for seats in the formal peace negotiations, eventually negotiating 60 percent of their demands to be included in the final peace agreement (Duncanson, 2016; Saiget, 2016).

While these efforts culminate in the advancement of women's formal power, it is notable that in many of the instances detailed, the efforts began with women utilizing their power in informal spaces—with grassroots organizing and informal networks. For example, in post-conflict Rwanda, the catalyst for seeking formal power began as women quickly took on new, informal roles outside of the household—to include subsistence farming, informal trading, and brickmaking, to name a few. In response to these new pressures and roles, women formed thousands of small and informal "self-help" groups across the country (Berry, 2018, 71). In many cases these self-help groups expanded into larger grassroots organizations that helped facilitate women's increased political participation—both in informal spaces, and in formal spaces through political training, mobilization, and running for elected office. Through this example, Berry (2018) shows how women were able to build small, individual stepping-stones based on pre-existing community networks that led to new community organizations, increased political space, and eventually greater representation of women in formal governance structures.

Women's Active Engagement in Conflict and Peace in Sudan

The following section applies the three pathways detailed above to examples of women's peace activities in Sudan. I do so to clearly identify and analyze how women have utilized their informal power to affect peace outcomes during one contemporary conflict which has occurred largely in informal spaces. While this brief section does not claim to cover all of the ways in which Sudanese women have engaged in contemporary peace and conflict in Sudan, it provides examples of three distinct ways in which Sudanese (and South Sudanese) women have engaged through informal pathways to achieve peace outcomes—with varying outcomes—since South Sudan's secession in 2011. The first example describes women's leadership and participation in Abyei peace councils and the Amiet Peace Market, through the pathway of Informal Social Networks, and eventually, through Formal Power. The second example relates to formal women's civil society organizations' attempts to access and influence the formal peace processes, with international support, through the pathway of Formal Power. The third example interrogates women's leadership in the popular uprisings of 2019 that led to the toppling of then-President Omar al-Bashir's 30-year dictatorship, through both the pathways of Informal Social Networks and Informal Social Movements.

As a brief overview of Sudan's contemporary conflicts, Sudan has been mired in political violence and civil war for the majority of its independence. After a devastating decades-long war between non-state actors in southern Sudan—led primarily by the Sudan People's Liberation Movement/Army (SPLM/A)—and the various formal and informal armed actors of the Government of Sudan—South Sudan gained its independence in 2011, following an internationally orchestrated peace process that culminated in the Comprehensive Peace Agreement of 2005. The Comprehensive Peace Agreement, however, did not address many of the underlying causes of the conflict—including systemic economic and political inequities between the center (Khartoum and the riverine Arab tribes) and the periphery (to include Darfur and the Two Areas of Southern Kordofan and Blue Nile). It also left the disputed area of Abyei between Sudan and South Sudan unaddressed. This resulted in continued conflict across informal spaces in Sudan and the disputed territory of Abyei, primarily between non-state actors such as armed communal groups and militias—some backed by the Government of Sudan or foreign actors—as well as with the participation of Sudan's Armed Forces. President Bashir's regime, sanctioned for links to terrorist organizations and atrocities in Darfur, intentionally kept formal institutions weak in order to consolidate power within his elite circles. After U.S. sanctions were lifted in 2017, increased pressures from the IMF, World Bank, and third-party donor states led Sudan to enact certain austerity measures and financial reforms that led to popular uprising that began on the streets of Khartoum in December 2018 (Becker et al., 2023). These popular uprisings were largely led by women who bore the brunt of the austerity measures, and eventually led to the ousting of President Bashir in a military coup, which, through a series of future juntas led to another full-scale civil war between the former Sudanese Armed Forces and the Rapid Support Forces militia (Burns, 2023).

Abyei Peace Councils and the Amiet Peace Market

At the time I visited Abyei in 2013, neither the women from the Ngok Dinka nor the Misseriya communities had formed cohesive movements, rather they drew upon their pre-existing social networks through their informal roles in subsistence and care labor to organize and express their interests in working toward peace outcomes. The women initially knew each other from local and communal activities, such as subsistence farming, gathering water or firewood, local trading, shared care labor, and community activities. The Ngok Dinka women used these social networks to begin organizing to discuss peace activities, such as meeting with Misseriya women and reopening local markets in which the two communities traded goods.

By 2016, the Ngok Dinka women formed the Abyei Women's Union to advocate for communal reconciliation, improved access to basic services, and women's participation in decision-making (IOM, 2018). These women played an instrumental role in mobilizing women to participate in a joint women's conference in 2016 between Ngok Dinka and Misseriya women, which became a cornerstone in a series of intercommunity dialogues that led to the eventual signing of a local peace agreement between leaders (albeit male leaders) of the two communities and the opening of Amiet Peace Market. Women were both instrumental in the success of the market and advocates for its opening and continuation. Both Ngok Dinka and Misseriya women reported the market as a principal means of their livelihoods, referencing the market "as a solid source of revenue and affordable food, with opportunities to head up businesses such as shops and restaurants" (Concordis International, 2016, 2020). While women's mobilization and advocacy for community reconciliation, joint trade, and women's increased participation in community peacebuilding were initially orchestrated through Informal Social Networks, there is evidence that some women eventually moved toward the pathway of Formal Power. The Abyei Women's Union secured support from and training from the International Organization for Migration (IOM) and the U.S. Agency for International Development (USAID) to hold the Abyei Women's Union Conference to develop action plans to improve their communities (IOM, 2018). As we can see in the case of Abyei, despite being very much on the margins of formal political power, women were able to claim ground in the middle of peace activities.

The Sudan Taskforce on the Engagement of Women

While many informal social networks and movements have been led and utilized by women in an effort to affect peace outcomes in Sudan, the Sudan Taskforce on the Engagement of Women (often referred to within Sudan's peace processes as simply the Taskforce), drew directly on the pathway of Formal Power to achieve their goals. The Taskforce was formed in 2013 by women who had already achieved some level of formal power within opposition political parties and formal civil society organizations. The women who made up the Taskforce already knew each other professionally through their political work and through a previous coalition of women community leaders from Sudan and South Sudan who had organized around the Comprehensive Peace Agreement process throughout the 2000s. The group consistently emphasized the importance of their power in channeling the concerns of women in more informal spaces—notably the conflict zones—into the formal peace processes. The Taskforce received funding from INGOs such as Inclusive Security for training, travel, and other material support to lobby for their participation in the formal peace processes, which at the time of its inception was led by the African Union High-level Implementation Panel. They were eventually included as official observers in the 2016 peace talks on Darfur and the Two Areas, though the talks did not produce any tangible results (Bigio, 2018; Sudan Taskforce on the Engagement of Women, 2014, 2017). While the Taskforce was consistently able to get an audience to express their positions with the mediators, international officials, and the warring parties, there were few overall peace dividends from these processes, much less successes for Sudanese women.

It is notable that in the case of formal women's civil society organizations in Sudan, and specifically the Taskforce, that attempts to utilize the pathway of Formal Power to put women directly in the center of formal processes were not overly successful in the sense that women gained little formal power. However, they were able to communicate the concerns of constituencies from the margins, as marginalized as the women remained from the formal processes. It is also important to contextualize their lack of success in the formal space with the overall lack of success of the formal processes in producing peace outcomes. This lends support to the underlying argument that conflicts occurring in informal spaces may require, at least in part, informal pathways to conflict resolution.

Women and the Popular Uprisings of 2018–2019

Under pressure from International Financial Institutions and donor states to remove subsidies and implement austerity measures, the Sudanese government stopped its long-running state-funded import of wheat in 2018. Additionally, as much of Sudan's economy operated in informal markets, Sudan was under pressure to correct its informal exchange rate which operated on average with a five times difference against the official exchange rate of the US dollar, creating myriad currency issues for foreign exchange (International Crisis Group, 2021). The removal of the wheat subsidies, along with the exchange rate adjustments, and the hardship this created for many Sudanese was the catalyst for what became four months of sustained civil protests in Khartoum that spread throughout the country to remove the authoritarian Bashir regime (Hassan, 2019). The uprising was largely led by women, with many accounts saying that women made up as much as two-thirds of the protestors in the street (Abdulbari, 2019). Women, who were structurally vulnerable given patriarchal power structures and limited formal economic rights, experienced the greatest hardships under the increasing austerity measures. Some women organized themselves through their informal networks as "tea ladies"—ubiquitous parts of Sudanese life on every street corner, yet unsanctioned and sometimes cracked down on by the Sudanese government. They also mobilized through pre-existing Sudanese Professional Associations that formed local resistance committees, to include women with formal and informal professions, and pre-existing women's cooperatives that had formed to serve the poor and the marginalized (Abusharaf, 2022; Ali, 2024; Gaafar & Shawkat, 2019).

As the protests came to a head, Sudan's military stepped in and ousted the long-running dictator President Omar al Bashir in April of 2019 (Lynch & Gramer, 2021). Following many tense weeks and months of military rule under a Transitional Military Council and continued popular protests for a civilian, democratic government, the civilian protestors represented by the Forces for Freedom and Change (FFC) and the military agreed to share power through a transitional government that was to maintain power until national, multiparty elections could be held in 2023 (Gavin, 2021). Women were excluded almost entirely from the formal negotiation process, which was supported by the international community (Abbas, 2020). Women, not holding significant formal economic or militarized power, were not deemed as necessary within the formal negotiations on the future of the country. As with the Taskforce, in the case of women participation in the popular uprisings of 2018–2019 in Sudan, we see that women had limited success through the pathway of Formal Power in attempting to access or influence the formal peace and transition processes which, as with previous formal processes, had little success in creating peace outcomes as the processes devolved into numerous military juntas and the eventual full-scale civil war which erupted in April 2023 (Burns, 2023). On the other hand, women had a significant impact through the pathways of Informal Social Networks and Informal Social Movements, in which women were able to use pre-existing social networks and develop new social movements to orchestrate nation-wide popular uprisings and the eventual ousting of one of the longest running dictators in Africa. As with the case of Abyei, we can see that women on the margins were able to utilize pathways of informal power to claim significant space in the middle of conflict and peace activities.

What Sudan's Lessons Tell Us About Women as Agents for Peace in Increasingly Informal Conflicts

While the case of Sudan may not be representative of all contemporary conflicts, it reinforces theoretical arguments about women's influence in both formal and informal spaces within contemporary peace and conflict. In the context of increasingly informal conflicts, women have been seen to draw on their myriad roles in informal markets and institutions—including utilizing previously existing informal social networks and intentionally organizing informal social movements—to achieve peace outcomes. Women were also seen to draw on sources of formal power in an attempt to achieve peace outcomes. It is notable, however, that despite making up the majority of the protestors during the popular uprising, women, holding little power in formal institutions in Sudan, were largely excluded from the formal peace negotiations which were supported by third-party states and international and multilateral organizations. This demonstrates how women were made vulnerable due to economic policies that devalued the informal economy and reduced social welfare protection, all while excluding them from the centers of power and decision-making. This dynamic can be seen to have both fomented the popular uprising which resulted in the ousting of a long-running wartime dictator, as well as to have diminished the chances for a formal, sustainable peace. Despite their relative lack of success in achieving peace outcomes in the formal institutions of peacemaking, women's roles in informal processes—from organizing and participating in local peace conferences and markets to national popular uprisings—have had significant impacts on both local and national-level political stability and violence in Sudan. In other words, women were able to claim significant space in the middle of peace activities from the margins.

Conclusion

This chapter has explored the increasingly prominent role of women in contemporary conflicts, emphasizing their overrepresentation in informal institutions and markets as both a response to structural marginalization and a source of agency in shaping conflict and peace outcomes. As modern wars increasingly unfold in informal spaces, women—historically excluded from formal political and economic institutions—have leveraged informal social networks, grassroots organizing, and informal economic participation to influence peace processes. Through the case of Sudan, this chapter examined three pathways through which women have sought to influence peace outcomes: Informal Social Networks, Informal Social Movements, and Formal Power. The findings from Sudan support the central argument of this chapter: in contexts where formal institutions are weak or absent, informal institutions and networks—often led or occupied by women—become central to both war and peace. Moreover, the growing informality of modern conflicts has made women's roles in peace and conflict activities increasingly important.

Future research would benefit from a more systematic examination of how women's power—both formal and informal—shapes contemporary conflicts and their resolution. Interrogating the impact of the informal pathways women utilize during conflict may help further elucidate the relationship between sustainable peace and women's meaningful participation and inclusion in modern conflict resolution. As demonstrated throughout this chapter, initial lessons and theoretical arguments from conflicts in former colonies of the Global South with weak institutions have demonstrated that women, often marginalized from formal institutions and markets, have trouble accessing and influencing formal peace processes. While women still seek formal avenues of power to influence such processes, they have also been shown to capitalize on their power from the margins to claim space in the middle of peace and conflict activities to improve their economic and political situation and affect broader community and national peace outcomes. This chapter has shown that women's roles in informal spaces are not peripheral, but rather fundamental, to the way modern conflicts unfold and are resolved.

References

Abbas, R. (2020, April 11). *A year after Bashir's fall, the struggle for Sudanese women continues*. The Wilson Center.

Abdulbari, N. (2019, April 12). *Why women led the uprising in Sudan*. The Washington Post.

Abusharaf, R. (2022, March 3). *The women of Sudan will not accept setbacks*. Brookings.

Adjei, M. (2019). Women's participation in peace processes: A review of literature. *Journal of Peace Education, 16*(2), 133–154. https://doi.org/10.1080/17400201.2019.1576515

Ali, N. (2024). *Khartoum's women street vendor cooperatives and the politics of care* (Middle East Report, 310).

Bayat, A. (2010). *Life as politics: How ordinary people change the Middle East*. Stanford University Press.

Becker, D., Aberg, J. H. S., & Burns, J. G. (2023). The will to do good and the clash of practices: Understanding sudanese sanctions relief. *International Politics, 60*(5), 1–24. https://doi.org/10.1057/s41311-023-00437-9

Berry, M. (2018). *War, women, and power: From violence to mobilization in Rwanda and Bosnia-Herzegovina*. Cambridge University Press.

Bigio, J. (2018, April 19). Five questions on the Sudan peace process. Council on Foreign Relations.

Bouta, T., Frerks, G., & Bannon, I. (2005). *Gender, conflict, and development*. World Bank Publications.

Brinks, D. M., Levitsky, S., & Murillo, M. V. (2019). *Understanding institutional weakness: Power and design in Latin American Institutions*. Cambridge University Press.

Burns, J. G. (2023, April 23). The violence in Sudan is partly our fault. *The New York Times*.

Cheldelin, S., & Eliatamby, M. (2011). *Women waging war and peace: International perspectives of women's roles in conflict and post-conflict reconstruction*. Continuum International Publishing.

Chenoweth, E. (2021). *Civil resistance: What everyone needs to know*. Oxford University Press.

Cohn, C. (2017). Beyond the 'women, peace and security agenda': Why we need a feminist roadmap for sustainable peace. *Consortium on gender, security, and human rights*.

Cohn, C. (2013). *Women and wars: Contested histories, uncertain futures*. Polity Press.

Cohn, C., & Duncanson, C. (2020). Whose recovery? IFI prescriptions for postwar states. *Review of International Political Economy, 27*(6), 1214–1234. https://doi.org/10.1080/09692290.2019.1677743

Concordis International. (2016). *The importance of the Amiet peace market*. https://concordis.international/news/the-importance-of-the-amiet-peace-market

Concordis International. (2020). *Advocates and protectors: The role of Abyei's women and youth in managing conflict and promoting sustainable peace*. https://concordis.international/reports/advocates-and-protectors-the-role-of-abyeis-women-and-youth-in-managing-conflict-and-promoting-sustainable-peace

Consortium on Gender, Security and Human Rights. (2017). *Feminist critiques of the sustainable development goals: Analysis and bibliography*. https://genderandsecurity.org/sites/default/files/Feminist_Critiques_of_the_SDGs_-_Analysis_and_Bibliography_-_CGSHR.pdf

Duncanson, C. (2016). *Gender and peacebuilding*. Polity Press.

Ellerby, K. (2016). A seat at the table is not enough: Understanding women's substantive representation in peace processes. *Peacebuilding, 4*(2), 136–150. https://doi.org/10.1080/21647259.2016.1192240

Foucault, M. (1980). *Power/knowledge: Selected interviews and other writings 1972–1977*. Pantheon Books.

Fuest, V. (2008). "This is the time to get in front": Changing roles and opportunities for women in Liberia. *African Affairs, 107*(427), 201–224. https://doi.org/10.1093/afraf/adn003

Gaafar, R., & Shawkat, O. (2019, February 12). *Sudanese women at the heart of the revolution*. AfricanFeminism.

Gavin, M. (2021, November 22). *The crisis in Sudan: What to know*. Council on Foreign Relations.

Hassan, M., & Kodouda, A. (2019). Sudan's uprising: The fall of a dictator. *Journal of Democracy, 30*(4), 89–103. https://doi.org/10.1353/jod.2019.0071

Holland, A. (2017). *Forbearance as redistribution: The politics of informal welfare in Latin America*. Cambridge University Press.

Hunt, S. (2011). Building a Peace Network. In S. Cheldelin & M. Eliatamby (Eds.), *Women waging war and peace: International perspectives of women's roles in conflict and post-conflict reconstruction* (pp. 99–116). Continuum International Publishing.

International Crisis Group. (2021, February 23). The rebels come to Khartoum: How to implement Sudan's new peace agreement. Briefing 168/Africa.

IOM. (2018, April 21). Women leaders take action to realize peace and development in Abyei.

Kaldor, M. (2012). *New and old wars: Organized violence in a global era*. Polity Press.

Kohli, A. (2020). *Imperialism and the developing world: How Britain and the United States shaped the global periphery*. Oxford University Press.

Krause, J., Krause, W., & Bränfors, J. (2019). Women's participation in peace negotiations and the durability of peace. *International Interactions, 44*(6), 985–1016. https://doi.org/10.1080/03050629.2018.1492386

Lynch, C., & Gramer, R. (2021, December 3). The battle for Khartoum exposes waning U.S. influence. *Foreign Policy.*

Lynch, C. (2013). Neoliberal ethics, the humanitarian international, and practices of peacebuilding. In J. Smith & E. Verdeja (Eds.), *Globalization, social movements, and peacebuilding* (pp. 47–68). Syracuse University Press.

Marriage, Z. (2013). *Formal peace and informal war: Security and development in Congo*. Routledge.

Matfess, H. (2017). *Women and Boko Haram: Beyond victimhood*. Zed Books.

McLeod, L., & O'Reilly, M. (2019). Critical peace and conflict studies: Feminist interventions. *Peacebuilding, 7*(2), 127–145. https://doi.org/10.1080/21647259.2019.1588457

Moran, M. H. (2012). "Our mothers have spoken": Synthesizing old and new forms of women's political authority in Liberia. *Journal of International Women's Studies, 13*(4), 51–66.

Moran, M. H. (2006). *Liberia: The violence of democracy*. University of Pennsylvania Press.

Mutsi, M. (2011). Countering the currents: Zimbabwe. In S. Cheldelin & M. Eliatamby (Eds.), *Women waging war and peace: International perspectives of women's roles in conflict and post-conflict reconstruction* (pp. 117–138). Continuum International Publishing.

Richmond, O. (2014). *Failed statebuilding: Intervention, the state, and the dynamics of peace formation*. Yale University Press.

Saiget, M. (2016). Women's participation in African peace negotiations: Cooperating with the UN agencies in Burundi and Liberia. *Peacebuilding, 4*(1), 28–40. https://doi.org/10.1080/21647259.2015.1099727

Smith, J., & Verdeja, E. (Eds.). (2013). *Globalization, social movements, and peacebuilding*. Syracuse University Press.

Stephen, L. (1997). *Women and social movements in Latin America: Power from below*. University of Texas Press.

Sudan Taskforce on the Engagement of Women. (2014). Statement and recommendations.

Sudan Taskforce on the Engagement of Women. (2017). Recommendations.

UN Women. (2015). *Transforming economies, realizing rights*.

CHAPTER 7

Fighting Like a Propagandist? How Al Qaeda and the Islamic State Conceptualize Their Battlefield

Marie Robin

Introduction

"Battlefield of the media," "cognitive warfare," "winning the hearts and minds:" an increasing number of expressions related to warfare, and used by media and practitioners alike, seemingly imply that words may act as weapons during wars. Following these notions, language and narratives are now wielded as strategic tools in conflicts, rather than merely serving as ancillary elements. In other words, it seems that communicants increasingly act at the middle of the battlefield with their words and narratives, and not just as supporting operators acting at the margins.

Recent conflicts certainly do not say anything different. In the context of Ukraine and in Bucha (Viginum, 2025), the Kremlin's strategy of

M. Robin (✉)
Institute of Security and Global Affairs, Leiden University, The Hague, The Netherlands
e-mail: m.p.c.e.robin@fgga.leidenuniv.nl

M. Robin et al. (eds.), *The Changing Fights and Fighters of Contemporary War*, https://doi.org/10.1007/978-3-032-05518-7_7

disseminating disinformation and orchestrating propaganda campaigns—characterized by narratives of "Nazi Ukrainians" and the "humiliation" of the Russian people—was central to justifying and to conducting the February 2022 invasion (Schmitt, 2022) and was framed as a propaganda or information war by many (Bond, 2023; Liebich, 2023). Similarly, the atrocities committed in Israel and Palestine are consistently paralleled by a contest of narratives, with each side framing their actions as a defensive response to the crimes of the other (Wajner, 2019). In the ongoing tensions between Rwanda and the Democratic Republic of the Congo, narratives related to accusations of resource exploitation and ethnic manipulation have also been weaponized to exacerbate regional tensions and shape the conflict's trajectory (Stearns, 2024). The critical role of narratives and their instrumentalization in the current conflict even led the nongovernmental organization Reporters without Borders to warn on the dangers of expanding the battlefield too much, calling on the Congolese authorities and M23 to "protect journalists and stop forcibly instrumentalizing them as propaganda tools," following attacks against over 50 newsrooms in the span of a year (Reporters without Borders, 2025). In Syria, Iraq, Nigeria and beyond, the propaganda efforts of jihadist groups have also been critical in mobilizing material and physical support and in directly facilitating military operations (Ingram et al., 2020).

If this is indeed the case, and if words are being "weaponized" in a manner that aids a belligerent in conducting their war and in achieving victory, it is plausible to argue that those who wield words in a conflict may themselves be considered participants in the conflict. In other words, those using words may arguably be framed as fighters. The core argument of this chapter is that jihadist terrorist groups, in opposition to our legal understandings found in international humanitarian law, implement a broad understanding of the "fighter" category, one that encompasses propagandists.

In a previous work, I have questioned, at the ethical level of the just war tradition, whether propagandists (specifically, civilian propagandists), should be included within the category of "combatants" (Robin, 2024). There, I had argued that, morally speaking, while propagandists contribute significantly to the conflict, they should not be categorized as combatants subject to lethal harm. Instead, I proposed that they be viewed as "indirectly participating civilians." This classification implies that they should not be deliberately targeted with lethal force, but they may be maximally exposed to "less-than-lethal harm," such as property destruction or privation of liberty. Ethically, they should still be protected as part of the "margins," and thereby not be seen as direct battlefield participants liable to lethal harm.

In this chapter, I seek to advance my previous inquiry in two distinct ways.

First, this chapter will focus on a specific case: the propagandists of al Qaeda (AQ) and the Islamic State (IS). Examining the Islamic State and al Qaeda is particularly pertinent because, maybe more than other belligerent groups, these organizations have developed sophisticated media apparatuses capable of communicating their cause, mobilizing fighters, and intimidating opponents across diverse communication formats and languages. For the over 40,000 foreign fighters who joined the ranks of the IS caliphate, exposition to propaganda contents has been identified as one of the many causes of their military engagement (Ayad, 2024; European Parliament, 2016). Very concretely, the AQ-affiliated US-Yemeni propagandist, Anwar al-Awlaki, has been identified as the primary inspiration behind more than twenty terrorist acts worldwide (Meleagrou-Hitchens, 2020). At its peak, 16 years ago, the al Qaeda organization operated over "5,600 websites, with 900 new sites, blogs, and forums appearing every year" (Ayad, 2024). Going even further in developing propaganda, at some point, the content released daily by the Islamic State's Al Hayat Media Foundation, including concrete guidelines on how to build bombs or how to hold a weapon, reached thousands of followers daily, throughout the world. Even after the territorial fall of the caliphate, propaganda contents continue to call on the revenge of the Umma and to strike so-called enemies of the Muslims (Djene, 2024), hoping to sustain the fight through the virtual world. Today, propaganda from both groups continues to incite violence from followers across the world. In fact, in the second half of 2024, three websites on the open web linked to the Islamic State movement attracted over 421,000 visitors, with more than 40 percent of the traffic being unique users (Ayad, 2025). This is only in addition to the flows generated by over 300 IS accounts on Facebook, 50 accounts on Instagram, TikTok, as well channels on WhatsApp, Telegram, Element, and accounts on X. This continuous online presence has tangible consequences, for example when, recently, an 18-year-old Chechen Frenchman inspired by jihadist online propaganda planned an attack (which was overturned by the French intelligence services) against the football events in Saint-Etienne, during the Paris 2024 Olympic Games (France info, 2024).

Second, this chapter shifts the perspective: rather than approaching the issue of propagandist participation from an ethical standpoint—as a neutral observer determining whether propagandists *should be* treated as "combatants" (i.e., whether they may be targeted)—I aim to explore this inquiry in an entirely inductive and case-driven way, integrally focusing on the jihadist actors' understanding of this issue. This chapter, therefore, deliberately chooses not to take a legal or ethical standpoint which would apply "our own" understanding of "combatant" categorization taken from international humanitarian law or the just war tradition. Instead, I want to analyze whether propagandists *themselves* perceive their role as that of fighters acting at the very heart of the battlefield, rather than in its peripheries. For this reason, in this article, I refrain from using the terminology of "combatant," closely associated with existing frameworks of international law, and instead use the word "fighter," less legally connoted and therefore more appropriate for this inductive endeavor. I do so to understand how these jihadist groups shape what they think battlefield participation means. Do they coin propagandists as fighters? Specifically, what do the propagandists say about their very own activities? Do they view themselves as engaged in combat? Do they claim to be employing weapons in a conflict and to be part of the center of the battlefield? In essence, do propagandists, through their own narratives, identify as fighters, and what conception of the battlefield do they themselves enforce? I am not interested in what a combatant should be from a legal or ethical standpoint, but rather on what the jihadist propagandists I investigate say a fighter is.

This line of inquiry is important for three reasons at least. First, because how actors talk about the battlefield has a direct impact on how this battlefield is shaped and fought on. Speech acts, narratives, and discourses—as demonstrated by scholars of framing and securitization theory among others—play a role in shaping the battlefield itself (Buzan et al., 1998). Articulating who the enemy is, who takes part in the fight, why the fight happens, and how it is to be conducted, participates in delineating the fight on the ground. This means, concretely, that the narratives that belligerent actors enforce about a security-related issue or a war (what people say the security issue is about) arguably contribute to shaping how a battlefield is constituted, how a war is fought, and in drawing its potential limits and boundaries (De Graaf & Dimitriu, 2015). In line with the argument developed in this book, this also means that what belongs to the middle and to the margins of a battlefield is not only fluid and moving, but it is also essentially contested at the discursive level. Defining who fights, and where, is an oppositional exercise where so-called conventional and nonconventional belligerents will enforce different conceptions of where the fight could and should happen (Robin, Theussen, Carlson this volume). Second, and going further, this means that if the communicators (here the jihadist propagandists) involved in the conflict assert that they are fighters because the conflict is also waged through words, then the battlefield may indeed be partly structured accordingly as a result, thereby necessitating a reconsideration of the war-peace continuum. If belligerents consider that there exists a "battlefield of the media" (Al-Zawahiri, 2005), what impact does it have on war doctrines and strategies, and on the military and media operations undertaken to counter these actors? The third reason why investigating what propagandists themselves say about their participation matters is that it sheds light into the strategic choices made by these groups, thus increasing our knowledge of how they pursue and fight for their cause. At a time where both groups have suffered severe military setbacks, and while they are in the process of reconfiguring their fight in various parts of the globe, investigating what they frame as important and efficient on the battlefield, including things that we might perceive peripheral, provides valuable insight into their potential future endeavors.

This chapter therefore explores the following questions: Do propagandists of the Islamic State and al Qaeda coin their role as that of a fighter? Do they put themselves at the heart of the battlefield, or rather at the margins, as support of the main participants?

I show that jihadist terrorist groups, unlike international humanitarian law, implement a broad understanding of the "fighter" category, one that encompasses propagandists. This analysis presents a novel contribution to the literature on the changing character of war by demonstrating that jihadist terrorist groups, through their own propaganda, extend the definition of a fighter to include propagandists within the ranks of the mujahidin (fighters). This expansion of the "fighter" category consequently leads to a corresponding broadening of what these groups consider to be "legitimate targets in war," as portrayed in their propaganda—resulting in an ever-expanding battlefield (Theussen this volume). Ultimately, the broadened conception of the fighter category fosters the notion of a societal war, wherein all segments of society are viewed as potential participants and targets.[1] This reconceptualization likely lowers the threshold for justifying lethal force and, as a result, may contribute to an increased incidence of casualties during conflicts. In essence, propagandists from al Qaeda and the Islamic State play a significant role in expanding the scope of the battlefield, by including themselves and others at its center stage, rather than at its margins.

Using the case of two notoriously "talkative" organizations, al Qaeda and the Islamic State, and using primary sources from both groups in French, English, and Arabic, I first show, in the first part of this article, that both al Qaeda and the Islamic State foster a narrative of *belonging*, whereby propagandists and the structures they belong in are presented as directly included within the military organization, participating in military strategies, decisions, and activities. In a second part, this article demonstrates that propagandists, by their very own activity, are presented as showing *partiality* in the conflict. Their positive contribution to jihad is regularly recognized by the propaganda productions of the groups. They are presented as positively helping one side of the conflict. Finally, the last section shows that al Qaeda and the Islamic State insist on the ability of propagandists to generate a negative *impact* on the opposing side which, when managed in a professional way by a particularly influential voice, is coined by these groups as—at least discursively—a "real" weapon against the opponents. In their productions, jihadist propagandists, ultimately, are also presented as having a detrimental impact on the opposing side, as "*harming*" the enemy. In their own view, propagandists thus fulfill core elements of what it means to be a fighter: they are part of the fighting organization, contribute to their own side achieving its ends, and cause their enemy harm; thus putting themselves in the middle of the battlefield (Fig. 7.1).

[1] Other propaganda narratives have also put forward a narrative of societal war. See for example (Barros & Thomas 2018; Moore 2018; Welch 2014).

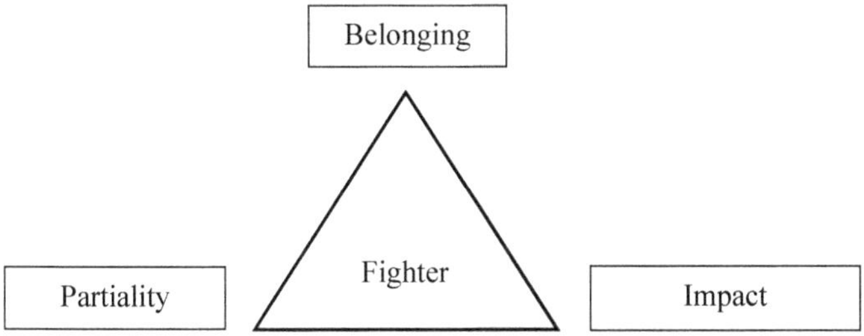

Fig. 7.1 Components of a jihadist "fighter"

The Propagandists' Belonging in Jihadist Military Organizations

I first observe that propagandists from both al Qaeda and the Islamic State present themselves as *belonging*: they picture themselves as an integral and essential part of the military cause itself, at the very heart of battlefield decisions, and activities.

The Strategic Integration of Propaganda: Embedding Media Operations Within Jihadist Military Structures

Al Qaeda

From its inception, al Qaeda recognized the strategic value of propaganda, integrating it tightly within its military training camps. In the Al-Mas'ada training camps of Peshawar, Pakistan (1979 onward), where recruits were trained before fighting Soviet troops, Osama bin Laden and Abdullah Azzam established a media desk headed by "Abu Mosad Reuters," symbolically named after the British news agency. Propaganda was not peripheral—it was seen as an integral component of al Qaeda's early military compounds, and media activities were conducted directly where military operations were decided and prepared. As Redda Sayam, a cameraman and producer who fought in Afghanistan, stated:

> We defeated the Americans using their own weapons and, by weapon, I mean the camera. Since Bosnia, Hollywood is not the only one able to present the image of an always-victorious Rambo – image that has no other purpose than that of rallying American youngsters. Now, we have our own movies to present an example to young Muslims. Now, we have

> the means to show the true face of Americans and the reality thanks to a truly Islamic information system. (El Difraoui, 2013, 120)

This small unit, which was initially directly embedded into military training compounds, later grew into a more independent (and more powerful) media committee (or information committee)—among the six committees led by the command council of the organization (*majlis al-shura*). The information committee was equipped to produce and distribute media globally and took upon itself to ensure that propaganda was woven into the fabric of military operations (El Difraoui, 2013). The media committee of al Qaeda included "special computer department and several subunits, such as a unit in charge of the editing of movies, the secretariat, the printing press, foreign relations, the photography branch, the phonetics branch, the translation branch, and the archive branches" (Gunaratna & Oreg, 2010, 1063), as well as the notorious Al-Sahab, the media production branch of al Qaeda, used to disseminate the propaganda of the organization across various medias (Holbrook, 2018). Most importantly for our investigation, the media committee, although separate from the military committee, was designed in a way that would allow a large fluidity and mobility with the latter. To make sure that media operations would be neatly embedded within the military strategy of the group, therefore, "senior members of al Qaeda's logistical and operational were members of the media committee at one point or another" (Gunaratna & Oreg, 2010, 1063). In fact, this fluid mobility between military and media roles led scholars as early as 2010 to advise that "authorities should pay close and thorough attention and place high supervision on present senior members of the media committee, such as Adam Gadahn or Muhammad Abaytah alias Abd al-Rahman al-Maghrebi, who might become the external operational planners of the near future" (Gunaratna & Oreg, 2010, 1064). Media operations within al Qaeda, therefore, are designed and conducted within military strategies.

The Islamic State

The Islamic State has gone even further, integrating propaganda into the core of its military apparatus and positioning propagandists as central figures within its strategic and operational structure. At the strategic level, propaganda falls partly under the purview of the *Amniyat*, the organization's elite intelligence service. The *Amniyat* oversees intelligence gathering, the planning and execution of attacks both locally and internationally, cyber operations, and propaganda; it represents the apex of the Islamic State's military hierarchy (Passot, 2018; Suc, 2018). The inclusion of propaganda within the *Amniyat*'s responsibilities therefore underscores the strategic importance that the Islamic State assigns to its media operatives. This strategic integration is evident in IS's external communication, such as its English-language magazine Dabiq, which notes that "the secularists and nationalists were now in a propaganda race with the mujahidin" (Islamic State, 2015b, 31), portraying propaganda as an entire field of confrontation. Because of this, jihadist fighter Abu Muharib in Somalia, in issue 12 of Dabiq, describes coordinated efforts to tightly synchronize media strategies with tactical military maneuvers and logistical planning: "there is a phase of coordination and cooperation currently being undertaken in order to achieve a synchronized media effort, tactical maneuvering of forces, and securing of logistics to achieve strategic aims" (Islamic State 2015b, 60). In the propaganda of the Islamic State, media and military operations, therefore, are depicted as planned in conjunction at the strategic level.

At the tactical and operational levels too, IS has established multiple officials, tasked with documenting military operations and acting directly on the frontlines, thus operating in close coordination with direct military operations (Nasr, 2016). From an early stage, IS ensured that GoPro cameras were mounted on soldiers' Kalashnikovs or RPG-7s, in addition to media operatives accompanying soldiers on the frontlines (Nasr, 2016). Beyond documentation, IS has also formed several *jihad al-iliktruni* brigades—military units tasked with cyber operations and communication, which extend beyond traditional military roles to include recruitment efforts, such as targeting women. IS's internal documents clearly emphasize the coordination between media and military operations. For example, the document *Responsibilities of Media Offices towards Military Media* mandates that "the official in charge of the media office and the publication brother should be attached to the military media" to ensure synchronization with military operations (Islamic State undated, 1). Similarly, the Central Media Office, in its document *Clarification regarding the media of the Islamic State*, advises,

> All media personnel within the wilayat should be linked with the media official of the office appointed by the Wali, may God preserve him, in order

> to have coordination between the soldiers of the caliphate in the areas of the wilayah, their emir, and the Central Media. (Islamic State undated, 2)

Overall, the Islamic State has placed its propagandists at the heart of its military strategy and battlefield, assigning them roles far beyond traditional media support who usually operate at the margins. These operatives are not only responsible for producing propaganda but are also actively involved and they participate in military planning and operations, working within the *Amniyat* and other military units. This fusion of media and military roles reflects the Islamic State's —and al Qaeda's—strategic prioritization of propaganda as a vital component of its military strategy.

The Militarization of Propagandists: Integrating Ideologues into the Jihadist Combat Apparatus

Further investigation reveals that it is not only the practice of propaganda that is integrated into the military vision of jihadist groups like al Qaeda and the Islamic State, but also the propagandists themselves, who are portrayed as integral members of the military ranks. In their official outlets, both the Islamic State and al Qaeda frequently feature portraits of prominent and charismatic members of their organizations where propagandists appear alongside notorious military commanders and celebrated martyrs. In these portraits, al Qaeda and the Islamic State elevate their propagandists to the status of charismatic figures, celebrated for their communication prowess and influence within the organization; propagandists are presented as mujahidin (fighters) with attributes such as bravery, strength, and heroic deed. Media and military operators from al Qaeda and the Islamic State, this section will show, are presented in a fluid fashion, going easily from one function to the other, and sharing similar attributes and qualities.

Al Qaeda

Several individuals move fluidly from propaganda to military operations. Within al Qaeda, the notorious Khaled Sheikh Mohamed—known as the brain behind the 9/11 attacks—acted in parallel as the chief of special operations (in charge of planning attacks) and as the head of the media committee, showing the close connection between both responsibilities in the eyes of the Majlis al-Shura. Additionally, Mustafa Ahmad al-Hawsawi, who acted as the financial intermediate between the 9/11 hijackers and

Khaled Sheikh Mohamed, was also part of the media committee, under the leadership of Khaled Sheikh Mohamed (Gunaratna & Oreg, 2010, 1063). This mobility reflects an understanding of both functions acting hand in hand, undetachable from each other.

A prime example of a propagandist being celebrated and portrayed as a mujahid is previously mentioned Anwar al-Awlaki, a U.S.-born radical cleric of Yemeni descent. Al-Awlaki was one of the most active members of al Qaeda in the Arabian Peninsula and served as the chief ideologue for this branch of the organization. Fluent in both English and Arabic, he distinguished himself as one of the earliest jihadists capable of effectively communicating the message of jihad in English, thereby reaching international audiences and inspiring numerous attacks in Western countries. Yet, Anwar al-Awlaki mostly did not engage directly in combat operations with the al Qaeda organization in Yemen, where he was active. Instead, he served as a charismatic leader and recruiter for the group. Due to his influential role, the United States deemed Awlaki a legitimate target and attempted to eliminate him on three occasions before succeeding on September 30, 2011. On May 22, 2013, the Obama Administration formally acknowledged that Anwar al-Awlaki had been killed in a drone strike, which sparked significant debate over the legal and ethical implications of targeting American citizens in the fight against terrorism (Rushe et al., 2011). Following Anwar al-Awlaki's death, al Qaeda's propaganda featured numerous eulogies in his honor. He was celebrated as a "mujahid" (combatant) praised for his bravery and his pivotal role in advancing jihad. The imagery associated with his death, which depicted him alongside both books and weapons, was steeped in military symbolism, drawing from the visual language traditionally reserved for fallen fighters. British propagandist Samir Khan, who was killed in the same drone strike as Awlaki was similarly depicted in eulogies as a "brother mujahid." The imagery surrounding Khan's death also featured the dual symbolism of books and weapons, reinforcing his portrayal as both a propagandist and a fighter within al Qaeda's ranks (Rushe et al., 2011).

The Islamic State

The same type of eulogies can be found in the propaganda shared by the Islamic State. In the eulogy "Story of a Martyr: The Mujahid Sheikh Abu Muhammad al-Furqan," published in 2021 in the group's Arabic newsletter Al-Naba, propagandists of the Islamic State recount the life of a media operative, Abu Muhammad, who not only became the amir for the Islamic State media operations under the *nom de guerre* Abu Sajjad but also oversaw covert operations in enemy territories. In Al-Naba, the Islamic State congratulates him:

> At the same time, he was directing the work of the covert (amni) unit working in the land of the idolaters after he assumed responsibility of the matter from the hand of Sheikh al-Adnani who became amir for the Delegated Committee in administering the wilayas of al-Sham after the killing of Sheikh Abu al-Harith al-Ansari (may God accept him). So, he followed up word with deed, and followed up the threat with implementation, for the soldiers of the Caliphate carried out attacks in the capitals of Crusader Europe and the cities of secular Turkey and the areas of the Sahwa forces, as they picked off the heads of the apostates, and terrified the hearts of the idolaters, and healed the hearts of a believing people. (Islamic State, 2021a)

His dual role in directing media and coordinating military operations exemplifies the extent to which media operatives are embedded within the IS military strategy and structure, showing how propagandists are depicted as an actual—and critical—part of the military system. And in fact, many of these individuals, in both groups, go indifferently from one form of participation to the other: for example the French propagandist Rachid Kassim who initially joined the Islamic State to undertake military actions. After a knee injury, however, Kassim initiates his propaganda activities at the end of 2015, becoming one of the most prolific propagandists of the group (Cogné, 2016), inspiring Larossi Aballa's attack against a policeman and his wife in Magnanville, France in 2016, and sharing direct guidelines to Adel Kermiche and Abdel Malik Petitjean who killed the priest Jacques Hamel in a church in Saint-Étienne-du-Rouvray, France, on 26 July 2016 (La Croix, 2017).

As it appears, the Islamic State is even more explicit than al Qaeda about its conceptualization of propagandists as fighters within the battlefield. Its 2016 *Media Operative, You are a Mujahid Too*, probably deserves to be quoted at length in that it explicitly showcases the Islamic State's information doctrine, as well as the status of its media operatives. In the document, the group declares that:

> To every media operative brother in the Islamic State, you should know and be convinced of the following fact, (that) the media is a jihad in the

> way of Allah (and that) you, with your media work, are therefore a mujahid in the way of Allah […] On the contrary, media operatives are at the forefront of the conflict, in the heart of the war, within the furnace of its battles. They participate alongside their brothers, fighting against the enemies of Allah on the Earth and raising aloft the flag of jihad. They share their daily bread and wander the land with them, sleeping rough alongside them… They are great. And lest it be forgotten, like their soldier brothers, their pure blood flowed, they tasted the ills of imprisonment in Crusader-apostate jails, they emigrated, supported and strove until the enemy recognized their clout. […] Have you not seen the photographer, how he carries a camera instead of a Kalashnikov and races before the soldiers in raids, welcoming bullets in his chest with open arms?! Have you not seen the brigades that disseminate videos and pamphlets? How they enter into the most dangerous and fortified areas to circulate the mujahidin's productions in the heart of the hypocrites' den?! Have you not seen how dedicated the media operative is in gathering intelligence on the enemy's movements and following the work of the brothers as they monitor the news of the enemy?! (Islamic State 2016b, 9, 17–18)

In this official Islamic State document, propagandists are presented as real soldiers, taking part in jihad to the same extent as military officers, including at the very frontline of military action. Propagandists, like conventional soldiers, are highlighted for their bravery and for their contribution to Allah's cause. On its cover, featured below, the document directly represents this *belonging* of the propagandists, at the core of danger and of the military action. Media operatives, here, belong in the battlefield and in the military apparatus (Fig. 7.2).

Because of the similarity in the qualities needed for both roles of media operative and fighter, not only is it that fighters can turn into propagandists, but it is also possible, conversely, for propagandists to undertake actions usually carried out by soldiers. The jihad-al-iliktruni brigades, for example, adhere to military discipline, use formal military titles and ranks, and maintain hierarchical relationships with other military divisions, operating closely with conventional military brigades (Milton, 2018). Islamic State media operatives, referred to as "media mujahidin," adopt a kunya (nom de guerre) upon joining the organization (Milton, 2018). Additionally because propagandists are no less than military soldiers, they are also entitled, like conventional soldiers, to undertake acts of violence. This is, for example, the case when that same Rachid Kassim, on 20 July 2016, just one week after the Nice attacks, appears in a video in

Fig. 7.2 Cover of media operative, you are a Mujahid, too

which he congratulates the assailant Mohamed Lahouaiej Bouhlel, before proceeding himself with the beheading of a hostage accused of espionage (Cogné, 2016). Like soldiers, propagandists are presented as entitled to carry out violence.

Surrounded by books and weapons, propagandists are not only operationally integrated into the military hierarchy, but they are also individually recognized as belonging to the ranks of mujahidin, able, for this reason, to undertake acts of physical violence. Their roles and accolades within propaganda materials reflect their integration into the military framework, illustrating that both the Islamic State and al Qaeda consider them essential, active members of their combat forces. In their propaganda, propagandists seemingly "belong" in the military apparatuses of their respective groups.

The Propagandists' Partiality and Contribution to Jihad

The second element visible in how propagandists of al Qaeda and the Islamic State depict themselves is their demonstrated partiality, meaning that they "fight" because they actively support one side of a conflict. Propaganda inherently embodies this partiality, as it is a strategic tool designed to persuade audiences and achieve specific political and strategic objectives. Propagandists explicitly align with one side: they operate strategically, advancing the interests of their affiliated side. Both al Qaeda and the Islamic State recognize and emphasize the significant, positive contribution of propaganda to their respective causes.

Al Qaeda

Al Qaeda's leadership, particularly Ayman al-Zawahiri, has underscored the critical role of propaganda in their strategy. Al-Zawahiri famously articulated that "more than half of this battle is taking place in the battlefield of the media," emphasizing that media warfare is crucial for winning the hearts and minds of their community (Al-Zawahiri, 2005), while urging that: "We must get our message across to the masses of the nations and break the media siege imposed on the jihad movement. This is an independent battle that we must launch side by side with the military battle" (Al-Zawahiri, 2005). Similarly, for Osama bin Laden (who, interestingly, is here quoted by the Islamic State, showcasing an apparent consensus between both groups about this issue), "There is a group of media operatives and companions of the pen that has a prominent and important role in steering the war, shattering the morale of the enemy and raising the spirits of the ummah" (Islamic State 2016b, 3). This perspective that combat is partly conducted through the pen is echoed in the influential manifesto *The Management of Savagery*, attributed to Abu Bakr Naji, which highlights the essential role of media in conveying the jihadist message to the Umma, explaining that "It only remains for us to create media information and effective (religious) propaganda so that this meaning may be conveyed to the Umma—all of the Umma—without complication beneath the shadow of that terrible battle whose foretokens have appeared" (Naji, 2005, 83). This demonstrates the perception within al Qaeda that propaganda is not merely supportive at the margins but directly contributes positively to advancing jihad. Carsten

Bockstette's seminal 2008 report, in which the author notes that "jihadist terrorists place a great deal of emphasis on developing comprehensive communication strategies in order to reach their desired short-, mid- and long-term goals and desired end states [with an] ability to develop and implement such sophisticated strategies shows their fanatic conviction and their professionalism" confirms that al Qaeda places significant emphasis on comprehensive communication strategies to achieve their objectives, highlighting the professionalism and conviction behind these efforts (Bockstette, 2008). Al Qaeda, thus, counts on propaganda to advance its cause and strengthen its side of the conflict; propagandists, in this sense, by showing partiality, help their side of the conflict.

The Islamic State

The Islamic State, among all the groups, is certainly the one that goes the furthest into glorifying the role of propaganda in jihad. Despite Abu Bakr al-Baghdadi's infrequent public appearances, his commitment to media operations is evident in the sophisticated and expansive propaganda machinery developed under his leadership. The Islamic State's strategic use of social media, and emotionally charged high-quality video content reflects a deliberate effort to engage and mobilize supporters, particularly among younger audiences, contrasting with al Qaeda's more traditional methods (Aggarwal, 2019). The Islamic State manual, *How to Survive in the West* (Islamic State, 2015a, 64), emphasizes the primacy of propaganda, stating that "media propaganda is the first step to justify what will happen later." It also identifies propaganda as "the most important aspect of guerrilla warfare because public support means the public will support your cause, give you money and men, and even hid you in moments of danger. 'You are the people,' that's what guerrilla warfare is. If the people turn against you, then you have lost the war" (Islamic State, 2015a).

Moreover, as previously discussed, the Islamic State's Arabic newsletter, Al-Naba, regularly eulogizes "martyrs" who have died for jihad, including propagandists.[2] This practice distinguishes propagandists from other non-fighting members of the caliphate, such as women, children, and

[2] Al-Naba is the weekly newsletter of the Central Media Office of the Islamic State. It was first published in 2014 and is still being published today. This Arabic newsletter aims at sharing local news, military operations, as well as international news. It also publishes religious articles, as well as advocacy documents.

the elderly, who do not typically receive such honors. Propagandists, however, are frequently the subject of tribute videos, martyrdom articles, and official acknowledgments from amirs, who publicly recognize their contributions to the jihad. In the previously mentioned eulogy for the propagandist Abu Muhammad al-Furqan, for instance, the Islamic State explicitly links propaganda to battlefield effectiveness, asserting that:

> The war of doctrines and ideas is no less important and fierce than the wars of iron and fire through which the armies fight each other and as a result of which skulls are smashed, blood is shed, and people are destroyed. Indeed, there is no exaggeration in saying that the war of ideas is the foundation on which most of the wars of iron and fire arise. (Islamic State, 2021a)

This sentiment is echoed in the case of Fabien Clain, a prominent French propagandist, who received direct recognition by none other than Abu Bakr al-Baghdadi for his role in the organization's efforts (Agence France Presse, 2019; Robin, 2024).

In sum, both al Qaeda and the Islamic State portray their propagandists as playing an indispensable, positive role in advancing their causes. They help. By actively supporting their respective sides, these propagandists present themselves as part of the "fight" due to their clear alignment with and contribution to the cause ("partiality"). I now turn to the final characteristic underlined by the jihadist propagandists about their activities and their relation to the battlefield: their capacity to inflict harm on the opposing side.

The Propagandists' Impact on the Opposing Side: Propaganda's Ability to Harm

I now show that propagandists from al Qaeda and the Islamic State depict propagandists not merely as a tool for spreading ideology, but also as a strategic weapon designed to weaken, and effectively *harm* the enemy. In so doing, the propagandists of al Qaeda and the Islamic State position themselves as fighters.

Al-Qaeda

Al-Qaeda's strategic documents underscore the "harmful" dimension of propaganda and its capacity to diminish the enemy. In *the Management of*

Savagery, Abu Bakr Naji directly associates the harm inflicted through combat with the harm caused by media operations, highlighting that both forms of "fighting" are essential to achieving victory. Naji writes that "Those who have not boldly entered wars during their lifetimes do not understand the role of violence and coarseness against the infidels in combat and media battles" (Naji, 2005, 73), reflecting his belief that media operations are a form of fighting (and of violence) capable of causing significant damage to the enemy. Naji further emphasizes the causal relationship between media operations and military success, stating that: "Understanding the media politics of the adversaries and dealing with them is very important in winning the military and political battle" (Naji, 2005). His perspective is here central to al-Qaeda's broader strategy, where propaganda is not just a tool for spreading ideology but is seen as a weapon that can weaken the enemy's resolve and effectiveness. Propagandists, in this view, are presented as central actors of the battlefield, able to harm the opponents, and not just as peripheral supportive operators.

It is widely acknowledged: al Qaeda propagandists have utilized various online platforms and social media to urge Muslims to participate in jihad (Ayad, 2024; El Difraoui, 2013). The most famous of them, Anwar al-Awlaki, impact wise, was directly linked to several significant attacks, including the 2009 Fort Hood shooting, the attempted bombing of Northwest Airlines Flight 253, the 2013 Boston Marathon bombing (Bergen, 2016), as well as the San Bernardino shootings and the Orlando nightclub attack (Shane, 2016). Through his influential voice, al-Awlaki was able to inspire numerous individuals to carry out attacks across different locations, thereby having a tangible and detrimental impact on the opposing side of the conflict. His ability to incite violence through his words arguably demonstrates the lethal potential of jihadist propaganda, positioning it as a weapon capable of causing real-world harm.

Propaganda not only recruits but it also provides operational guidance which can facilitate direct harm. Al Qaeda, throughout the years, has shared many textbooks, sometimes gathered in "encyclopedias" of several hundred pages such as the encyclopedia of jihad (*mawsu'*et al. *-jihad*), the encyclopedia of weapons (*mawsu'*et al. *-asliha al-kubra*), the encyclopedia of planning (*mawsu'*et al.- *'idad*). There, individuals would receive direct information on how to conduct attacks, how to build bombs, or how to use a knife with the intent to kill. In 2003 and 2004, when the physical camps of the organization had been destroyed in Afghanistan, the group even sought to move its training programs online, by creating a magazine, titled *mu'askar al-battar* (Camp al-Battar), designed as a virtual training camp for "wannabe jihadists" (Hecker, 2015, 22).

Al Qaeda propagandists depict their activities as having a clear harmful impact on the other side by showing their role in recruiting assailants, in sharing operational advice and guidance on how to wage this violence, and in directly calling onto violent acts to be committed. Within the Islamic State too—for example when the modalities of the car bombing attack in Notre-Dame exactly correspond to the guidelines provided by propagandist Rachid Kassim—propaganda is understood as having the ability to harm.

The Islamic State

The Islamic State has been explicit in its recognition of propaganda as a weapon. As analyzed by British researcher Charlie Winter, "for the Islamic State, the mainstream media is considered to be an effective weapon that, if leveraged correctly, has 'far-reaching' power that can exceed that of the most powerful bombs" (Winter, 2017, 3). In its propaganda, IS places propaganda and the narratives it develops, as one of the frontlines of the group, in order to harm and weaken their opponents. In its information doctrine, *Media Operative, you are a mujahid too*, the group quotes two hadiths: "Strive against the polytheists with your money, your bodies and your tongues" (Islamic State, 2016b, 7) and "satire is more grievous to them than the hurt of an arrow" (Islamic State, 2016b, 27). This is done to present propaganda as part of the greatest "forms of the rite of jihad" (Islamic State, 2016b). Propaganda, it contends, can harm the opponent as much as a conventional weapon, if not more. Because of this harmfulness of propaganda, in its Dabiq magazine, the group warns that its opponents are not only engaging in military combat but also in "fighting the Islamic State ideologically, politically, and through propaganda" (Islamic State 2015b). This recognition equates propaganda efforts with traditional military assaults, signaling that the Islamic State understands propaganda not as a peripheral activity but as a weapon with the direct potential to harm. This is for example the case when it mentions the existence of "media trenches" (Islamic State, 2014a, 43–44) or when it states that "this is the punishment for one who merely attempts to divide the Muslim Jama'ah—the Khilafah—through propaganda and arms." In doing so, the Islamic State promises a similar punishment to those harming the group militarily than those doing it through propaganda (Islamic State, 2016c, 8).

Tellingly, the fact that propaganda can harm clearly appears in jihadist training manuals. The Islamic State's *How to Survive in the West* goes so far as to claim that propaganda is "the most important aspect of guerrilla warfare," arguing, as previously underlined, that "if the people turn against you, then you have lost the war" (Islamic State 2015a, 64). By equating a loss in public perception with losing the war, the Islamic State thus elevates propaganda to the status of a decisive weapon in the jihadist arsenal. Various issues of Dabiq also contribute to this elevation of propaganda as a decisive weapon. For instance, in its issue 12, the Islamic State describes how its media fighters are engaged in an ideological battlefield that complements the physical battlefield. The magazine states that "just as the strong military campaign of the soldiers of the Khilafah was crushing the forces of disbelief on the physical battlefield, the strong media campaign launched by the media soldiers of the Khilafah on the ideological battlefield continued to crush and destroy every specious argument invented by the jihad claimants and those infected with the diseases of irja and hizbiyyah" (Islamic State, 2015b, 40).[3] This framing, in addition to further elevating the status of propagandists within the organization, also highlights the perceived efficacy of media operations in weakening the enemy's resolve and legitimacy. Such is also the case in its French-language magazine Dar al-Islam, where the group republished an analysis by French analyst Cédric Mas. Mas argued that the Islamic State "makes a military and operational use of propaganda, which is not only a means to legitimize or to recruit, but veritably an operational and autonomous mode of action against its enemies" (Islamic State, 2016a). The Islamic State endorsed this analysis, adding commentary that further insisted, with pride, on the militarization of its propaganda activities (Islamic State, 2016a, 88–89). This endorsement underscores the

[3] As it is used here, irja refers to the Murji'ah movement, a theological doctrine which argues that judgment of faith should be left to God. The Islamic State rejects this doctrine, contending that some actions are so grave (abandoning the caliphate for example) that they amount to apostasy and can remove a person from Islam. Hizbiyyah means partisan-ism. It has to do with issues of factionalism within the Muslim community (having different parties or groups within the Muslim community), which the Islamic State sees as un-Islamic. The Islamic State instead insists on Muslim unity under a single leader and interpretation of faith, which they claim to represent as the only legitimate Islamic authority.

group's pride in its ability to use propaganda as a means of inflicting harm on its adversaries, blurring the lines between media operations and traditional combat.

The Islamic State's treatment of Western journalists also illustrates the group's view of propaganda as a weapon. The execution of Steven Sotloff, for instance, a US-Israeli journalist captured by the Islamic State in 2013, was justified not as an act of retribution against an innocent civilian, but as a necessary action in the media war against Islam's enemies. The group portrayed Sotloff as a participant in the broader media struggle against the caliphate, i.e., as a fighter, arguing that his work for Western and Jewish publications made him a fighter in the ideological war (Islamic State 2014a). According to the group,

> The case of Steven Sotloff contains a direct refutation against those who portray western journalism and humanitarian aid as purely innocent, for this man was a Jew and citizen of the Jewish state. In addition to his work for crusader media including Time, National Interest, Foreign Policy, the Christian Science Monitor, and the Long War Journal, he also "freelances" for two Jewish publications—the Jerusalem Report and the Jerusalem Post. *The war against Islam for the sake of taghut is a media war as well as a military and intelligence struggle.*

This rationale not only justifies the killing of journalists but also reinforces the Islamic State's view that media figures are fighters (and thus legitimate targets in the conflict). This reframing moves propagandists from the margins to the center of the battlefield, signaling a profound shift in how jihadist groups conceptualize warfare in the digital age.

All in all, both al Qaeda and the Islamic State depict their propagandists as wielding a form of power that is inherently harmful to the enemy. By framing propaganda as a weapon capable of causing significant damage, these groups elevate their media operatives to the status of fighters, whose efforts are essential to the overall war effort. The jihadist understanding of propaganda as a weapon challenges conventional distinctions between fighters and civilians, suggesting that those who engage in ideological and media battles are as integral to the war effort as those who take up arms.

Conclusion

This chapter examined how propagandists within al Qaeda and the Islamic State depict themselves in their own documents. It demonstrated that these propagandists see themselves not as peripheral supporters of military operations but as integral members of the fighting organization as these groups envision it. Through their communication activities, they situate themselves at the heart of the battlefield, alongside traditional combatants. For both groups, words are not merely tools for persuasion but weapons of war. Propagandists propose three narratives about their relationships' to the battlefield: they belong to a military structure (belonging), directly contribute to organizational objectives (partiality), and inflict harm on the enemy (impact).

By elevating propagandists to the status of fighters, al Qaeda and the Islamic State challenge the traditional notion of the battlefield as well as that of the fighter, suggesting that modern warfare's core has expanded to include ideological, rather than purely physical, combat. Both al Qaeda and the Islamic State deliberately position their media operatives as essential fighters, using propaganda as a strategic weapon to inflict psychological, ideological, and operational harm. This shift challenges conventional, legal distinctions between combatants and civilians, redefining the battlefield to encompass the ideological harm.

What are the broader implications of recognizing this self-depiction of propagandists as fighters? How does this contribute to our understanding of the evolving nature of warfare? And what is the significance of acknowledging the shift from the margins to the center of the battlefield of these jihadist propagandists in jihadist thought?

Several key conclusions can be drawn. First, at the ethical level, recognizing that al Qaeda and the Islamic State portray propagandists as fighters signals a significant expansion in the definition of combat. This redefinition lowers the threshold for what constitutes participation in warfare. As demonstrated by other studies, both groups have worked to broaden the categories of individuals and actions considered part of the fight (Benotman & Malik, 2016; Morris, 2024). This trend weaponizes all aspects of society, blurring the lines between civilians and fighters. The result is a movement toward "total war," where even speech is framed as combat, eroding the distinction not only between fighters and civilians, but also between wartime and peacetime activities. This has profound implications for international norms and humanitarian law, as it risks normalizing perpetual conflict and complicates efforts to safeguard non-combatants (Dörmann, 2005; Kinsella, 2005).

Second, within the broader context of social movement and guerrilla warfare literature, this shift in the role of propagandists highlights a key trend in terrorism studies: the strategic use of rhetoric, such as the bandwagon effect, by insurgent groups. By portraying anyone—especially media operatives—as essential to the war effort, these groups enhance recruitment. They offer potential members the opportunity to perceive their contributions, however modest, as pivotal to the group's success. This narrative creates a sense of inclusivity, empowering supporters to view even non-physical actions as vital forms of participation in warfare.

Third, and perhaps most significantly, this chapter contributes to the broader discussion on the changing character of war. The fact that propagandists within al Qaeda and the Islamic State view themselves as fighters underscores a critical evolution in modern conflict. The distinction between fighter and civilian is increasingly difficult to maintain (Kinsella, 2011). Propagandists, once relegated to the periphery, now arguably occupy the core of the battlefield, blurring the legal principle of distinction that traditionally separated combatants from non-combatants. This development challenges existing frameworks in international law and forces a reconsideration of how combatant status is defined in asymmetric warfare (Kinsella, 2011; Robin, 2024).

From this, a practical and operational question arises: why would propagandists, typically perceived as civilians operating in relative safety, willingly present themselves as fighters? By adopting this identity, they expose themselves to greater danger, as they arguably accept to become subject to lethal force under the principle of distinction in armed conflict. This paradox invites further investigation. While this chapter has shown that propagandists depict themselves as fighters, it raises the question of whether this self-representation serves strategic purposes beyond self-aggrandizement. Does adopting the identity of a fighter enhance their credibility, inspire greater loyalty among followers, encourage additional followers into joining in what is now presented as part of the highest form of jihad (Winter, 2017, 11), or deter adversaries? Or does it reflect an ideological commitment so profound that the risk of being targeted is seen as a necessary sacrifice in the service of the cause? These questions suggest avenues for future research, particularly regarding the motivations and strategic calculations behind this embrace of vulnerability in jihadist propaganda.

References

Primary sources

Agence France Presse. (2019, April 29). *L'EI diffuse une vidéo de son 'chef' pour la première fois depuis cinq ans L'Express*. https://www.lexpress.fr/monde/l-ei-diffuse-une-video-de-son-chef-pour-la-premiere-fois-depuis-5-ans_2075542.html

Al-Zawahiri, A. (2005). *Letter to Abu Musab al-Zarqawi*.

Cogné, G. (2016, September 12). Qui est Rachid Kassim, soupçonné d'inciter les jihadistes français à passer à l'acte ? *France Info*. https://www.francetvinfo.fr/faits-divers/terrorisme/policiers-tues-a-magnanville/qui-est-rachid-kassim-soupconne-de-mettre-les-jihadistes-francais-en-contact_1821511.html

Djene, E. (2024, January 16). Extrême-Nord: l'État islamique exécute 4 civils chrétiens en représailles au conflit israélo-palestinien. *Actu Cameroun*.

Holbrook, D. (2018). *Al-Qaeda 2.0: A critical reader*. Oxford University Press.

Islamic State. (2014a, October 11). Dabiq 4. The Failed Crusade. *Al Hayat Media Center*.

Islamic State. (2014b, July 27). Dabiq 2. The Flood. *Al Hayat Media Center*.

Islamic State. (2015a). *How to survive in the West. A Mujahid guide*.

Islamic State. (2015b, November 18). Dabiq 12. Just Terror. *Al Hayat Media Center*.

Islamic State. (2015c, May 21). Dabiq 9. They Plot and Allah Plots. *Al Hayat Media Center*.

Islamic State. (2016a). Dar al-Islam 8. Attentats sur la voie prophétique (Attacks on the Prophet's path). *Al Hayat Media Center*.

Islamic State. (2016b). Media Operative, You are also a Mujahid. *Al-Himmah Publication*. In Ingram, H. J., Whiteside, C., & Winter, C. (Eds.) (2020), *The ISIS Reader. Milestone Texts of the Islamic State Movement* (pp. 215–225). Hurst & Company.

Islamic State. (2016c). Dabiq 13. The Rafidah from Ibn Saba' to the Dajjal. *Al Hayat Media Center*.

Islamic State. (2021a, May). Story of a Martyr: The Mujahid Sheikh Abu Muhammad al-Furqan. Part 1. *Al-Naba Newsletter*, issue 285.

Islamic State. (2021b, May). Story of a Martyr: The Mujahid Sheikh Abu Muhammad al-Furqan. Part 2. *Al-Naba Newsletter*, issue 287.

Islamic State. (n.d.a). *Responsibilities of Media Offices towards Military Media*.

Islamic State. (n.d.b). *Clarification regarding the media of the Islamic State*.

Joscelyn, T. (2019, September 17). Abu Bakr al-Baghdadi praises the Islamic State's global operations. *Long War Journal*. https://www.longwarjournal.org/archives/2019/09/abu-bakr-al-baghdadi-preaches-patience-to-his-so-called-caliphates-soldiers.php

La Croix. (2017, February 11). *Le djihadiste français Rachid Kassim visé par la coalition en Irak.*
Marighella, C. (1971). *Minimanual of the urban guerrilla.* Pattern Books.
Naji, A. B. (2005). *The management of Savagery.* Harvard University.
Rushe, D., McGreal, C., Burke, J., & Harding, L. (2011, September 30). Anwar al-Awlaki death: US keeps role under wraps to manage Yemen fallout. *The Guardian.* https://www.theguardian.com/world/2011/sep/30/anwar-al-awlaki-yemen?newsfeed=true

References

Aggarwal, N. K. (2019). *Media persuasion in the Islamic State.* Columbia University Press.
Ayad, M. (2025, February 12). A decade after the 'Caliphate': The state of the Islamic State online. *Institute for Strategic Dialogue.* https://www.isdglobal.org/digital_dispatches/a-decade-after-the-caliphate-the-state-of-the-islamic-state-online/
Ayad, M. (2024, September 13).From message boards to TikTok: al-Qaeda's two decades of internet exploitation. *Institute for Strategic Dialogue.* https://www.isdglobal.org/digital_dispatches/from-message-boards-to-tiktok-al-qaedas-two-decades-of-internet-exploitation/
Barros, A., & Thomas, M. (Eds.). (2018). *The civilianization of war. The changing civil-military divide, 1914–2014.* Cambridge University Press.
Benotman, N., & Malik, N. (2016). The children of Islamic State. *Quilliam Foundation, 7*, 1–100.
Bergen, P. (2016). *The United States of Jihad. Investigating America's homegrown terrorists.* Crown Publishers.
Bockstette, C. (2008). *Jihadist terrorist use of strategic communication management techniques. Occasional Paper Series, George C. Marshall, European Center for Security Studies,* 20.
Bond, S. (2023, February 28). How Russia is losing—And winning—The information war in Ukraine. *NPR.*
Braddock, K. (2020). *Weaponized words: The strategic role of persuasion in violent radicalization and counter-radicalization.* Cambridge University Press.
Buzan, B.; Wæver, O., & de Wilde, J. (1998). *Security. A new framework for analysis.* Lynne Rienner.
Dörmann, K. (2005). The legal situation of 'unlawful/unprivileged combatants.' *International Review of the Red Cross, 85*(849), 45–74.
El Difraoui, A. (2013). *Al Qaïda par l'image.* Presses Universitaires de France.
European Parliament. (2016, March). Foreign fighters—Member State responses and EU action, *Briefing.* https://www.europarl.europa.eu/EPRS/EPRS-Briefing-579080-Foreign-fighters-rev-FINAL.pdf

France info. (2024, September 11). *Attentats déjoués pendant les JO, menace terroriste en France... Le 8h30 franceinfo d'Olivier Christen.*

De Graaf, B., & Dimitriu, G. (2015). Shaping societies for war: Strategic narratives and public opinion. In De Graaf, B. & Dimitriu, G. (Eds.), *Strategic Narratives, Public Opinion and War* (pp. 31–42). Routledge.

Gunaratna, R., & Oreg, A. (2010). Al Qaeda's organizational structure and its evolution. *Studies in Conflict & Terrorism, 33*(12), 1043–1078.

Hecker, M. (2015, June). Web social et djihadisme: Du diagnostic aux remèdes, *IFRI: Focus stratégique, 57.*

Hussein, H. (2016, March 18). La vengeance, mythe mobilisateur de Daesh, *Les cahiers de l'Islam. Revue d'études sur l'islam et le monde musulman.*

Ingram, H. J., Whiteside, C., & Winter, C. (2020). *The ISIS reader. Milestone texts of the Islamic state movement*. Hurst & Company.

Kinsella, H. M. (2011). *The image before the weapon.* Cornell University Press.

Kinsella, H. M. (2005). Discourses of difference: Civilians, combatants, and compliance with the laws of war. *Review of International Studies, 31*(1), 163–185.

Liebich, A. (2023, May 13). The Propaganda War over Ukraine: Unanimity, on Both Sides? *Global Challenges*. https://globalchallenges.ch/issue/13/the-propaganda-war-over-ukraine-unanimity-on-both-sides/

Meleagrou-Hitchens, A. (2020). *Incitement: Anwar al-Awlaki's Western Jihad.* Harvard University Press.

Milton, D. (2018, August). Pulling back the curtain. An inside look at the Islamic State's Media Organization. *Combating Terrorism Center at West Point.*

Moore, A. W. (2018). *Bombing the city. Civilian accounts of the Air War in Britain and Japan, 1939–1945*. Cambridge University Press.

Morris, A. M. (2024). Who becomes a foreign fighter? Characteristics of the Islamic State's Soldiers. *Terrorism and Political Violence, 36*(2), 246–264.

Nasr, W. (2016). La violence, une fin ou un moyen pour l'État islamique ? *Inflexions, 31*(1), 47–53.

Passot, O. (2018). L'activité de renseignement des groupes jihadistes, *Étude de l'IRSEM*, 60.

Payne, K. (2009). Winning the Battle of Ideas: Propaganda, Ideology and Terror. *Studies in Conflict and Terrorism, 32*(2), 109–128.

Reporters without borders. (2023, February 13). Conflict in the DRC: Over 50 attacks on newsrooms and journalists recorded in North Kivu in less than a year.

Robin, M. (2024). Words rather than swords analysing the ethical status of propagandists in warfare. *Review of International Studies, 50*(6), 1046–1065.

Schmitt, O. (2022, June 16). 'Il ne faut pas humilier la Russie'. La formule et ses implications politico-stratégiques. *Le Rubicon.*

Shane, S. (2016, July). The enduring influence of Anwar al-Awlaki in the Age of the Islamic State. *CTC Sentinel*,*9*(7).
Stearns, J. K. (2024, August 21). Rwanda-Congo: The war of narratives. *Center on International Cooperation*. https://cic.nyu.edu/resources/rwanda-congo-the-war-of-narratives/.
Suc, M. (2018). *Les Espions de la terreur*. Harper Collins.
Viginum. (2025). *War in Ukraine. Three years of Russian information operations*. Secrétariat général de la défense et de la sécurité nationale.
Wajner, D. F. (2019). 'Battling' for legitimacy: Analyzing performative contests in the Gaza flotilla paradigmatic case. *International Studies Quarterly, 63*(4), 1035–1050.
Walzer, M. (1977). *Just and unjust wars*. Penguin.
Welch, D. (2014). *Germany and Propaganda in World War I: Pacifism, Mobilization and Total War*. I.B. Tauris.
Winter, C. (2017). Media Jihad: The Islamic State's doctrine for information warfare. *International Center for the Study of Radicalization*.

CHAPTER 8

Politics of Exclusion in Military Organizations: The Institutional Position of Drone Pilots

Vicky Karyoti

Introduction

The modern battlefield is no longer an open, clearly delineated space where warfare takes place, nor a time during which hostilities occur between two or more belligerents under an agreed—either explicitly codified in law, or implicitly by custom—set of rules of engagement and understanding of the strategic goals and what is at stake. As discussed in chapters in this book, this new battlefield can have tremendous effects on the legal regimes that govern and control armed conflict and on the ethical principles underpinning it. While these effects are understandably felt by the non-combatant population, the majority of the hostilities from the side of the West is being carried out either by military professionals or private contractors (Asaro, 2013; Galliott, 2013; Phelps, 2021; Zehfuss,

V. Karyoti (✉)
Royal Danish Defence College, Copenhagen, Denmark
e-mail: vaka@fak.dk

M. Robin et al. (eds.), *The Changing Fights and Fighters of Contemporary War*, https://doi.org/10.1007/978-3-032-05518-7_8

2012). When the margins of the battlefield are closing in, who and what is a military professional change.

Drones—armed and unarmed—have been used for over two decades by NATO states in circumstances and environments that do not merit the labels of "battlefield" and "international armed conflict," thereby proving that such usage is one of the factors that further push the margins outwards (Karyoti, 2022).[1] At the same time, both the greater society and the military profession itself have certain understandings of drone pilots as less than other military professionals. Drone pilots routinely request to be reassigned, or they abandon their profession entirely, and various Air Forces around the world have to worry about drone pilot retention. The traditional professional soldier—the combatant wearing arms on a battlefield—now seemingly appears as a remote combatant pushing buttons in a North American desert (Calhoun, 2011; Jackman, 2023; Miron et al., 2023). Drone pilots are under fire both from voices inside their institution, and the larger society for not "being a real soldier," Popular depictions and journalistic reports of drone attacks[2] focus on civilian casualties—as they should—but there is an underlying assumption that drone pilots and crews do not care about civilians, that they did not take all the precautions they could to avoid them, or that their deaths do not weigh heavy on them (Karyoti, 2021a; News Wires, 2024). As one drone pilot told me during an interview, "I might not risk my life, but I risk my soul".

This contradiction both serves to further obfuscate the clarity of the battlefield margins and soldier definitions, and to demoralize military professionals on the basis of their tasks and status in their own professional group. Let us make no mistake: drone pilots are military professionals, at least in NATO states. They enter the military force either through the same system as everyone else (France), or by starting with a separate career path, specific to drones (USA Air Force) (Phelps, 2021). But more questions occur when one starts looking into what a drone pilot is. Contrary to popular beliefs and media representations, operating a drone is not akin to "playing a video game" on a laptop in a comfortable office thousands of miles away from the battlefield (Fino, 2019; Gregory, 2011; Hijazi

[1] It appears as a kind of circular logic: drones are being used in non-traditional battlefield environments, and since drones' activities fall outside of the scope of the "battlefield", they obfuscate the margins even further.

[2] Examples of such depictions are the 2017 short films *Sentinel* and *Slaughterbots*, as well as various documentaries, such as the 2016 *National Bird*.

et al., 2019). Or rather, it is not just that; such simplification stems from a lack of knowledge on how military drones work, and what is required for their function and completion of tasks.

The gamification of the drone as shown in the public imaginary has contributed to the widespread belief that very little expertise or professionalism is required for their operation, that drone pilots themselves are as far from being a "real pilot" as anyone playing on a flying simulator at home, and that this means that drone pilots and entire drone crews are not bound and judged by either the regulations that govern other military professionals or by the standards of the entire professional group (Molenkamp et al., 2024). As a result, the very identity of the drone pilot as a professional is not only questioned but outright dismissed.

This chapter analyzes the impact new technologies have on the battlefield through the lens of the military profession: what makes a professional of the battlefield, what does not, and how the introduction of new military technologies can influence the individual professional's self-understanding as one. By focusing on drone pilots in various NATO states—such as the USA and France—and examining the concept of the military profession through a sociological analysis of the makeup, inner workings, and boundaries of the concept, I unpack the factors that contribute to a soldier's recognition as a professional. I defend the argument that a change in the margins of the battlefield does not change the foundations for the individual's self perception as a professional and a combatant, nor for their institution's policies. The thesis of this chapter is that even if there is a shift of the margins of the battlefield, and oftentimes armed forces engage in operations that are either in grey zones regarding their topicality and temporality, both the legal and self-understandings of professionalism remain as they were. Not only because it is for the benefit of the continuous respect of international humanitarian law, but because such understandings are built on foundations that are not negated by shifts in the types of war we fight (Moskos et al., 2000).

Drones & Modern Warfare

While military drones are hardly an invention of the twenty-first century, dating back to World War One, their widespread use, especially for lethal purposes, has spiked since the attacks on 9/11, and the subsequent War on Terror (Alston & Joel, 2011; Karyoti, 2021a; Miron et al., 2023). Much of the discourse surrounding military drones, and in particular lethal drones and drone strikes, concerns the ethical and legal issues arising from their use. Some of these issues start from the use of drones in civilian settings, meaning not in clearly defined battlefield environments, against targets whose status as combatants is at best disputed and at worst entirely rejected. This trend relates to the overarching theme of this book, as the shift of the margins of the battlefield unquestionably includes drone operations.

More than two decades after the attacks on 9/11 and the War on Terror, drones are not only being used but are considered an integral part of modern warfare. In the ongoing—as by the writing of this book—war in Ukraine, drones are used by both Russia and Ukraine as part of the hostilities (Fenbert, 2024) (see Theussen in this volume). Ukraine considers drones as the weapon of choice for states with asymmetrical capabilities against stronger enemies: "Unmanned systems [...] are almost the only tool for withdrawing from military operations of a positional form" (Valerii Zaluzhny cited by Psaropoulos, 2024).

The war in Ukraine demonstrates a situation where drones are being used within the temporal understanding of a war, but not in the geographic sense as the strikes occur in urban environments (News Wires, 2024). But the usage of armed drones is not limited to this war; only in the first two months of 2024, the USA has carried out attacks via drones in Yemen and Iraq (Al Deng, 2024; Guerin & Bachega, 2024; Jazeera, 2024). In both cases, drone attacks have taken place in civilian areas, affecting the local population and infrastructure. The victims most often include children, and the attacks are sometimes not even preceded by a warning (Klippenstein & Grim, 2024).

But the idea of what a military drone is should be clear: it is a tool for military purposes, whether surveillance and data collection, or delivery of lethal force. While commercially available, off-the-shelf drones are also being used in contemporary warfare, the drone pilots this chapter focuses on are tasked with operating larger, military-only types of aircraft (Seibt, 2024). They resemble manned aircraft in many ways: design, size, and personnel required (Asaro, 2013). For example, the MQ1-Predator and MQ9-Reaper are the most frequently used drones by the US, both of which belong to the MALE (medium altitude long endurance) drones. This means they are used for military purposes, deployed in operations and theatres of conflict (Kunertova, 2019). In some respects, a military drone like the Reaper requires different teams of professionals for its function; a team for launching and landing, the drone operators themselves, and weapons specialists—also called weapons officers in certain countries—in the case of armed drones. There are surveillance experts tasked with following a single target for weeks or even months at a time (Phelps, 2021).

It is important to note that drones are not the only tools or technologies that are or have been controversial on the basis of the legality and ethicality of their use. The closest neighboring technology, Lethal Autonomous Weapon Systems (LAWS) have stirred up heated debates for as long as they have existed as an idea in the imaginings of roboticists and war theorists (Altmann & Sauer, 2017; Heyns, 2016; Johnson & Axinn, 2013; Klincewicz, 2015; Lieblich & Benvenisti, 2016; Mindell, 2015; Roff, 2014; Sharkey, 2016; Singer, 2009, 2010; Walsh, 2015). The two technologies are quite similar in a lot of their technical specifications, as they both reduce or eliminate the need for human presence close to the line of fire. While still not widely used, LAWS take the concept of distance one step further by promising to take out the need for human supervision for the majority—or indeed the entirety—of their functions (Leys, 2018; Lyall, 2020; Scharre, 2019). They also present a continuity of current military technology, because automation technology can be incorporated into drones, possibly in the future removing the need for human operation and supervision. Cyber warfare poses questions of legality and ethicality as well, as the means of that type of warfare also obfuscate the temporality and topicality of hostilities (Dipert, 2010; Libicki, 2016).

Why then, if drones are not the only example of a technology being controversial, is drone warfare so contested? I support that this is largely due to two reasons: the amount and intensity of the use of drones in the past two decades and today, and the contradiction that they pose for a professional group to consider drone pilots and their crews as much part of their internal hierarchy as fighter pilots and other combat personnel. As mentioned, drones have been such an integral part of modern warfare, that they have characterized Barack Obama's US Presidentship (Heatherly, 2014; Kennedy & Rogers, 2015) but especially the ongoing—as of 2025—conflict between Russia and Ukraine. The extended use of drones in this conflict has been showcased by the extensive damage Ukrainian drones caused on Russian bombers, as well as the Crimean bridge, both of which occurred within a few days from eachother in June 2025 (Gozzi, 2025a, 2025b). This intensity, paired with the visibility of their use have made the public not only aware of them as military weapons, but as symbols of extrajudicial executions (Chapa, 2015; Phelps, 2021).

I analyze the second reason for the extent of the controversy around drones by examining the concept of professions and professionalism and then applying it to the case of drone pilots. In the next section I discuss who is a professional, and what it takes—and means—to have membership in a professional group, and whether drone pilots are indeed military professionals, and the reason this categorization matters.

Profession: A Historical Concept

Historically, a profession is different from other jobs, called "occupations" (Cook, 2004; Cribb & Gewirtz, 2015; Johnson, 1972). The term referred to a different kind of occupation, one that was distinguished from others because of its societal importance, entry systems and requirements, and rules that governed its tasks (Freidson, 1983). The occupations which were considered "professions" were: the medical, the legal, the clerical, and the military. They had exclusive authorization to perform their tasks, which is true to this day: only a surgeon is authorized to perform medical operations, an individual has to obtain a law license to practice law, priests are ordained and stationed according to the structure and operating rules of their respective denomination, and it is only military professionals who are authorized for the management of violence in the state's conflicts (Cribb & Gewirtz, 2015; Freidson, 1983).

While some of these observations are still true today as they were centuries ago, the boundaries of these professions and their tasks are a great deal blurrier now. For example, the state police are tasked with maintaining order in society, and for the execution of its tasks it is recognized that it has the right to use violence. While a surgeon is the one who can legally perform surgery, an operation is carried out by professionals with other titles and tasks: anesthesiologists, resident and trainee doctors, nurses (Cribb & Gewirtz, 2015). If a person suffers from a medical emergency on an airplane, any specialty of medical professional will suffice to be accepted to come to their aid, not just a pathologist or a nurse. Specifically in the military profession, these lines have become increasingly more flexible with the use of private contractors, non-commissioned officers, local civilian personnel as translators etc. (Elsea et al., 2008). This blurring of clear demarcation lines can further the narrative that the categorization of military personnel as the "professional" group, and especially which subgroups within it carry that label, is challenged.

Such obfuscation is generally seen as valid due to the societal understanding and acceptance of today's complexity (Moskos et al., 2000). The multiplicity of the different types of tasks within a profession is mitigated by the creation—either consciously or unconsciously—of subgroups within the larger professional group, usually corresponding to the specific task for which each subgroup is responsible (Hughes, 1958). Further subgroups might also be created according to ranks, as divided due to differences and changes in class, developments which have been central to the understanding of the military profession as such (Huntington, 1957).

Historically, the division of the military profession in subgroups according to tasks or ranks corresponded to social divisions of class; either because the existence of an aristocratic class was demanded by the existence of certain, more prestigious tasks—such as the cavalry—or because the execution of those tasks demanded a certain amount of capital, both monetary and social (Badsey, 2016). In other words, not only several aristocratic and land-owning groups were created for the execution of tasks, as was the case for the exchange of military service to monarchs for land and wealth, but to execute tasks required resources, as was the case for chariots in ancient kingdoms, or mounted knights during the Medieval and Renaissance periods (Ellis, 2004). That historical division was translated into high status; while evident that the aristocratic class already owned vast amounts of social capital—a different term for status—just undertaking those prestigious tasks awarded even higher status. Put differently, membership to these subgroups was awarded according to existing status, but it also reproduced status to the individuals within them (Dafoe et al., 2014; King, 2013).

Later, with the professionalization of the military during the seventeenth and eighteenth centuries, such divisions did not fade but simply widened to include the newly formed middle class, consisting mostly of descendants of city merchants and state employees (Badsey, 2016; Denison, 1913). While still not having the vast resources of the aristocratic class, this influx of relatively wealthy individuals resulted in creating even more subgroups, corresponding to the tasks these individuals could undertake. Each of these subgroups had its own traditions, subculture, symbols of inclusion, shibboleths, and rituals (Farley, 2019; Ruffa, 2017; Soeters, 2018).

Different military institutions around the world have different requirements and processes for the various tasks and positions within them. For example, the US Air Force has established a separate training and career track for drone pilots, separate from other types of pilots (Phelps, 2021; Royakkers & van Est, 2010). This leads to the creation of new professional groups, and even the fragmentation of the group into smaller subgroups, even within the armed forces of the same state. US Air Force officers are a professional group, but it can be fragmented into smaller subgroups, like US Air Force fighter pilots, or indeed engineers, medical personnel, and of course drone pilots. It also means that while there is a set of rules and requirements that apply to everyone within the professional group, in many cases there are variations for each different subgroup (Karyoti, 2022).

I would argue that, even in cases where all officers start from the same institutions and same training—as is the case for the French armed forces—the allocation of individuals to different subgroups according to their tasks means that while the requirements for entry and training and general rules of behavior apply to every individual, all subgroups then have different rules of behavior, as well as standards of performance. These are relevant to a number of factors: the tasks for which the subgroup is responsible, the subgroup's history and tradition, and its relevant placement within the overall hierarchy of the organization (Cook, 2004).

Professions are also characterized by the existence of very rigid set of rules for behavior, and requirements of training and education for their members, and the military profession is no exception. (Dunivin, 1994; Freidson, 1983; Hughes, 1958; Soeters, 2018; Wilson, 2007). Historically, these rules have been established by the local government—and later, state government—along with the state mandate for the military profession: the management of violence for defense purposes (Huntington, 1957; Janowitz, 1960). This is intuitively understood by comparing again to the medical profession: not anyone can or should practice medicine, without the proper training, adherence to rigid rules, and robust oversight from the professional institutions as mandated by the state (Johnson, 1972). Similarly, the management of violence—as defined by Samuel Huntington to be the function and mandate of the military professional—requires the existence of a strict hierarchy, extensive processes for the oversight of professional activities, and the creation and offering of specialized training (Huntington, 1957; Moskos et al., 2000).

Modern language has shifted the meaning of the term "professional." Acting "professionally" means to act in an ethical way, with the interests of one's clients at heart, and with a clear demarcation from the individual's private life (Cook, 2004). While these are certainly attributes inherent in a professional—in the traditional understanding of the term—they are not integral to the definition or identity of one. This means that, even if a private contractor might behave in ways that are widely considered to be "professional", in terms of warfare analysis they are not included in that group. This is not a moral or normative assessment of their activities and conduct, but an observation relevant to an objective definition. Conversely, a military professional can maintain their professional status even if they conduct in unethical or unprofessional ways, relevant to the severity of the transgression. Some actions lead to less harsh punitive measures, while others can lead to dishonorable discharge and loss of professional status (Cook, 2004). I further discuss individual conduct in the next section.

It is important to emphasize that distinction between the traditional and modern use of the terms in this analysis, as aphorisms of who is not a professional are thrown around based on moral and normative assessments of the modern battlefield. But these terms mean something different for the professionals themselves, and adherence to the criteria set for each professional group becomes a matter of utmost importance in warfare. From this analysis we can understand that there are three types of criteria: social, legal, and self-assessment criteria, which can overlap or diverge. For example, the social type of criteria does not only refer to the public opinion, but the internal social dynamics as well, with military professionals assessing the conduct of their colleagues accordingly, thereby both enacting and reproducing these criteria, and function as gatekeepers of the professional group. Finally, actions that might be seen as unethical by the public—such as the use of certain types of weapons or the engagement in hostilities in urban areas—can be wholly legitimate in a legal sense.

Drone Pilots as Military Professionals

Let us turn our attention back to drone pilots and their membership in the military profession. In order to examine whether a change on what it means to be a professional soldier, and whether the margins of the battlefield from a military professional standpoint are occurring, this section will focus on what being a drone pilot entails, as part of their professional military duties. Then, it synthesizes this analysis with the previous discussion on the concept of professionalism, to discuss the circumstances and conditions under which a military professional might lose their "professional" status, and finally how that applies to drone pilots.

For many military professionals, the risk to life and limb is inherent to the very essence of their professional duties (Contratto, 2011; Galliott, 2013; Toner, 1995). While there are certainly numerous specialties and tasks in the military that do not entail said risk, such as engineering, logistical support, research, and communications among others, the individuals tasked with these do not enjoy the same recognition and status as combat personnel (Karyoti, 2021b). Drone pilots exist in a grey space between combat personnel—especially since they often carry out lethal attacks—and working from such distance from the battlefield that their very identity as military professionals of the same caliber is contested. The fact that drone pilots routinely complain about suffering from Post-Traumatic Stress Disorder is met with disbelief and further ridicule: what have drone pilots to be traumatized about (Hijazi et al., 2019)? Their physical self is not in danger, so it does not make sense.

The reality of the drone pilot and their crews is entirely different from the widespread idea about their function. To demonstrate this, I want to draw a comparison to another aircraft, one which is considered a "real" combat aircraft with a "proper" pilot: the F-16. In battlefield situations, the F-16 pilot is certainly put in physical danger and risk to life and limb. But other than engaging in dogfights, F-16 pilots do not observe the effects of their operations nearly as close as drone pilots. Similarly, B-52 crews that engage in bombing, remain quite far away from their targets, and disengage after the mission has been completed. That is not the case for armed drone attacks: not only do they depend on weeks-long surveillance of targets, but drones are also up and close to the attacks and their aftermath, especially since they have to observe and report the results of the operation (Bryant, 2017; Edney-Browne, 2017; Gilbert et al., 2018; Jackman, 2023).

Another element of drones' operations that is left out of the popular discussions about drones is locality. Not all NATO states that engage in drone warfare conduct their operations remotely from dedicated drone facilities, as is the case on US territory. France, for example, deploys drones in the same area of operations with other units (Jackman, 2023; Karyoti, 2022; Phelps, 2021). That means that drone personnel are stationed alongside other Air Force personnel, sharing facilities and amenities with combat pilots, helicopter pilots, search and rescue pilots, medical personnel, logistics personnel, engineers etc. Effectively, this results in fewer chances for drone personnel to feel isolated, a separate and cut-off subgroup, a different class of citizen (Hijazi et al., 2019). Conversely, drone facilities in the US are reported to be of lower quality than their combat counterparts, including professionals complaining that the hours of the day during which they must conduct their missions which take place on the other side of the planet usually occur during night-time in local time zones. This means that they cannot utilize the facilities as they are closed when they would have time to enjoy them (Hijazi et al., 2019). It might seem trivial, but many drone pilots live on these bases either permanently or for many months at a time. Such circumstances result in exclusionary practices, no matter how unintentional they may be.

Furthermore, the existence of a separate career path for drone pilots means that, even as professionals within the same service—such as the Air Force—and professional group—"pilot" —their divergence from the rest of the pilot group is being reinforced and reiterated. In the services which operate on this separate trajectory for drone pilots, if one does not make the cut for the fighter pilot trajectory is seen as lesser in abilities and overall talent. The popular image of the combat pilot reproduces that idea: the combat pilot has been perceived as one of the most prestigious jobs in the military profession since the advent of combat aviation (Schultz, 2018). They have been referred to as the "knights of the air", borrowing the term "knight" which itself carries a centuries-long tradition of prestige and high status (Fino, 2017). The individuals who are not judged to be satisfactory enough for that training and career trajectory do not only enjoy the status awarded to pilots, but are furthermore seen as less exactly because they were not "good enough" (Karyoti, 2022). All these factors can contribute to a sense of alienation, demoralization, and lack of certainty in one's self-understanding and identity (Hardison et al.,

2017). But a professional's identity is meant to be built on strong foundations, especially military professionals who are aware of the risks to both their physical self and their mental state as part of their job (Toner, 1995).

The question that naturally arises is: what would shake that professionalism, then? What would be the factors and circumstances that could potentially cause a reframing and redefinition of what it means to be a professional soldier? And are those potentially transformative factors a possibility in the near future? In order to address these questions, I return to the discussion on what a professional is. As analyzed above, it is not a moral judgement on one's conduct, but that does not mean that either the inclusion of one in a professional group or the very definition of the profession are immutable. Therefore, there are two different questions to be considered: when can an individual—rather than a professional group or subgroup—no longer be a professional? And when does the profession lose its privileged status and the individuals within it can no longer be understood as professionals?

The first question is not relevant to this analysis, as it is an issue of individual choices and conduct which might violate societal expectations of how a professional should execute their function. Acting in ways which break the social contract of a profession to the greater society can and should lead to an examination of one's professional conduct and possible loss of professional status, whereas what is being addressed here is a possibly systemic issue regarding entire professional groups and the society at large. Individual soldiers and officers failing at adhering to established rules of their professional tasks do not alter the overall structure—including definitions, set of criteria for inclusion, and internal culture—of any professional group (Toner, 1995). That is not to say that group behavior, which is comprised of individual behaviors, cannot in any way cause such a transformation. But that behavior should not only be large and systematic, but also consciously and deliberately with the purpose of causing said transformation.

Drone pilots, as a new professional subgroup, adhere to said professional standards, and therefore this is not a case of transforming the larger subgroup. Not only are drone pilots not behaving in such a way that can be considered largely violating the mandate and boundaries of their professional tasks, but they have repeatedly expressed their dissatisfaction with how they are viewed and treated both by their colleagues, and the society as well (Edney-Browne, 2017; Gilbert et al., 2018; Hardison et al., 2017; Miron et al., 2023). Therefore, the question of individual behavior—even at a group level—is irrelevant to this discussion.

The second question is the core of this analysis: when and under what circumstances can a professional group or subgroup lose its status as one? Additionally, who can effectively decide that such a change has taken place? Is it the profession itself or does society have a say in it? As military professionals, drone pilots have to adhere to specific rules and standards for their duties, they are still bound by the same regulations and procedures as the entire military profession (Asaro, 2013; Chappelle et al., 2019). So long as they are recognized as official members of the armed forces, their identity as military professionals cannot be denied.

Regardless of the narrative that the grey zone kind of operations in which drone pilots take part negates their professionalism, I argue that a violation of rules of engagement and international law—if such occurs—does not erase one's professional identity (Cook, 2004). Quite the opposite; the narrative that a drone pilot is not a professional can have destructive effects on the respect for the law of armed conflict, as military professionals must adhere to very rigid regimes, and violations of said regimes leads to punitive measures, something which is significantly less possible in the case of unlawful combatants (Solis, 2010).

Conclusion

It can be argued that the shift in the margins of "military operations" and the battlefield mirrors the shift in the margins of professionalism described above. When the boundaries of who can be considered a military professional and under what circumstances shift, they can have a significant impact on the respect and application of international law, as well as public opinion's view of these professionals, and the self understanding of military organizations and the identity of its members. As we have seen, professionalism and membership in a professional group comes not only with high status, but with increased responsibilities and a robust system for ensuring adherence to established rules of conduct. Furthermore, being a professional soldier comes with its own societal expectations of ethical and honorable conduct, and engaging in warfare that is seen as illegitimate or unethical can worsen the public opinion on one's profession and further demoralize them (Chamayou, 2013; Cook, 2004).

At the same time, with the numbers of military professionals who are disillusioned with their job on the rise, and retention rates on the decline, it is imperative for military organizations to ensure not only that their members remain satisfied with their work—and in fact, remain *in* their work—but also continue to be considered as much professional as the rest of the force.

As demands for drone personnel are at an all-time high, and exodus numbers are on the rise, implementing measures to address internal discrepancies as well as dissatisfaction amongst drone pilots and crews becomes an imperative for the functionality of these institutions and the effectiveness of completing their missions (Svan, 2019). Some measures that have been deployed include monetary bonuses, medals of honor awarded for remote operations, and general pay rises for drone pilots who remain in their position for a pre-determined amount of time (Finnerty, 2022; Jackman, 2023).

These policies and attitudes can become lessons for other countries to emulate, in order to prevent the issue described above: job dissatisfaction and low retention rates. Additionally, this general idea of addressing such issues by investigating psychological reasons for exiting that stem of the professionals' identity, as well as tangible incentives for remaining in service can be applied to other subgroups within the military profession that might be forming with the movements of the battlefield and warfare margins. It is therefore in the best interest not only of various military organizations but of their respective societies, to maintain this belief that drone pilots and indeed any member of the armed forces taking part in military operations, are indispensable and integral elements of the state's military power.

References

Al Jazeera. (2024, February 1). *US military targets 10 Houthi drones in new Yemen strikes*. Al Jazeera. https://www.aljazeera.com/news/2024/2/1/us-military-targets-10-houthi-drones-in-new-yemen-strikes

Alston, P., & Joel, A. (2011). The CIA and targeted killings beyond borders. *Harvard National Security Journal* (Forthcoming, NYU School of Law, Public Law Research Paper No. 11-64).

Altmann, J., & Sauer, F. (2017). Autonomous weapon systems and strategic stability. *Survival, 59*(5), 117–142. https://doi.org/10.1080/00396338.2017.1375263

Asaro, P. M. (2013). The labor of surveillance and bureaucratized killing: New subjectivities of military drone operators. *Social Semiotics, 23*(2), 196–224. https://doi.org/10.1080/10350330.2013.777591

Badsey, S. (2016). *Doctrine and reform in the British Cavalry*. Routledge.

Bryant, B. (2017). Letter from a sensor operator. In L. Parks & C. Kaplan (Eds.), *Life in the age of drone warfare*. Duke University Press.

Calhoun, L. (2011). The end of military virtue. *Peace Review, 23*(3), 377–386. https://doi.org/10.1080/10402659.2011.596085

Chamayou, G. (2013). *A theory of the drone*. The New Press.

Chapa, J. O. (2015). Drones and the ethics of targeted killing. *Journal of Military Ethics, 14*(3–4), 284–286. https://doi.org/10.1080/15027570.2015.1127719

Chappelle, W., Goodman, T., Reardon, L., & Prince, L. (2019). Combat and operational risk factors for post-traumatic stress disorder symptom criteria among United States air force remotely piloted aircraft "Drone" warfighters. *Journal of Anxiety Disorders, 62*(June 2018), 86–93. https://doi.org/10.1016/j.janxdis.2019.01.003

Contratto, M. R. (2011). *The decline of the military ethos and profession of arms: An argument against autonomous lethal engagements* (Air War College Maxwell Paper, 62).

Cook, M. L. (2004). *The moral warrior: ethics and service in the U.S. military*. State University of New York Press.

Cribb, A., & Gewirtz, S. (2015). *Professionalism*. Polity Press.

Dafoe, A., Renshon, J., & Huth, P. (2014). Reputation and status as motives for war. *Annual Review of Political Science, 17*, 371–393. https://doi.org/10.1146/annurev-polisci-071112-213421

Deng, C. (2024, February 1). U.S. hits Houthi targets in Yemen, citing threat to ships. *The Wall Street Journal*. https://www.wsj.com/world/middle-east/u-s-hits-houthi-drone-station-in-yemen-citing-threat-to-ships-91031180

Denison, G. T. (1913). *A history of cavalry from the earliest times, with lessons for the future*. Macmillan.

Dipert, R. R. (2010). The ethics of cyberwarfare. *Journal of Military Ethics, 9*(4), 384–410. https://doi.org/10.1080/15027570.2010.536404

Dunivin, K. O. (1994). Military culture: Change and continuity. *Armed Forces & Society, 20*(4), 531–547. https://doi.org/10.1177/0095327X9402000403

Edney-Browne, A. (2017). Embodiment and affect in a digital age: Understanding mental illness among military drone personnel. *Krisis, 1*, 18–32.

Ellis, J. (2004). *Cavalry: The history of mounted warfare*. Pen & Sword Military Classics.

Elsea, J. K., Schwartz, M., Nakamura K. H. (2008). *Private security contractors in Iraq: Background, legal status, and other issues American law division foreign affairs, defense, and trade division private security contractors in Iraq: Background, legal status, and other issues*. CRS Report for Congress, Congressional Research Service USA.

Farley, R. (2019). US Air Force culture, 1947–2017. In P. R. Mansoor & W. Murray (Eds.), *The culture of military organizations* (pp. 426–448). Cambridge University Press.
Fenbert, A. (2024, February 12). *Air Force: Ukraine downs 14 drones, 1 missile overnight*. The Kyiv Independent. https://kyivindependent.com/air-force-ukraine-downs-14-drones-1-missile-overnight/
Finnerty, R. (2022). *US Air Force continues cash bonuses amid multi-year pilot shortage*. FlightGlobal. https://www.flightglobal.com/fixed-wing/us-air-force-continues-cash-bonuses-amid-multi-year-pilot-shortage/148238.article
Fino, S. (2019). Automation in air warfare: Lessons for Artificial Intelligence today. In A. Gilli (Ed.), *The brain and the processor: Unpacking the challenges of human-machine interaction* (pp. 27–43). NATO Defense College.
Fino, S. A. (2017). *Tiger check: Automating the US Air Force fighter pilot in air-to-air combat, 1950–1980*. Johns Hopkins University Press.
Freidson, E. (1983). The theory of professions: State of the Art. In R. Dingwall & P. Lewis (Eds.), *The sociology of the professions—Lawyers, Doctors and others* (pp. 13–27). Macmillan.
Galliott, J. C. (2013). Killing by remote control: The ethics of an unmanned military. *Journal of Military Ethics, 12*(3), 278–280. https://doi.org/10.1080/15027570.2013.848090
Gilbert, E., Adey, P., Akhter, M., Suchman, L., Wall, T., Weber, J., Parks, L., & Kaplan, C. (2018). Life in the age of drone warfare. *The AAG Review of Books, 6*(3), 206–217. https://doi.org/10.1080/2325548X.2018.1471945
Gregory, D. (2011). From a view to a kill. *Theory, Culture & Society, 28*(7–8), 188–215. https://doi.org/10.1177/0263276411423027
Gozzi, L. (2025a, June 2). *How Ukraine carried out daring 'Spider Web' attack on Russian bombers*. BBC. https://www.bbc.com/news/articles/cq69qnvj6nlo
Gozzi, L. (2025b, June 4). *Ukraine says it hit Crimea bridge with underwater explosives*. BBC. https://www.bbc.com/news/articles/cz708lpzgxro
Guerin, O., & Bachega, H. (2024, February 8). *US drone strike kills Iran-backed militia leader in Baghdad*. BBC. https://www.bbc.com/news/world-middle-east-68235311
Hardison, C., Aharoni, E., Larson, C., Trochlil, S., & Hou, A. (2017). Stress and dissatisfaction in the Air Force's remotely piloted aircraft community: Focus group findings. In *Stress and dissatisfaction in the Air Force's remotely piloted aircraft community: Focus group findings*. https://doi.org/10.7249/rr1756
Heatherly, M. C. (2014). Drones: The American controversy. *Journal of Strategic Security, 7*(4), 25–37. https://doi.org/10.5038/1944-0472.7.4.3
Heyns, C. (2016). Autonomous weapons systems: Living a dignified life and dying a dignified death. In N. Bhuta, S. Beck, R. Geiβ, H.-Y. Liu, & C. Kreβ

(Eds.), *Autonomous weapons systems: Law, ethics, policy* (pp. 3–20). Cambridge University Press. https://doi.org/10.1017/CBO9781316597873.001

Hijazi, A., Ferguson, C. J., Richard Ferraro, F., Hall, H., Hovee, M., & Wilcox, S. (2019). Psychological dimensions of Drone warfare. *Current Psychology, 38*(5), 1285–1296. https://doi.org/10.1007/s12144-017-9684-7

Hughes, E. C. (1958). *Men and their work*. Forgotten Books.

Huntington, S. P. (1957). *The soldier and the state: The theory and politics of civil-military relations*. Vintage Books.

Jackman, A. (2023). 'Manning' the 'unmanned': Reapproaching the military drone through learning the/to drone. *Political Geography, 104*, 1–11. https://doi.org/10.1016/j.polgeo.2023.102894

Janowitz, M. (1960). *The professional soldier: A social and political portrait*. Free Press.

Johnson, A. M., & Axinn, S. (2013). The morality of autonomous robots. *Journal of Military Ethics, 12*(2), 129–141. https://doi.org/10.1080/15027570.2013.818399

Johnson, T. J. (1972). *Professions and power*. Macmillan.

Karyoti, V. (2021a). *9/11's legacy of drone warfare has changed how we view the military*. The Conversation.

Karyoti, V. (2021b). *Politics of exclusion in military institutions*. University of Southern Denmark.

Karyoti, V. (2022). Drones and their pilots—Technology and social hierarchies within the French Air and Space Force. *Vortex, 3*, 79–91.

Kennedy, C., & Rogers, J. I. (2015). Virtuous drones? *International Journal of Human Rights, 19*(2), 211–227. https://doi.org/10.1080/13642987.2014.991217

King, A. (2013). Professionalism. In A. King (Ed.), *The combat soldier: Infantry tactics and Cohesion in the twentieth and twenty-first centuries* (pp. 338–375). Oxford University Press. https://doi.org/10.1093/acprof

Klincewicz, M. (2015). Autonomous weapons systems, the frame problem and computer security. *Journal of Military Ethics, 14*(2), 162–176. https://doi.org/10.1080/15027570.2015.1069013

Klippenstein, K., & Grim, R. (2024, February 5). *White house falsely declared it warned Iraq of impending airstrikes*. The Intercept. https://theintercept.com/2024/02/05/white-house-iraq-airstrikes-john-kirby/

Kunertova, D. (2019). *Military drones in Europe: The European defense market and the spread of military UAV technology*. University of Southern Denmark.

Leys, N. (2018). Autonomous weapon systems and international crises. *Strategic Studies Quarterly, 12*(1), 48–73.

Libicki, M. C. (2016). Is there a cybersecurity Dilemma? *The Cyber Defense Review, 1*(1), 129–140.

Lieblich, E., & Benvenisti, E. (2016). The obligation to exercise discretion in warfare: Why autonomous weapons systems are unlawful. In N. Bhuta, S. Beck, R. Geiβ, H-Y Liu, & C. Kreβ (Eds.), *Autonomous weapons systems: Law, ethics, policy* (pp. 245–283). Cambridge University Press. https://doi.org/10.1017/CBO9781316597873.011

Lyall, J. (2020). *Divided armies*. Princeton University Press. https://doi.org/10.1515/9780691194158

Mindell, D. A. (2015). *Our robots, ourselves: Robotics and the myths of autonomy*. Viking.

Miron, M., Whetham, D., Auzanneau, M., & Hill, A. (2023). Public drone perception. *Technology in Society, 73*, 1–17. https://doi.org/10.1016/j.techsoc.2023.102246

Molenkamp, A., Weerdesteijn, M., & Smeulers, A. (2024). A playstation mentality to killing? Adverse psychological consequences in drone pilots and the stigmatization thereof in the military. *Armed Forces and Society* (pp. 1–20). https://doi.org/10.1177/0095327X241236221

Moskos, C. C., Williams, J. A., & Segal, D. R. (2000). *The postmodern military: Armed forces after the cold war*. Oxford University Press.

News Wires. (2024, February 10). *Deadly Russian drone attack hits Kharkiv petrol station*. France24. https://www.france24.com/en/europe/20240210-deadly-russian-drone-attack-hits-kharkiv-petrol-station

Phelps, W. (2021). *On killing remotely: The psychology of killing with drones*. Little, Brown and Company.

Psaropoulos, J. (2024, February 7). *Ukraine's Zaluzhny Touts drones as path to victory; Russia suffers strikes*. Al Jazeera. https://www.aljazeera.com/news/2024/2/7/ukraines-zaluzhny-touts-drones-as-path-to-victory-russia-suffers-strikes

Roff, H. M. (2014). The strategic robot problem: Lethal autonomous weapons in war. *Journal of Military Ethics, 13*(3), 211–227. https://doi.org/10.1080/15027570.2014.975010

Royakkers, L., & van Est, R. (2010). The cubicle warrior: The marionette of digitalized warfare. *Ethics and Information Technology, 12*(3), 289–296. https://doi.org/10.1007/s10676-010-9240-8

Ruffa, C. (2017). Military cultures and force employment in peace operations. *Security Studies, 26*(3), 391–422. https://doi.org/10.1080/09636412.2017.1306393

Scharre, P. (2019). *Army of none: Autonomous weapons and the future of war*. W.W. Norton & Company.

Schultz, T. P. (2018). *The problem with pilots: How physicians, engineers, and airpower enthusiasts redefined flight*. Johns Hopkins University Press.

Seibt, S. (2024). *Les "drones dragons" ukrainiens crachent leur feu sur les positions russes*. France24. https://www.france24.com/fr/europe/20240909-les-drones-dragons-ukrainiens-crachent-leur-feu-sur-les-positions-russes
Sharkey, N. (2016). Staying in the loop: Human supervisory control of weapons. In N. Bhuta, S. Beck, R. Geiβ, H-Y Liu, & C. Kreβ (Eds.), *Autonomous weapons systems: Law, ethics, policy* (pp. 23–38). Cambridge University Press. https://doi.org/10.1017/CBO9781316597873.002
Singer, P. W. (2009). *Wired for war: The robotics revolution and conflict in the twenty-first century*. Penguin Books.
Singer, P. W. (2010). The ethics of Killer applications: Why is it so hard to talk about morality when it comes to new military technology? *Journal of Military Ethics, 9*(4), 299–312. https://doi.org/10.1080/15027570.2010.536400
Soeters, J. (2018). Organizational cultures in the military. In G. Caforio & M. Nuciari (Eds.), *Handbook of the sociology of the military* (pp. 251–272). Springer. https://doi.org/10.1007/978-3-319-71602-2_13
Solis, G. D. (2010). *The law of armed conflict: International humanitarian law in war*. Cambridge University Press.
Svan, J. H. (2019, October 29). *Air Force recognizes drone pilots with new medal.* Stripes. https://www.stripes.com/branches/air_force/air-force-recognizes-drone-pilots-with-new-medal-1.605089
Toner, J. H. (1995). *True faith and allegiance—The burden of military ethics*. University Press of Kentucky.
Walsh, J. I. (2015). Political accountability and autonomous weapons. *Research and Politics, 2*(4), 1–6. https://doi.org/10.1177/2053168015606749
Wilson, P. H. (2007). Defining military culture. *The Journal of Military History, 72*(1), 11–41. https://doi.org/10.1353/jmh.2008.0041
Zehfuss, M. (2012). Killing civilians: Thinking the practice of war. *British Journal of Politics and International Relations, 14*(3), 423–440. https://doi.org/10.1111/j.1467-856X.2011.00491.x

CHAPTER 9

Explaining European Military Engagement in the Fight Against Daesh

Patrick A. Mello

Introduction

In their introduction to this volume the editors argue that the actors, battlefields, and practices of war have seen substantial change in recent decades. What used to be located at the margins of armed conflict has become mainstream, as traditional boundaries of warfare have eroded (Robin et al., 2024). Against this backdrop, and drawing on previously published work (Mello, 2022), the current chapter examines European involvement in the anti-Daesh coalition in Syria and Iraq, aiming to account for the observed variance in countries' military contributions to the fight against Daesh.[1] Among other potential explanations it has

[1] This chapter is based on my article "Incentives and Constraints: A Configurational Account of European Involvement in the anti-Daesh coalition" (Mello, 2022). While the article provided a set-theoretic analysis with QCA, this chapter summarizes prevalent explanations and the empirical patterns of military involvement.

P. A. Mello (✉)
Department of Political Science and Public Administration, Vrije Universiteit Amsterdam, Amsterdam, The Netherlands
e-mail: p.a.mello@vu.nl

M. Robin et al. (eds.), *The Changing Fights and Fighters of Contemporary War*, https://doi.org/10.1007/978-3-032-05518-7_9

been suggested that the extent to which EU citizens from a given country joined Daesh as *foreign fighters* could help account for a country's response and willingness to participate in the ad hoc coalition against Daesh. The foreign fighters phenomenon prompts a number of intricate political and legal questions and it adds further complexity to contemporary warfare (see also Carlson in this volume).

In the fall of 2014, US President Barack Obama announced the formation of a multinational military coalition, aiming to "degrade and ultimately destroy" the terrorist threat that emanated from the so-called "Islamic State" in Iraq and Syria (WH, 2014).[2] Several months later, international diplomats met in Brussels to pass a joint declaration that laid out the aims in the global fight against the Daesh terrorist group, especially with regard to the support of "military operations, capacity building, and training," and addressing the humanitarian crisis in the region (DoS, 2014). In 2015, following a series of Daesh-related terrorist attacks in France, including a bombing at the *Bataclan* concert hall in Paris, and prior attacks against the satirical journal *Charlie Hebdo*, the French government for the first time invoked Article 42 (7) of the European Union's Lisbon Treaty, requesting EU member states' solidarity and assistance in the fight against Daesh (EP, 2015). Shortly thereafter, Resolution 2249 was passed in the UN Security Council, where Daesh was condemned for "its continued gross systematic and widespread attacks directed against civilians" and member states were called upon to "take all necessary measures in compliance with international law." Notably, while Resolution 2249 entailed the phrase "all necessary measures," it was not adopted under Chapter VII of the UN Charter and hence it is questionable whether it should be seen as authorization of the use of force against Daesh (for a legal assessment of the resolution, see Akande & Milanovic, 2015).

Since its formation in 2014, the multinational coalition against Daesh has been joined by 82 countries and five international organizations (as

[2] The terrorist group is variously referred to as ISIL (Islamic State in Iraq and the Levant), ISIS (Islamic State in Iraq and al-Sham), IS (Islamic State), or Daesh (*al-Dawla al-Islamiya fil Iraq wa al-Sham*). While the US government primarily uses the term "ISIL," the French and British governments have made it their policy to refer to "Daesh" since this term does not legitimize the group as an "Islamic state" and it further carries negative connotations in Arabic (Connable et al., 2017).

of January 2025).[3] By March 2019, the last Daesh-occupied parts of Syria were taken by forces supported by the multilateral military coalition.[4] However, the military involvement in the anti-Daesh coalition has been characterized by substantial variance, particularly among the EU member states. Whereas several EU countries assumed leading roles in the anti-Daesh airstrikes, other countries limited their contributions to the provision of training for local forces, often within the Kurdish Training and Coordination Center (KTCC) in Erbil, and still others merely expressed their political support for the aims of the coalition, or showed no involvement whatsoever. For example, while the UK and France took leading roles in the airstrikes, Germany and Italy limited their involvement to air support and the training of local forces, while Spain just did the latter. Others, like Austria, Bulgaria, and Slovakia endorsed the anti-Daesh coalition but did not provide material support. How to account for this variation among EU countries' contributions to the anti-Daesh coalition? This chapter proposes five approaches culled from the literature, and examines how these approaches suggest and foreclose answers to that question.

Prior work has examined the initial phases of the multinational military coalition and identified conceivable explanations for the observed variance among Western countries' military involvement (Haesebrouck, 2018; McInnis, 2016; Saideman, 2016), whereas other studies have concentrated on accounting for the contributions of individual countries (Doeser & Eidenfalk, 2019; Massie, 2019; Pedersen & Reykers, 2020). Against this backdrop, this chapter conducts a comparison of EU member state involvement in the military coalition. When the Lisbon Treaty's mutual defense clause was invoked in 2015, this constituted a historical first. Hence, it is of particular policy relevance to conduct a comparison of EU member states and their involvement in the anti-Daesh coalition. With its focus on the nexus between domestic and international politics, the chapter also speaks to the dynamics of multinational

[3] Among others, the aims of the anti-Daesh coalition have been supported by international organizations such as the European Union, the Arab League, NATO, INTERPOL, and the Community of Sahel-Saharan States.

[4] As of December 2024, Daesh-related groups were still active in Syria, where they attempted to exploit the security vacuum that occurred after the fall of the Assad regime. For a recent analysis, see: https://acleddata.com/2024/12/11/syria-which-groups-have-been-fighting-each-other-and-where/ (accessed January 8, 2025).

military coalitions where what used to be at the margins of the battlefield is moving closer to the center of attention, in line with the broader aims of this volume as outlined in the introduction (Robin et al., 2024). Multinational military coalitions have become widespread in international security, since almost all contemporary conflicts happen in the context of coalitions, alliances, or under the auspices of international organizations (Auerswald & Saideman, 2014; Karlsrud & Reykers, 2020; Kreps, 2011; Mello & Saideman, 2019; Rynning et al., 2021; Schmitt, 2019; von Hlatky, 2013; Weitsman, 2014). At the same time, the erosion of the state's monopoly on the use of force is not a new phenomenon (Kaldor, 1999; Mello, 2010), but the Syrian civil war underscored how "foreign fighters" can impact conflict dynamics and domestic political calculations in combatants' home countries (O'Connor & Piketty, 2020; TSC, 2017).

Drawing upon a framework I developed for a set-theoretic analysis (Mello, 2022), this chapter explores the motivations for EU member states' military participation in the anti-Daesh coalition. Specifically, I examine five potential explanations for the observed military involvement, which are conceived of either as *incentives* for military participation or as *constraints* that counteract such involvement. These include (1) the extent to which EU citizens from a given country joined Daesh as foreign fighters, (2) the value that a country places on its alliance relationship, (3) the political position of its government on a left–right dimension, (4) the extent to which of parliament is involved in decisions on military deployments, and finally (5) an indicator of the degree to which citizens perceive terrorism and foreign fighters as challenges to their country's security. Empirically, the chapter starts out with a summary of EU member states' contributions to the military coalition against Daesh, whose involvement included participation in the air strikes, air support, training provision to local forces, and mere political and/or logistical support for the coalition. Notably, the coalition was also characterized by withdrawals and re-entries of some of its members and these temporal aspects naturally present a challenge for explanatory endeavors (cf. Rynning et al., 2021).

My results provide a differentiated picture, demonstrating that none of the five explanatory factors can individually account for the observed variance. However, certain factors show up prominently across many of the countries that were involved militarily in the anti-Daesh coalition and others arguably served as effective constraints against military involvement. Specifically, countries with foreign fighters in Iraq and Syria and those who highly value their alliance relationship with the US were particularly prone to become involved militarily. Conversely, the chapter underscores the policy relevance of institutional constraints such as ***parliamentary veto rights*** because most of the parliaments of countries that were involved in the airstrikes of the anti-Daesh coalition include no formal parliamentary involvement on matters of military deployment policy (Peters et al., 2011); Ruys et al., 2019). This resonates with prior work that has emphasized that parliamentary veto rights can constrain democracies' war involvement if certain preconditions are met (Dieterich et al., 2015; Mello, 2019; Wagner, 2018), which further underlines the political importance of this institutional constraint.

The chapter progresses as follows. The next section examines EU member states' military contributions to the anti-Daesh coalition. This is followed by a concise review of the literature on alliance formation and coalition warfare. The main part of the chapter introduces five explanatory factors and applies these to the (then) EU-28 with the UK and these countries' involvement in the anti-Daesh coalition. The chapter concludes by summarizing its findings and their implications in the broader context of this edited volume.

Military Contributions to the Multilateral Coalition Against Daesh

The multilateral military coalition was formed under US leadership in September 2014 (WH, 2014),[5] following an official request from the Iraqi government. From its inception, the military campaign against Daesh was limited to Iraqi territory and only subsequently, throughout 2015–2016, expanded to Syrian territory. The combat intensity peaked in mid-2017, a time for which the British NGO "Airwars.org" reported civilian deaths from coalition airstrikes of up to 2,600 individuals in Iraq

[5] General information and details on individual countries' contributions can be found on the official coalition website: https://theglobalcoalition.org (accessed February 22, 2024).

Table 9.1 EU-28 contributions to the Anti-Daesh coalition

Primary contribution	*Countries*
Air strikes	Belgium, Denmark, France, Netherlands, United Kingdom
Air support	Germany, Italy, Poland
Training local forces	Czech Republic, Estonia, Finland, Hungary, Latvia, Lithuania, Portugal, Romania, Slovenia, Spain, Sweden
Logistical support	Cyprus, Greece
Political support	Austria, Bulgaria, Croatia, Luxembourg, Slovakia
No involvement	Ireland, Malta

and 1,300 in Syria.[6] Table 9.1 summarizes the primary military contributions of the then EU-28 member states (including the UK before Brexit).

The table essentially entails three groups of countries. The first group comprises those states that actively took part in the airstrikes, either through the bombing of targets in Iraq and Syria (the UK, France, Belgium, Denmark, and the Netherlands) or by providing air support to those conducting the airstrikes (Germany, Italy, and Poland). Yet it should be noted that individual contributions in this category were made at different points in time. While France and the UK took part in airstrikes from September 2014 onward, Belgium, Denmark, and the Netherlands only followed a month later. In November 2014, Italy deployed reconnaissance aircraft to the coalition, while Germany only followed in similar support functions in December 2015, and Poland even later in June 2016, also with reconnaissance aircraft.

The second group includes countries that restricted their contribution to the training of local forces, mainly at the Kurdish Training Coordination Center (KTCC) in Erbil in Northern Iraq, but also in other locations. While most of these deployments were small-scale training missions, several countries deployed substantial numbers of training personnel (between 30 and 500 soldiers, including Hungary, Finland, Portugal, Romania, Spain, and Sweden), whereas others contributed merely a

[6] These estimates draw on varying quality of reporting. For the timeframe observed in this chapter, Syrian casualty data reached a high level of confidence, indicated by confirmation from several different sources and/or declarations of responsibility by one of the belligerents. Detailed assessments of the impact of coalition airstrikes can be attained at: https://airwars.org/conflict/coalition-in-iraq-and-syria/ (accessed February 22, 2024).

handful of officers to instruct local forces (the Czech Republic, the Baltic countries, and Slovenia). Finally, the third group contains countries that provided no material contributions beyond logistics (Cyprus and Greece granted overflight and basing rights) or declarations of political support (Austria, Bulgaria, Croatia, Luxembourg, and Slovakia). Two countries did not provide official endorsements for the anti-Daesh coalition (Ireland and Malta).

Accounting for Military Contributions to the Anti-Daesh Coalition

Under which conditions are military coalitions formed and why do states decide to join them? The academic literature variously emphasizes the importance of threat perception (Walt, 1987), alliance membership (Snyder, 1997), alliance value (Davidson, 2014), international hierarchy (Lake, 2009), military effectiveness (Kreps, 2008), or diplomatic embeddedness (Henke, 2017) as some of the primary reasons why states decide to join military coalitions. Besides these general factors—which apply to a broad set of contemporary military missions and are not specific to the anti-Daesh coalition—in the context of the latter it may arguably have mattered that many countries did not want to echo their dismal experiences from the protracted military campaigns in Afghanistan and Iraq (Rynning et al., 2021, Saideman, 2016; Schmitt, 2019).

Furthermore, studies have repeatedly shown that *domestic politics and institutions* have considerable influence on decision-making processes, especially in security policy (Mello, 2014; Milner & Tingley, 2015). Decisions on military deployments are commonly decided at the cabinet table, which means that these decisions are exposed to *party politics* (Haesebrouck & Mello, 2020; Hofmann & Martill, 2021; Rathbun, 2004; Wagner et al., 2017), particularly in countries with coalition governments (Oppermann & Brummer, 2020). Governments also operate under legal and institutional constraints, which may require advance *parliamentary approval* of decisions on military deployments (Peters & Wagner, 2011; Ruys et al., 2019). What is more, most democratic leaders closely observe *public opinion*, which can thus constitute an additional constraint against war involvement (Baum & Potter, 2015; Everts & Isernia, 2015). Building on this body of work, this chapter investigates five potential explanations for the observed variance among EU member states:

threat perceptions, *alliance considerations*, *political partisanship*, *institutional constraints*, and *public opinion*. These factors were selected not only because of their frequent appearance in the literature on military interventions but also due to their theoretical and empirical relevance in shaping policy outcomes. The enduring influence of these variables has been demonstrated across a range of contexts, from the post-Cold War era to more recent interventions, suggesting their applicability to understanding variance in EU member state behavior. Moreover, each factor represents a distinct yet interconnected dimension of decision-making: threat perceptions reflect external pressures, alliance considerations capture strategic interdependencies, political partisanship highlights domestic ideological divides, institutional constraints underscore legal frameworks, and public opinion embodies societal influence. While alternative explanations undoubtedly exist, these five factors offer a comprehensive and empirically substantiated framework for exploring the complexities of military deployment decisions. The theoretical premises of these lines of argument will be introduced in the next sections.

Threat Perception

If one adopts a realist perspective, then the primary driver of why states join military coalitions or why they intensify their alliance cooperation is their threat perception (Walt, 1987). The emergence of the "Islamic State" together with increased terrorist activity in Europe and beyond surely increased governments' willingness to "do something" to tackle this new phenomenon (Gerges, 2016), particularly after the events in Paris in January 2015, when terrorists killed 12 people during their attack on the satirical journal *Charlie Hebdo* (though this was claimed by al Qaida), and particularly after the series of terrorist attacks of November 2015, which included the bombing at the *Bataclan* concert hall where 130 people were killed (claimed by the Islamic State), which prompted the French government to invoke Article 42 (7) of the European Union's Lisbon Treaty and call upon European solidarity to combat Daesh.

These events were compounded by reports about steady flows of foreign fighters arriving in Iraq and Syria to join Daesh (UNODC, 2019). Though estimates vary, most reports agreed in their assessment that a considerable portion of the more than 25,000 foreign fighters who had joined Daesh came from Western Europe, containing large numbers of people from France, Germany, and the UK, as well as smaller numbers from Belgium, Denmark, the Netherlands, and Sweden (Dodwell et al., 2016; TSC, 2017).[7] Because some of these foreign fighters had perpetrated extreme acts of violence in territory held by Daesh, and since others have engaged in terrorist activities in third countries, the eventual return of these foreign fighters to their countries of origin was perceived as a serious security threat to many European countries. In sum, the external threat perspective indicates that states with considerable numbers of foreign fighters in Iraq and Syria had a particular incentive to contribute militarily to the anti-Daesh coalition.[8]

To which extent can the foreign fighters phenomenon help to account for the observed patterns in military participation? Table 9.2 shows data on citizens from EU member states who went to join Daesh in Iraq or Syria. The data stems from the Soufan Center and Global Strategy Network (TSC, 2017). Due to the nature of the phenomenon, the reported numbers represent estimates, though most figures have been confirmed in later investigations (see UNODC, 2019). In September 2015, about 30,000 foreign fighters from over 100 countries were estimated to have joined Daesh at various points in time. About 5,000 of these individuals came from EU member states. This provides a fairly clear-cut empirical pattern: 12 EU countries had citizens who joined Daesh as foreign fighters, many of these countries also experienced deaths from jihadi-motivated terrorist attacks on their own soil (GTD, 2018). Of those eight countries that participated in the airstrikes (see Table 9.1), seven also had foreign fighters in Iraq and Syria (the sole exception here is Poland, a country for which no foreign fighters were reported). Yet, we also see that countries like Sweden, Austria, and Spain, and to a lesser extent Finland and Bulgaria, had substantial numbers of foreign fighters but their involvement in the anti-Daesh coalition was limited to the provision of training to local forces (Spain, Sweden, and Finland) or mere political support (Austria and Bulgaria).

[7] For an analysis of the economic drivers of Daesh's recruitment of foreign fighters, see Brockmeyer et al. (2018). The role of women in Daesh is examined in Loken and Zelenz (2017).

[8] This is not to imply that these dynamics were necessarily at play in all EU member states with foreign fighters. Arguably, states had the option to engage in other ways with the challenge of foreign fighters, besides military involvement in the anti-Daesh coalition.

Table 9.2 EU-28 Nationals as foreign fighters in Iraq and Syria

Country	*Foreign fighters*	*No recorded foreign fighters*
France	1910	Croatia, Cyprus, Czech Republic, Estonia, Greece, Hungary, Ireland, Latvia, Lithuania, Luxembourg, Malta, Poland, Portugal, Romania, Slovakia, Slovenia
Germany	915	
United Kingdom	850	
Belgium	478	
Sweden	300	
Austria	296	
Netherlands	280	
Spain	204	
Denmark	145	
Italy	110	
Finland	80	
Bulgaria	10	

Source: The Soufan Center and the Global Strategy Network (2017)

Alliance Membership

A different line of argument focuses on the role of alliance membership as a motivating factor for decisions on whether to join a military coalition. Here, scholars typically emphasize the value that states place on their alliance relationship as an important driver of decisions about military contributions (Davidson, 2014, 2020; Massie, 2019). This is similar, but not identical to established arguments on alliance dependence (Bennett et al., 1997; Snyder, 1997).[9] Accordingly, states may value their membership in an alliance or their bilateral relationship with an alliance leader for diverse reasons (Lanoszka, 2022). These may be rooted in their security needs, but the reasons can also originate from status seeking (Pedersen & Reykers, 2020), reputational concerns (Oma & Petersson, 2019), or financial incentives (Henke, 2019; Newnham, 2008). For instance, most Eastern European countries—especially Poland and the Baltic states—place great value on their membership in NATO and on their close relations with the US, because this provides a credible security

[9] Alliance dependence arguments traditionally emphasize the countervailing fears of abandonment and entrapment that states operate under when considering military participation (Bennett et al., 1997; Snyder, 1984). By contrast, arguments on alliance value further include considerations of prestige-enhancement, which can also serve as motivating factors for decisions on military involvement (Davidson, 2011).

assurance against threats from neighboring Russia (Doeser & Eidenfalk, 2019). Other countries, including Denmark, the Netherlands, and the UK, conventionally regard close relations with the US as a means to secure international influence and standing (Ringsmose, 2010).[10] In his application of such arguments to NATO, Ringsmose (2010, 331) distinguishes between what he terms "Article 5ers" and "Atlanticists." The first group includes states that perceive threats and insecurity and hence underscore NATO's mutual defense clause. The latter group entails countries that conventionally uphold "special relationships" with the US. Generally speaking, countries in both of these groups would be expected to lend political support and contribute to military operations led by the US, even under conditions where the mission is happening outside the formal organizational framework of NATO, as in the case of the anti-Daesh coalition.

Are there discernable patterns for the relationship between alliance membership and coalition involvement? When we examine formal alliance membership in NATO, it is apparent that all eight EU countries that participated in the air strikes are also NATO members. Yet, while this may have been a necessary condition, it was not sufficient for military involvement in the coalition since numerous European NATO members did not contribute beyond the provision of training or political support (including Bulgaria, Estonia, Greece, Portugal, and Spain, among others). Besides formal alliance membership, we could also examine alliance dependence. Here, the Baltic states and Poland are clearly among those who are most dependent on NATO due to their conflictive neighborhood with Russia. Hence these EU countries arguably have the most pronounced interests in securing a steadfast partnership with the US and therefore they would seek to maintain their status as loyal NATO members. Poland did eventually contribute with air support, providing tactical reconnaissance throughout the second half of 2016. Estonia, Latvia, and Lithuania each contributed a handful of officers to train local forces. To some extent, these contributions reflect the capabilities of the involved countries, because the Baltic states do not possess fighter jets they could have deployed while Poland does have a sizable air force. However, due to the Russia-Ukraine war and tensions on their Eastern borders, these Eastern European countries emphasized that their attention had to remain in their

[10] On alliance value considerations in Canada, see von Hlatky and Massie (2019).

immediate neighborhood, rather than deploying sizable military forces to Syria and Iraq (Doeser & Eidenfalk, 2019, 19).

Parliamentary Veto Rights

There is an emerging literature that centers on the role of parliaments in security policy and which explores the impact of particular forms of institutional constraints, such as parliamentary veto rights and constitutional restrictions on security policies in democracies (Dieterich et al., 2015; Mello & Peters, 2018; Peters & Wagner, 2011; Raunio, 2014; Raunio & Wagner, 2015). Research in this vein highlights that military deployment decisions are often dependent upon structural and procedural restrictions, and also that parliaments are important collective actors in security policy, mainly, but not exclusively, under conditions where parliaments enjoy a formal veto right over military deployment decisions (Coticchia & Moro, 2020; Kaarbo & Kenealy, 2016; Kesgin & Kaarbo, 2010; Mello, 2019; Oktay, 2018; Strong, 2015, 2018). Even though it is acknowledged that mandatory parliamentary involvement can also yield unintended consequences, as in undermining the desired democratic deliberation (Lagassé & Mello, 2018), the general expectation is that where legislatures have a say on military operations this imposes an additional hurdle for war involvement. Certainly, this should not be regarded as an absolute constraint. But whenever the public is strongly opposed to a planned military involvement, then one would not expect contributions to be approved by parliament.[11] Besides, because of the fusion between government and opposition in parliamentary democracies, preferences opposed to military engagement will typically be anticipated by governments. Hence, more often than not, the government of the day will refrain from submitting a motion when there is reason to expect a parliamentary veto on the military deployment issue.[12]

[11] An example is the Iraq War of 2003, where the combination of parliamentary veto rights and public opposition nearly always served as an effective constraint on war involvement (Dieterich et al., 2015).

[12] In August 2013, the most prominent case of a parliamentary veto happened in the British House of Commons, where MPs voted against Prime Minister Cameron's proposal to engage militarily in Syria (Kaarbo & Kenealy, 2017; Strong, 2018).

How do parliamentary veto rights relate to European involvement in the anti-Daesh coalition? For this institutional constraint, the key criterion is whether parliament enjoys the right to debate and decide upon military operations before the armed forces are deployed.[13] Drawing on comparative data on parliamentary war powers (Dieterich et al., 2015; Wagner, 2018; Wagner et al., 2010), 18 of the EU-28 members have parliamentary veto rights that apply to missions like the ad hoc coalition formed against Daesh. Notably, six out of eight countries that were involved in the air strikes did not feature parliamentary veto rights. This suggests that these have served as an effective *constraint* on executive decision-making, as only two countries with a legislative veto on military deployments, Denmark and Germany, participated in the airstrikes, and the latter restricted its military involvement to air support functions, arguably for political reasons. In Denmark, the broad political support for expeditionary warfare and involvement in US-led coalitions arguably outweighed the institutional constraint posed by mandatory parliamentary involvement (Jakobsen & Rynning, 2019).

Party Politics

The realist assumption that "politics stops at the water's edge" has long held sway over IR thinking on party politics and security policy (Gowa, 1998; Milner & Tingley, 2015). However, an emerging literature shows that ideological differences between parties on the left and right of the aisle also affect the way these formulate security policy and how they implement it once elected to government (Coticchia & Vignoli, 2020; Hofmann, 2013; Hofmann & Martill, 2021; Mello, 2014; Rathbun, 2004; Wagner et al., 2017; Wenzelburger & Böller, 2020). For example, the study by Wagner et al. (2017) finds that while rightist parties are generally more supportive of military operations, there is a curvilinear relationship with lower levels of support towards both ends of the political spectrum. Yet, when investigating governments' actual involvement in military operations, Haesebrouck and Mello (2020) find that "left-wing governments were more inclined to participate" (2020, 581). Against this mixed evidence, it is challenging to derive clear-cut expectations on

[13] Besides formal institutional rights it is also important to consider political preferences. Arguably, only the combination of both must be present for a parliamentary veto to be exercised (Mello, 2012).

party politics for the anti-Daesh coalition. As outlined in the previous section of this chapter, multilateral coalition warfare is multi-faceted and involvement can range from participation in the airstrikes to the training of local forces and mere logistical support. On the other hand, the military effort of the anti-Daesh coalition was decidedly "robust," and it took place outside the organizational frameworks of NATO or the EU. On this basis, we may assume that rightist governments were, by-and-large, more supportive of making military contributions than their leftist counterparts.

How does party politics relate to military involvement? To estimate the political positions of the EU-28 governments on a left–right scale in political space, I use data from the ParlGov database (Döring & Manow, 2018), which originates from the Chapel Hill Expert Survey (CHES, Bakker et al., 2015). Because many of the observed countries have coalition governments, I use a weighted left–right score for the overall government, based on parties' individual scores and their parliamentary seat shares. The general left–right variable in the CHES data runs from 0 (extreme left) to 10 (extreme right). The results do not yield a discernable relationship between party politics and military involvement. If we focus on the eight countries that participated in the air strikes, we can see that these are positioned across the political spectrum with French (Hollande) and Italian (Renzi) governments to the left, Denmark (Thorning-Schmidt) left-of-center, centrist governments in Belgium (Di Rupo) and Germany (Merkel), and center-right governments in the Netherlands (Rutte) and Poland (Tusk), and the UK (Cameron) on the political right. This confirms the notion that the anti-Daesh coalition, with its combination of strategic and humanitarian aims, was not a partisan intervention that received support primarily from one side of the political aisle.

Public Opinion

For theories on the democratic peace and democratic conflict behavior more generally, public opinion and citizens' attitudes are central building blocks (Doyle, 1983; Everts & Isernia, 2015; Ozkececi-Taner, 2017). This reasoning rests on the idea of a "public constraint," which goes back to Kant's well-known proposition that ordinary citizens would decide against war if they had a say in the decision. This assumes that ordinary citizens would be the ones who have to shoulder the burdens of warfighting (Kant, 2007, 100). However, when we apply this argument to contemporary contexts, we may question whether citizens' attitudes truly constitute a constraint on government policy, primarily because the population is not equally affected by the human and material costs of war (Kriner & Shen, 2010). That being said, studies have shown that, when certain requirements are met, public opinion can indeed stop governments from unpopular military engagements. For example, Dieterich et al. (2015) find that war-averse publics combined with institutional constraints—such as parliamentary war powers mentioned above—prevented the involvement of many European countries in the Iraq War. In more general terms, Baum and Potter (2015) underline that public opinion and media access are central variables to understand democratic constraints on foreign policy. Hence, public support or its absence can be seen as a key contributing factor for explaining decisions on military engagements, in addition to institutional factors such as parliamentary veto rights.

What were public attitudes towards the fight against terrorism and Daesh? Early in 2015, the European Commission requested a Special Eurobarometer survey. The survey was conducted in March 2015, when the terrorist attacks on *Charlie Hebdo* in Paris (January 7) were still fresh on people's minds (EC, 2015), even though these were claimed by al-Qaeda and not linked to the Islamic State. The Eurobarometer collected responses from about 28,000 Europeans across all EU member states. One survey question asked: "Would you say that the following challenges to the internal security of the EU are likely to increase, decrease or remain unchanged over the next years? Terrorism (including the 'foreign fighters' phenomenon)" (EC, 2015, T20). On average, 68% of the respondents said that the security challenge from terrorism and foreign fighters was likely to increase, with responses from individual countries ranging from 42% in Latvia and 44% in Lithuania to 79% in Germany and 80% in the Netherlands. Table 9.3 summarizes the survey results. We can see that most of those countries that participated in the airstrikes also featured high threat assessments. Out of those, the lowest rates were found in Poland (60%) and Italy (68%), but even these countries still had large shares of respondents who regarded terrorism and foreign fighters as an increasing security challenge. While certainly not conclusive, these survey results can be taken as evidence of a "permissive attitude" among the public when it came to questions of military involvement, at least in those countries that decided to become involved in the airstrikes against Daesh.

Table 9.3 EU-28 Attitudes on foreign and security policy

EU-28 and share of respondents who believed that terrorism and foreign fighters pose increased security challenges for the EU (Special Eurobarometer, EC 2015			
Netherlands	80%	Greece	68%
Austria	79%	Italy	68%
Cyprus	79%	Slovenia	68%
Germany	79%	Czech Republic	65%
Malta	79%	Poland	60%
Luxembourg	78%	Slovakia	60%
Finland	77%	Hungary	57%
France	75%	Bulgaria	52%
Belgium	73%	Estonia	52%
Sweden	73%	Croatia	51%
Denmark	72%	Spain	49%
United Kingdom	71%	Romania	48%
Portugal	70%	Lithuania	44%
Ireland	69%	Latvia	42%

Conclusion

Resonating with the broader aims of this volume to identify how phenomena formerly located at the *margins* of the battlefield have moved closer to the *middle* (Robin et al., 2024), this chapter examined the dynamics of multinational military coalitions. Specifically, the chapter examined EU contributions to the military coalition against Daesh in Iraq and Syria. Following a concise (and necessarily selective) review of the broader literature on alliances and coalitions, the chapter explored a set of five potential explanatory factors, which were conceived of either as *incentives* towards military contributions or as *constraints* that work against military involvement. While certainly not conclusive, the results highlight the importance of threat perceptions and alliance membership, as well as the policy relevance of institutional constraints, specifically parliamentary veto rights in liberal democracies. With regards to the former, all EU members that took part in the airstrikes against Daesh did so either under the presence of a threat, as when some of their own citizens had joined Daesh as foreign fighters, or due to considerations of alliance membership. This broadly resonates with work informed by realism (Davidson, 2014; Pedersen & Reykers, 2020). However, it is also evident that domestic factors should not be disregarded, particularly institutional constraints such as parliamentary war powers (Peters & Wagner, 2011; Ruys et al., 2019). It appears that these have posed effective *constraints* on executive decision-making, since merely two countries with a parliamentary veto on military deployments, Denmark and Germany, took part in the airstrikes, and the latter country restricted its military participation to air support functions, arguably for political reasons. In Denmark, the traditional political support for expeditionary warfare and participation in US-led coalitions possibly outweighed the institutional constraint posed by mandatory parliamentary involvement (Jakobsen & Rynning, 2019).

Evidently, and this seems to be a larger trend that extends beyond operation "Inherent Resolve," governments value the added legitimacy of parliamentary approval, also in states where parliament does not enjoy formal involvement in security policy and where there is no obligation on governments to subject missions to parliamentary debate and vote. For instance, this occurred in Belgium and the UK, where involvement in the anti-Daesh coalition was debated and voted upon by parliament (Fonck et al., 2019; Strong, 2018). Remarkably, party politics and partisanship did not yield distinct patterns. In line with prior studies' results, this should not be too surprising, because the anti-Daesh coalition did not constitute a traditional leftist military mission, such as a humanitarian military intervention, nor was it subject to purely strategic considerations, which the political right would support. Instead, the anti-Daesh coalition contained elements of both types of missions, and hence clear-cut partisan patterns could not be expected. Nonetheless, as Hofmann and Martill (2021, 322) recognize in their recent review, "party politics is more variegated in its effects than we might wish to accept." Therefore, the lack of a clear-cut pattern of party politics should not be interpreted in a way that partisanship had no influence on decision-making for the anti-Daesh coalition.

With its emphasis on comparing European military contributions and five explanatory factors, it was beyond the chapter's scope to investigate the multidimensional nature of the efforts against Daesh. Future studies could seize upon this with comparisons of capacity building efforts and humanitarian aid in the region. Besides, the human security dimension of the airstrikes deserves close scrutiny, for instance by examining the conditions under which civilian deaths occurred or by comparing the accountability mechanisms of the involved EU member states.[14] Finally, one further aspect that deserves treatment is the temporal dimension of coalition warfare (Rynning et al., 2021), by taking into account the entry and exit of several allies as the military campaign evolved, also because we know that coalition withdrawal often occurs as a function of domestic politics. Recent studies have covered this phenomenon at the individual case level, for instance for the war in Iraq (McInnis, 2019; Mello, 2020), and it would be valuable to explore if similar dynamics occurred in the anti-Daesh coalition. Finally, as mentioned in the introduction, the US-led coalition was supported by 82 states and five international organizations. Prospective studies could investigate the involvement of other groups of countries, beyond the EU context, for instance in Sub-Saharan Africa or the MENA region, and also by comparing the involvement of democracies and non-democracies in the coalition.

References

Akande, D., & Milanovic, M. (2015). The constructive ambiguity of the security council's ISIS resolution, *EJIL:Talk*! *21*, 16–05.

Auerswald, D. P., & Saideman, S. M. (2014). *NATO in Afghanistan: Fighting together, fighting alone*. Princeton University Press.

Bakker, R., De Vries, C., Edwards, E., Hooghe, L., Jolly, S., Marks, G., Polk, J., Rovny, J., Steenbergen, M., & Vachudová, M. A. (2015). Measuring party positions in Europe: The chapel hill expert survey trend file, 1999–2010. *Party Politics, 21*(1), 143–152.

Baum, M. A., & Potter, P. B. K. (2015). *War and democratic constraint: How the public influences foreign policy*. Princeton University Press.

Bennett, A., Lepgold, J., & Unger, D. (Eds.). (1997). *Friends in need: Burden-sharing in the Gulf War*. St. Martin's Press.

Brockmeyer, A., Do, Q-T, Joubert, C., Jelil, M. A., & Bhatia, K. (2018). *Transnational terrorist recruitment: Evidence from Daesh personnel records* (Policy Research Worling Paper 8381). World Bank Group.

Connable, B., Lander, N., & Jackson, K. (2017). *Beating the Islamic State: Selecting a new strategy for Iraq and Syria*. RAND Corporation.

Coticchia, F., & Moro, F. N. (2020). Peaceful legislatures? Parliaments and military interventions after the Cold War: Insights from Germany and Italy. *International Relations (online first)*. https://doi.org/10.1177/004711781 9900250.

[14] The UK-based NGO "Airwars.org" has collected a host of data on both aspects.

Coticchia, F., & Vignoli, V. (2020). Italian political parties and military operations: An empirical analysis on voting patterns. *Government and Opposition, 55*(3), 456–473.

Davidson, J. W. (2020). *America's entangling alliances: 1778 to the present*. Georgetown University Press.

Davidson, J. W. (2014). Heading for the exits: Democratic allies and withdrawal from Iraq and Afghanistan. *Democracy and Security, 10*, 251–286. https://doi.org/10.1080/17419166.2014.946017

Davidson, J. W. (2011). *America's allies and war: Kosovo, Afghanistan, and Iraq*. Palgrave Macmillan.

Dieterich, S., Hummel, H., & Marschall, S. (2015). Bringing democracy back in: The democratic peace, parliamentary war powers and European participation in the 2003 Iraq war. *Cooperation and Conflict, 50*(1), 87–106. https://doi.org/10.1177/0010836714545687

Dodwell, B., Milton, D., & Rassler, D. (2016). *The Caliphate's global workforce: An inside look at the Islamic State's foreign fighter paper trail*. West Point: United States Military Academy, Combating Terrorism Center.

Doeser, F., & Eidenfalk, J. (2019). Using strategic culture to understand participation in expeditionary operations: Australia, Poland, and the Coalition against the Islamic state. *Contemporary Security Policy, 40*(1), 4–29.

Döring, H., & Manow, P. (2018). Parliaments and Governments Database (ParlGov): Information on parties, elections and cabinets in modern democracies. http://www.parlgov.org

Department of State, DoS. (2014). *Joint statement issued by partners at the Counter ISIL coalition ministerial meeting*. Washington, DC.

Doyle, M. W. (1983). Kant, Liberal Legacies, and Foreign Affairs. *Philosophy and Public Affairs, 12*(3), 205–235.

European Commission, EC. (2015). *Europeans' Attitudes towards security* special Eurobarometer 432, Wave EB83.2, Brussels.

European Parliament. (2015). *The EU's mutual assistance clause: First ever activation of article 42*(7) *TEU*. Brussels.

Everts, P., & Isernia, P. (2015). *Public opinion, transatlantic relations and the use of force*. Palgrave Macmillan.

Fonck, D., Haesebrouck, T., & Reykers, Y. (2019). Parliamentary involvement, party ideology and majority-opposition Bargaining: Belgian participation in multinational military operations. *Contemporary Security Policy, 40*(1), 85–100. https://doi.org/10.1080/13523260.2018.1500819

Gerges, F. A. (2016). *A history of ISIS*. Princeton University Press.

Gowa, J. S. (1998). Politics at the Water's edge: Parties, voters, and the use of force abroad. *International Organization, 52*(2), 307–324.

Global Terrorism Database, GTD. (2018). National consortium for the Study of Terrorism and Responses to Terrorism (START), University of Maryland, GTD 1970–2017 data file. https://www.start.umd.edu/gtd

Haesebrouck, T. (2018). Democratic participation in the air strikes against Islamic State: A qualitative comparative analysis. *Foreign Policy Analysis, 14*(2), 254–275.

Haesebrouck, T., & Mello, P. A. (2020). Patterns of political ideology and security policy. *Foreign Policy Analysis, 16*(4), 1–22. https://doi.org/10.1093/fpa/oraa006

Henke, M. E. (2019). Buying allies: Payment practices in multilateral military coalition-building. *International Security, 43*(4), 128–162.

Henke, M. E. (2017). The politics of diplomacy: How the United States builds multilateral military coalitions. *International Studies Quarterly, 61*(2), 410–424.

Hofmann, S. C. (2013). *European security in NATO's shadow: Party ideologies and institution building*. Cambridge University Press.

Hofmann, S. C., & Martill, B. (2021). The party scene: New directions for political party research in foreign policy analysis. *International Affairs, 97*(2), 305–322.

Jakobsen, P. V., & Rynning, S. (2019). Denmark: Happy to fight, will travel. *International Affairs, 95*(4), 877–895.

Kaarbo, J., & Kenealy, D. (2017). Precedents, parliaments, and foreign policy: Historical analogy in the house of commons vote on Syria. *West European Politics, 40*(1), 62–79. https://doi.org/10.1080/01402382.2016.1240408

Kaarbo, J., & Kenealy, D. (2016). No, Prime Minister: Explaining the house of commons' vote on intervention in Syria. *European Security, 25*(1), 28–48. https://doi.org/10.1080/09662839.2015.1067615

Kaldor, M. (1999). *New and old wars: Organized violence in a Global Era*. Stanford University Press.

Kant, I. (2007). *Political writings*. Cambridge University Press.

Karlsrud, J., & Reykers, Y. (2020). Ad hoc coalitions and institutional exploitation in international security: Towards a typology. *Third World Quarterly, 41*(9), 1518–1536. https://doi.org/10.1080/01436597.2020.1763171

Kesgin, B., & Kaarbo, J. (2010). When and how parliaments influence foreign policy: The case of Turkey's Iraq decision. *International Studies Perspectives, 11*(1), 19–36. https://doi.org/10.1111/j.1528-3585.2009.00390.x

Kreps, S. E. (2011). *Coalitions of convenience: United States military interventions after the cold war*. Oxford University Press.

Kreps, S. E. (2008). When does the mission determine the coalition?: The logic of multilateral intervention and the case of Afghanistan. *Security Studies, 17*, 531–567. https://doi.org/10.1080/09636410802319610

Kriner, D. L., & Shen, F. X. (2010). *The casualty gap: The Causes and consequences of American wartime inequalities*. Oxford University Press.

Lagassé, P., & Mello, P. A. (2018). The unintended consequences of parliamentary involvement: Elite collusion and Afghanistan deployments in Canada and Germany. *British Journal of Politics and International Relations, 20*(1), 135–157. https://doi.org/10.1177/1369148117745681

Lake, D. A. (2009). *Hierarchy in international relations*. Cornell University Press.

Lanoszka, A. (2022). *Military alliances in the twenty-first century*. Polity Press.

Loken, M., & Zelenz, A. (2017). Explaining extremism: Western women in Daesh. *European Journal of International Security, 3*(1), 45–68.

Massie, J. (2019). Why Canada goes to War: Explaining combat participation in US-led coalitions. *Canadian Journal of Political Science, 52*(3), 575–594.

McInnis, K. J. (2019). Varieties of defection strategies from multinational military operations: Insights from operation Iraqi freedom. *Contemporary Security Policy, 40*(1), 116–133. https://doi.org/10.1080/13523260.2018.1506964

McInnis, K. J. (2016). *Coalition contributions to countering the Islamic state*. Congressional Research Service.

Mello, P. A. (2022). Incentives and constraints: A configurational account of European involvement in the Anti-Daesh coalition. *European Political Science Review, 14*(2), 226–244. https://doi.org/10.1017/S1755773921000333

Mello, P. A. (2020). Paths towards coalition defection: Democracies and withdrawal from the Iraq War. *European Journal of International Security, 5*(1), 45–76. https://doi.org/10.1017/eis.2019.10

Mello, P. A. (2019). National restrictions in multinational military operations: A conceptual framework. *Contemporary Security Policy, 40*(1), 38–55. https://doi.org/10.1080/13523260.2018.1503438

Mello, P. A. (2014). *Democratic participation in Armed conflict: Military involvement in Kosovo, Afghanistan, and Iraq*. Palgrave Macmillan.

Mello, P. A. (2012). Parliamentary peace or partisan politics? Democracies' participation in the Iraq War. *Journal of International Relations and Development, 15*(3), 420–453.

Mello, P. A. (2010). In search of new wars: The debate about a transformation of war. *European Journal of International Relations, 16*(2), 297–309.

Mello, P. A., & Peters, D. (2018). Parliaments in security policy: Involvement, politicisation, and influence. *British Journal of Politics and International Relations, 20*(1), 3–18. https://doi.org/10.1177/1369148117745684

Mello, P. A., & Saideman, S. M. (2019). The politics of multinational military operations. *Contemporary Security Policy, 40*(1), 30–37.

Milner, H. V., & Tingley, D. (2015). *Sailing the Water's edge: The domestic politics Of American foreign policy*. Princeton University Press.

Newnham, R. (2008). 'Coalition of the Bribed and Bullied?' U.S. Economic linkage and the Iraq war coalition. *International Studies Perspectives,* 9(2), 183–200.
O'Connor, S., & Piketty, G. (2020). Introduction—Foreign fighters and multinational armies: From civil conflicts to coalition wars, 1848–2015. *European Review of History: Revue Européenne D'histoire, 27*(1–2), 1–11. https://doi.org/10.1080/13507486.2019.1709048
Oktay, S. (2018). Chamber of opportunities: Legislative politics and coalition security policy. *British Journal of Politics and International Relations, 20*(1), 104–120.
Oma, I. M., & Petersson, M. (2019). Exploring the role of dependence in influencing small-states' alliance contributions: A reputation mechanism argument and assessment. *European Security, 28*(1), 105–126.
Oppermann, K., & Brummer, K. (2020). Who gets what in foreign affairs? Explaining the allocation of foreign ministries in coalition governments. *Government and Opposition, 55*(2), 241–259. https://doi.org/10.1017/gov.2018.19
Ozkececi-Taner, B. (2017). Domestic politics and foreign policy. In W. R. Thomson (Ed.). *Oxford Research Encyclopedia of Politics*. Oxford University Press.
Pedersen, R. B., & Reykers, Y. (2020). Show them the Flag: Status ambitions and recognition in small state coalition warfare. *European Security, 29*(1), 16–32.
Peters, D., & Wagner, W. (2011). Between military efficiency and democratic legitimacy: Mapping parliamentary war powers in contemporary democracies, 1989–2004. *Parliamentary Affairs, 64*(1), 175–192. https://doi.org/10.1093/pa/gsq041
Peters, D., Wagner, W., & Glahn, C. (2011). *Parliamentary control of military missions: The case of the EU NAVFOR AtalantaRECON* (Online Working Paper [2011/24])
Rathbun, B. C. (2004). *Partisan interventions: European party politics and peace enforcement in the Balkans*. Cornell University Press.
Raunio, T. (2014). Legislatures and Foreign Policy. In M. Shane, T. Saalfeld, & K. Strøm (Eds.), *The Oxford handbook of legislative studies* (pp. 543–566). Oxford University Press.
Raunio, T., & Wagner, W. (2015). Legislative-executive relations in foreign and security policy: A framework for analysis. Manuscript.
Ringsmose, J. (2010). NATO burden-sharing redux: Continuity and change after the Cold War. *Contemporary Security Policy, 31*(2), 319–338. https://doi.org/10.1080/13523260.2010.491391
Robin, M., Theussen, A., & Carlson, K. (2024). Introduction: The changing movements of war. In M. Robin, A. Theussen, & K. Carlson (Eds.), *From the*

margins to the middle: The changing fights and fighters of contemporary war (pp. xx–xx). Palgrave Macmillan.

Ruys, T., Ferro, L., & Haesebrouck, T. (2019). Parliamentary war powers and the role of international law in foreign troop deployment decisions: The US-led coalition against "Islamic State" in Iraq and Syria. *International Journal of Constitutional Law, 17*(1), 118–150.

Rynning, S., Schmitt, O., & Theussen, A. (Eds.). (2021). *War time: Temporality and the decline of western military power*. Brookings.

Saideman, S. M. (2016). The Ambivalent Coalition: Doing the Least One Can Do Against the Islamic State. *Contemporary Security Policy, 37*(2), 289–305. https://doi.org/10.1080/13523260.2016.1183414

Schmitt, O. (2019). More allies, weaker missions? How junior partners contribute to multinational military operations. *Contemporary Security Policy, 40*(1), 70–84. https://doi.org/10.1080/13523260.2018.1501999

Snyder, G. H. (1997). *Alliance politics*. Cornell University Press.

Snyder, G. H. (1984). The security Dilemma in Alliance politics. *World Politics, 36*(4), 461–495.

Strong, J. (2018). The war powers of the British parliament: What has been established and what remains unclear? *British Journal of Politics and International Relations, 20*(1), 19–34. https://doi.org/10.1177/1369148117745767

Strong, J. (2015). Why parliament now decides on war: Tracing the growth of the parliamentary prerogative through Syria, Libya and Iraq. *British Journal of Politics and International Relations, 17*(4), 604–622. https://doi.org/10.1111/1467-856X.12055

The Soufan Center and the Global Strategy Network, TSC. (2017). *Beyond the Caliphate: Foreign fighters and the threat of returnees* New York, NY.

United Nations Office on Drugs and Crime, UNODC. (2019). *Foreign terrorist fighters: Manual for Judicial Training Institutes South-Eastern Europe* Vienna.

von Hlatky, S. (2013). *American allies in Times of War: The great asymmetry*. Oxford University Press.

von Hlatky, S., & Massie, J. (2019). Ideology, Ballots, and Alliance: Canadian participation in multinational military operations. *Contemporary Security Policy, 40*(1), 101–115. https://doi.org/10.1080/13523260.2018.1508265

Wagner, W. (2018). Is there a parliamentary peace? Parliamentary veto power and military interventions from Kosovo to Daesh. *British Journal of Politics and International Relations, 20*(1), 121–134. https://doi.org/10.1177/1369148117745859

Wagner, W., Herranz-Surrallés, A., Kaarbo, J., & Ostermann, F. (2017). The party politics of legislative-executive relations in security and defence policy. *West European Politics, 40*(1), 20–41.

Wagner, W., Peters, D., & Glahn, C. (2010). *Parliamentary war powers around the world, 1989–2004. A new dataset*. Centre for the Democratic Control of Armed Forces.

Walt, S. M. (1987). *The origins of alliances*. Cornell University Press.

Weitsman, P. A. (2014). *Waging war: Alliances, coalitions, and institutions of interstate violence*. Stanford University Press.

Wenzelburger, G., & Böller, F. (2020). Bomb or build? How party ideologies affect the balance of foreign Aid and defence spending. *British Journal of Politics and International Relations, 22*(1), 3–23.

White House, Office of the Press Secretary, WH. (2014, September 10). *Statement by the President on ISIL* Washington, DC.

CHAPTER 10

Transitional Justice for European Foreign Fighters? What Colombia's Transitional Justice Mechanism (JEP) Teaches

Kerstin Bree Carlson

Introduction

It would seem unlikely that sectarian strife in Syria could impact European constructions of the social contract, the rights and duties that states and citizens owe each other. Yet this has been one consequence of the prolonged conflict in Syria. Events including the stalled Arab spring in Syria in 2011 and the violence practiced by the Assad regime drew tens of thousands of concerned Muslims, and others, to the Levant to contest Assad's rule.[1] It is estimated that 40,000 foreigners traveled to the Levant to participate in the construction of a Muslim caliphate, to

[1] See Mohamedou (2018) recognizing the myriad factors that drove the rise of Islamicism generally and the Islamic State in particular.

K. B. Carlson (✉)
Roskilde University, Roskilde, Denmark
e-mail: carlson@ruc.dk

The American University of Paris, Paris, France

M. Robin et al. (eds.), *The Changing Fights and Fighters of Contemporary War*, https://doi.org/10.1007/978-3-032-05518-7_10

resist Assad, or both. Approximately 6000 Europeans were among them (see Mello, this volume). Many of these "foreign fighters" participated in jihadi groups resisting the Assad regime, the most successful of which was the Islamic State (IS). At its height, in late 2014, IS controlled approximately 100,000 square kilometers of territory (Jones et al., 2017), an area larger than the UK. It also successfully sponsored terror attacks in Europe that killed hundreds. In 2019, IS was territorially defeated and its surviving adherents were collected in camps in Syria and Iraq. In Syria, these camps are run by Syrian Kurds, who began negotiating with foreign states to repatriate non-Syrian nationals. While many states repatriated their nationals, most European states resisted, citing security concerns. This has led to an impasse, where at the time of this writing tens of thousands of IS adherents and their families are indefinitely imprisoned; more than half of them are children. It has also birthed a new jurisprudence of citizenship revocation in many European states, as states seek to address the foreign fighter dilemma by severing ties to their jihadi-sympathizing citizens. Citizenship revocation of European Muslims racializes citizenship in contravention of liberal rights guarantees (Choudhury, 2017; Sayyid, 2022). It alters which European citizens have what Hannah Arendt famously coined as "the right to have rights" (Arendt, 1973). In this way, we can see that the conflict in Syria has had repercussions that include European constructions of the social contract.

Do European nationals have a right to be repatriated, and do European countries have a duty to recognize even those citizens who may constitute a security threat? This question has been considered by several national courts as well as the European Court of Human Rights (ECtHR). This latter court ruled in 2022 that while states may not refuse entry to their nationals at the border, there is no right of repatriation that obligates states to assist their citizens repatriate (H.F. and Others v France, 2022). Moreover, the rules regarding whom states recognize as their citizens, and how, remain the provenance of individual states, and international obligations apply only in broad, general terms.[2] In multicultural Europe, many of the foreign fighters who traveled to Syria are Muslims with inherited cultural ties to a second country in addition to their European citizenship (Ip, 2020). Several European countries are making use of foreign fighters' dual citizenship to revoke their European citizenships, either

[2] One such example is the 1961 Convention Against Statelessness, which requires signatory states not render their citizens stateless. See discussion in Carlson 2024.

via criminal prosecution or through administrative action (Bolhuis & Wijk, 2020; Laine, 2017). Citizenship revocation is condemned by rights organizations, including the Council of Europe, which flatly instructs member states not to do it (Council of Europe, 2019). The practice is nonetheless expanding, meaning there are increasing numbers of foreign fighters seeing their citizenship revoked, including children and minors (Carlson, 2024; Casey, 2021; Prener, 2023; Rothmaier, 2019). The practice is also metastasizing, beginning to encompass crimes other than terror committed by dual citizens (Hamilton, 2019). Criminal law is thus transformed into a means of policing and "purifying" citizenship within the polity, exiling unwanted citizens (Choudhury, 2017; Naqvi, 2022; Tripkovic, 2021; Wacquant, 2009). Liberal nationalism's middle is being moved to the margin, as ethno-nationalist conceptions of statehood and belonging are being juridified through criminal law. This constitutes a reversal of the liberal, secular, Republican methods of recognizing citizenship that have been expanding in Europe following the Second World War (Tamir, 1995).

This chapter contrasts the conceptual and rights challenges that citizenship revocation for terror is posing in multicultural Europe against an innovative South American institution, Colombia's *Jurisdicción Especial para la Paz* (Special Jurisdiction for Peace, "JEP"). The JEP was instituted under the historic 2016 peace accord signed between the Colombian government and the *Fuerzas Armadas Revolucionarias de Colombia* ("FARC"), a leftist guerilla group that fought the Colombian state for more than 50 years. The JEP is a hybrid court that focuses on restorative justice.[3] Its investigatory and judicial work aims to fulfil a broader institutional goal of unifying politically opposed groups within a shared construction of statehood and belonging. This aim positions the JEP within the field of transitional justice, the practice of addressing past injustice in order to build a liberal, rights-respecting polity (Ambos & Peters, 2022; Bell, 2009). The chapter argues that Colombia's JEP offers a template to European states as regards (re)constructing a liberal rights order in the center (middle) of governance. This is because while European countries are denationalizing their citizens by labeling them terrorists, Colombia is renationalizing former guerilla rebels (aka terrorists) as citizens. At the heart of the lesson that Colombia's JEP offers is a

[3] The JEP also retains a punitive, not purely restorative, capacity in cases where restorative justice fails; see discussion in Section II.

politics of recognition; the chapter will theorize and apply this notion to the European foreign fighter phenomenon.

The chapter is structured in three parts. The first section maps what the chapter describes as Europe's illiberal response to its foreign fighters, effectively a response of non-recognition.[4] It engages with TWAIL (Third World Approaches to International Law) scholarship, postcolonial theory, and critical terrorism studies to situate, contextualize, and examine how European illiberalism towards racial and religious minorities in the European statehood project has intersected with the foreign fighter phenomenon. The first section argues that when it comes to liberal statehood, there are more parallels between Colombia and European states than are typically acknowledged. This is because like Colombia, Europe arguably has never practiced a uniform liberal human rights governance available to all its citizens; the foreign fighter phenomenon and illiberal responses thereto serve as an example of this inequality.

The second section journeys to Colombia to examine how liberal, rule-of-law ideals are being innovatively applied through its ad hoc peace institution, the JEP. This section describes the methods the JEP is using as it deliberately seeks to transform the Colombian state around an inclusive model of belonging that affords rights to all, what historian Heather Cox Richardson (2025) summarizes as the "liberal consensus": "'liberal' because it use[s] the government to protect individual freedom, and 'consensus' because it enjoy[s] wide support." It also draws parallels between the Colombian case and European foreign fighters. When the peace was forged after five decades of warfare, former combatants were quite unpopular in the Colombian mainstream. Indeed, a referendum on the 2016 peace accords failed when put to voters, as Colombians rejected peace accords in the name of law and order, convinced that the peace was too soft on terrorists, by which they meant the former FARC (Lafuente, 2016). Yet the peace ultimately constructed has been quite innovative in the ways that it foregrounds restorative, rather than retributive, justice, expanding citizenship protections to groups long excluded from the benefits of the polity, specifically the Colombian rural peasantry from which the FARC drew its recruits (Rojas Andrade & Merchán Duque, 2023). This is one reason that the JEP claims that it is pushing beyond traditional

[4] This can even be characterized as "anti-knowledge," as terror theorist Lisa Stampnitzky (2013) articulates it, discussed in greater detail in the first section.

transitional justice practices to model *transformative* justice, a process with the capacity to effectuate structural change.[5]

Finally, in the third section, the chapter considers what a transitional justice regime, applied to European foreign fighters, might offer, and why it is preferable to the status quo in Europe. Here the chapter draws on facts and ideas presented in the first two sections to address the ethnonationalist, racist constructions that challenge European liberalism and are revealed by European nations' terror laws. It argues that transitional justice, a toolkit for liberalism (Sharp, 2018), could offer principles, tools, and methods for perfecting a liberal, rights respecting governance space in European countries. Rule of law liberalism seems to have fallen out of favor across Europe, pressed from the middle to the margins by the increasing popularity of populist, ethno-nationalist, and neo-fascist politicians. By borrowing lessons from an innovative Colombian institution, the chapter suggests how European states might bring the rights obligations at the heart of liberalism's social contract back to the middle of statecraft and governance through applying transitional justice at home.

Europe: Reifying the Citizen/Terrorist Exclusion

The refugee camp Al Hol sits in North-eastern Syria, an area currently controlled by Syrian Kurds. It has existed for decades. With the fall of the IS self-proclaimed califate in 2019, the camp was fenced in and inhabitants found themselves in a permanent open-air prison. As of this writing, approximately 50,000 people are living in the brutal, barren Al Hol.[6] Several thousand are foreigners (*i.e.,* not from Syria), hundreds are European, and more than half of the entire population are children. Conditions in Al Hol are notoriously terrible (Gopal, 2024). Summers are dusty and hot; in the winter, temperatures fall below freezing. There are worms in the water and open sewers in the streets. Violence is rife; Islamic State recruits and punishes, and dozens of murders every year claim children, men, and women alike (ANHA, 2024).

[5] Discussion during "Harms" workshop for JEP employees, Bogota Colombia Feb 2024, notes on file with author.

[6] Most of the residents of Al Hol are women and children. The information regarding where, and how many, male fighters are imprisoned in the region is less precise. The U.S. State Department cites between 4000–5000 imprisoned male fighters (Betts 2022).

For more than a decade, residents in Al Hol have been the responsibility of the Syrian Kurds who control the region. Negotiations regarding repatriating foreigners to their countries of origin have been mostly inconclusive. There are no plans to disband the camp. Meanwhile, thousands of children grow towards adulthood in some of the bleakest circumstances imaginable.

Europe as a region is strongly committed to liberal values including human rights. European states and the European Union are vehement proponents of both international law as well as international order constrained by law. European states are committed to vigorous procedural protections regarding criminal law due to the structural inequalities that arise when the state's force is pitted against an individual. Yet despite these ideological, political, and legal commitments, European states have resisted calls to repatriate their citizens from Al Hol to process them in home courts.[7] The many Europeans who remain imprisoned, including children, are deprived of even the most basic human and civil rights recognized throughout Europe. We can all agree that children are not responsible for the crimes of their parents. Yet children trapped in Al Hol have been characterized by some European political actors as security threats in their own right, "cubs of the caliphate" who are possibly radicalized and dangerous (Dagres, 2021). This position seems incommensurate with articulated European rule of law values and procedures, particularly in the way that it suggests collective responsibility or other challenges to the individualization of guilt and criminal law's concomitant presumption of innocence.

For those foreign fighters who do make it home to Europe, many are put on trial and sentenced to prison terms. Criminal trials are ongoing, and the review of the jurisprudence produced by European courts against foreign fighters is still in its infancy (Carlson, 2023; Duffy, 2018; Ip, 2020; Rothmaier, 2019). Generally speaking, however, these processes have been critiqued on a number of vectors, including the imprecision of the legal categories that are applied, the difficulty of collective facts regarding the alleged crimes committed by the defendants, and the variability of sentences (Ahmed, 2023; Anwar, 2022; Besnier & Weill, 2019; Cahn & Alix, 2017; Garapon & Rosenfeld, 2016). Children are of course not tried, but they are often separated from their primary caregivers

[7] 9 February 2025 Webinar, Mazloum Abdi, Commander-in-Chief of Syrian Democratic Forces (SDF) (notes on file with author).

(their mothers), even in jurisdictions that otherwise permit flexible jail arrangements for parents.[8] In some jurisdictions, like Denmark, citizenship revocation has been normalized and widely applied (Carlson, 2024). This of course also impacts the children of foreign fighters, either by threatening their citizenship, or removing their parent, or both.

The social contract at the base of the liberal state is constructed on what Hannah Arendt (1973) famously summarized as "the right to have rights." By redefining the who and how of recognized rights, European terror and treason trials are challenging liberal rights recognitions at the center of European statehood.

The Foreign Fighter Phenomenon: Who, Why, What

Today's "foreign fighters" are foreigner nationals who traveled to Syria/ the Levant to support revolutionary groups. The contemporary foreign fighter phenomenon began in earnest with the onset of the Syrian civil war in 2011.[9] Before this date, there were small numbers of foreigners training or otherwise participating in hostilities in the Levant or Afghanistan. At the outbreak of the Syrian civil war in 2011, there was an exodus of European foreign fighters who traveled to Syria. For some, this was a response to the tyranny of President Assad. For others, the possibilities of building a Muslim state answer possibilities opened, but undelivered, by the Arab spring (Moaveni, 2019; Mohamedou, 2018; Razack, 2008).

The Arab Spring was brutally repressed in Syria, and reports of Assad's death squads and torture practices were widely reported in European media. Dozens of armed groups sprang up, disbanded, joined forces, changed names. Some of these groups were Western allies, receiving Western funds. Some of these groups changed status in relation to Western allyship. And of course, one of these groups was the Islamic State

[8] For example, women and children repatriated to Denmark were immediately separated, even though Denmark has the capacity to accommodate families in controlled environments and even where professionals urged that separation from their primary caregivers would only further traumatize vulnerable children. Interview with Repatriate the Children representative, August 2023, notes on file with author.

[9] Of course, "foreign fighters" are hardly a new phenomenon, as external allied participants, in the form of paid mercenaries or fellow believers in a common cause, have been present in many conflicts. See Flores (2016).

(IS), a jihadi movement which rose to prominence as it emerged from and ultimately challenged Al Qaeda (Mohamedou, 2018; Wood, 2017).

The foreign fighter phenomenon reached its peak between 2012–2015, as IS was emerging as the dominant jihadi group in the Levant. In 2014, the "caliphate" was declared, with IS' leader Abu Bakr al-Baghdadi declaring himself leader of all Muslims worldwide. Awareness of the IS threat in the European theater was highlighted by the jihadi terror attacks carried out in France in 2015 and 2016. In January 2015, the Kouachi brothers, trained in an Islamicist facility in Yemen, broke into the offices of the satirical journal *Charlie Hebdo* on a day when the editorial staff was holding its meeting, killing 11 journalists and security personnel. In November 2015, coordinated attacks at Stade de France and the 10th Arrondissement, including the Bataclan nightclub, killed 150 people. On Bastille Day in 2016, an IS-affiliate drove a truck down the promenade in Nice, killing 86 people. With these terror attacks, the punitive ideology that IS had been inflicting in its territorial holdings in the Levant, both against conquered peoples as well as its own members, was brought home to a European audience on European territory.

By 2016, both the UN and its member states had aggressively passed laws criminalizing participation or other support for terror groups (Ramraj et al., 2012) (see Mello in this volume). This made it possible to prosecute Europeans attempting to travel to Syria as well as to prosecute those who had been in Syria and returned home (Andersson et al., 2018; de Graaf, 2019; Weill, 2020). Hundreds of prosecutions were held in European courts, and a terror law jurisprudence began to emerge. This jurisprudence is retributive rather than restorative. This is significant, because European criminal law generally performs a communicative (restorative) rather than retributive or solely punitive function (Duff, 2001; Garland, 2002; Lacey, 2016). By being so retributive, terror law prosecutions distinguish themselves from other European criminal law practices. Because terror in Europe has become synonymous with Muslim extremism, this has had the effect of turning European Muslims into "suspect communities" (Ahmed, 2023; Fadil et al., 2019; Ragazzi, 2016). This turn in criminal justice practices arguably exacerbates existing structural racism in Europe (Kundnani, 2023; Sayyid, 2004, 2022). It also represents a lost opportunity, where state resources that could be put towards the rehabilitation and integration of criminal defendants are invested in retribution and ostracism instead (de Graaf, 2019; de Graaf & Schmid, 2016).

The well-documented case of Shamina Begum is illustrative. Begum was a British national who was groomed by IS operatives as a teenager. Together with two other school friends, the 15-year-old snuck away from her family in 2015. From London, the girls flew to Turkey and then passed overland into Syria. Shortly after arriving in Syria, Begum married a Dutch IS fighter, Yago Riedijk. She lived in territory controlled by IS until the fall of Raffah, in March 2019, after which she turned up in Al Hol camp. There she gave a controversial interview with a British journalist where she expressed a desire to return to Britain (she was close to birthing her third child, who subsequently died in Al Hol; none of Begum's three children survived), but also made unapologetic comments about IS ideology and politics (Loyd, 2019). The UK refused to repatriate her and revoked her citizenship; in 2024, her last legal challenge failed, and she remains as of this writing, stateless, in Al Hol (Phillips, 2024).[10]

Begum became infamous, in certain circles, as the face of non-repentant jihadist treachery, largely due to her unwillingness to repudiate IS during an interview with UK journalists. The question of how to understand Begum drove season 2 of the podcast series *I'm Not a Monster: The Shamima Begum Story* (Baker, 2023). Over 9 regular episodes, followed by updates as her case wound its ways through UK courts, the host challenged the construction of Begum as a dangerous terrorist nihilist. The 15-year-old Begum was radicalized online in a phenomenon that has been recognized as grooming, a predatory practice. When directed at children, the criminality usually rests entirely with the groomer; the groomed can be recognized as victims. In Begum's case, the online groomer was actually a Canadian asset (Loyd, 2019; Williams, 2023). Begum, however, has been left to assume full responsibility, as the adult she has now become, for actions taken against her as a child by other adults, including security authorities in Britain's allied countries. Begum's case follows a pattern that researchers call "adultification" where minority children are perceived as more adult and less innocent than white children of their same age (Cooke & Halberstadt, 2021).

[10] In a bitter irony, Begum's capacity to claim Dutch citizenship through her husband, who as of this writing seems to still be alive, housed in a non-disclosed jail in Kurdish-controlled Syria, is nullified by the fact that she was a minor when she married him, so their marriage is not recognized in the Netherlands.

European States and the Resistance to Repatriation

The Begum case brings home the question: what can and should European states do with their foreign fighters and IS adherent nationals, either at home or abroad? At the level of law, European states are required to recognize participation in terror as a crime. This follows United Nations' Security Council Resolution 2178 (2014) which mandated that states criminalize terror participation. Across Europe, participation in recognized terror organizations like IS has been criminalized. Sentences vary from months to years, depending on the jurisdiction. In addition to recognizing terror as a crime, several European jurisdictions also equate terror crime with treason. Considering IS adherence as "treason" rather than "terror" opens up wider possibilities for state action. Treason is a loyalty crime directed against the state and is treated distinctly from other forms of criminal deviance. For example, many state signatories to the Convention on the Reduction of Statelessness include "treason" as a sole exception to citizenship protection (Carlson, 2024). Citizens who betray their countries, these exemptions reason, can take up residence in the countries their acts have served, *i.e.,* where their "true loyalty" lies; their citizenship therefore need not be protected, and may be made forfeit. The distinction between terror and treason as crimes thus resides in the ways that punishment is meted out and belonging imagined. Where terror is crime, the crime is punished via prison and the rehabilitated citizen eventually reenters the polity, which is their country where they belong; this follows liberal constructions regarding the purpose and scope of criminal law (Duff, 2001). Where terror is treason, the criminal is transported/deported and ceases to be an individual recognized by the state as a citizen, as they belong to another country (Choudhury, 2017; Seemann, 2020).

This construction is born out in the Danish citizenship revocation jurisprudence for terror. In Denmark, the recognition of dual citizenship, combined with terror laws passed in 2002 and 2006 which imagined citizenship revocation as a possible response to a terror conviction, opened the door for citizenship revocation.[11] In the past two decades,

[11] Indeed, it seems possible and even plausible that countries that have recently changed their dual citizenship laws such as Denmark (2015) and Norway (2018) have done so in order to permit convicted terror actors to be excommunicated (Midtbøen 2019). See discussion in Carlson 2024.

Danish jurisprudence indicates that citizenship revocation for terror is the expected outcome for any Danish dual citizen, regardless of the terror infraction for which they are charged (Carlson, 2024).

Denmark's citizenship revocation practice is not singular; the practice is evolving and several European countries link citizenship revocation to terror prosecution for dual citizens (Bauböck & Paskalov, 2015). In the UK, citizenship revocation is possible for dual citizens convicted even of non-terror crime (Gentleman, 2020). In Italy, it is permitted towards specific natural citizens (the children of immigrants born in Italy) (Vedaschi & Arianna, 2019). In France, it is officially rejected but still often practiced via technical loopholes, a process Lepoutre (2020) calls a "grey hole" in terms of citizens' rights. The Council of Europe condemns citizenship revocation for crime (Council of Europe, 2019) as illiberal. In continental Europe, Denmark leads the development of citizenship revocation policy, and we see that more and more European states are considering it (Prener, 2023).

Equivocations in European Human Rights Law: HF and Others v France (ECtHR 2022)

While citizenship revocation is still the exception rather than the norm across European jurisdictions, repatriation is not a typical practice, either. The question of states' obligations regarding repatriation of their citizens was raised, and set aside, in the 2022 judgement by the European Court of Human Rights (ECtHR), *HF and Others v France*. The case was brought by the families of several French women who had traveled to Syria and now were imprisoned in camps there, unable to return to France without French assistance, and not receiving any replies regarding such assistance when they contacted French authorities. France is one of the countries that has had a varied response to its IS-adherents. Between 2019 and 2021, France repatriated several IS-adherents "on a case by case" basis.[12] This included the repatriation of 35 minors who were either orphans or whose parents consented to their repatriation unaccompanied by the parents as well as 16 mothers in 2022.[13]

[12] H.F. v France (2022) para 26.

[13] Id. Para 28.

The *HF and Others v France* judgment effectively defines a legal no-man's land, an ungovernable legal space where rights exist but the ECtHR cannot operate. The ECtHR recognized the difficulties of the French citizens imprisoned in Syrian camps, trapped in a limbo which they cannot address without the assistance of their states of citizenship. Regardless, the ECtHR found it was unable to protect the rights of French citizens detained in Kurdish-run camps in Syria. It ruled that France must answer the requests made by families of IS-adherents, but not that France must accede to them. This is effectively an administrative rebuke, instructing France how to run its processes but staying silent regarding rights-respecting conclusions to those processes.

In conclusion

A central promise made by liberalism is an anti-natalist, anti-racist agenda of non-discrimination regarding immutable characteristics. Liberalism expands our understanding of "immutable characteristics" to include gender identity, sexuality, and religious affiliation. These characteristics are included in basic freedoms, like freedom of speech and conscience, that form the foundation of the right to have rights, and which must be protected from state attack or other forms of discrimination. This pluralism of views and traits, Arendt argued, is a necessary antidote to totalitarianism (Arendt, 1973; Stonebridge, 2024).

The discussed terror law practices and judicial responses to them challenge the assumptions underwriting liberal order because they are racialized and because they implicate immutable characteristics such as dual citizenship identities. Moreover, these challenges are not being seriously addressed in terror law processes. Terror researcher Lisa Stampinsky calls this "anti-knowledge," where observers of terror engage in:

> An active refusal of explanation itself [...] knowledge and inquiry that entail knowing the terrorist are proscribed. It is though the language of evil creates a "black box" around the terrorist, which creates its own explanation: terrorists commit terrorism because they are evil. Any further attempt to pursue alternative explanations, thereby seeking to break the black box of "evil" is seen as a profanation, even a sacrilege. The roots of the politics of anti-knowledge is hence that, if terrorists are evil and irrational, then one cannot—and indeed should not—know them (Stampnitzky, 2013, p. 189)

In this way, terror itself is rendered an immutable characteristic, albeit one that for reasons of state security we must not tolerate. By fixing terror not as an act or crime but rather as a way of being that is outside of politics, behavior, and therefore also criminal law, European institutions have moved away from liberal ideals themselves, moving the liberal consensus to the margins in areas deemed to relate to state security (Carlson, 2023). As we see from the expansive possibility for terror to include gang or other criminal behavior, these securitized areas are only growing in size. This constitutes an expanding European illiberalism. The next section introduces a contrasting institutional framework addressing arguably similar challenges but recentering liberal rights consensus ideals.

Colombia: Turning Terrorists into Citizens

In 2016, a peace accord four years in the making was signed between the Colombian government and the *Fuerzas Armadas Revolucionarias de Colombia* (FARC), ending more than five decades of civil war. The accord was built on a 6-part, integrated system of "Truth, Justice, Reparation and Non-Repetition" ("SIVJRNR"). The parts are interrelated and must be considered holistically (Olasolo & Ramirez Mendoza, 2017). One element of the SIVJRNR consists of the creation of an innovative transitional justice mechanism (Special Jurisdiction for Peace, "JEP" in Spanish). The JEP has developed an innovative blend of amnesty, rehabilitation, and punishment as it adjudicates terrorism and collective crimes carried out both by the state and rebel actors (Liévano, 2024; Pinzón, 2020; Tarapués Sandino, 2020). This plays out along two tracks, one restorative, based on cooperation and designed to maximize social repair, including through its sanctions. The second is punitive, looking like regular criminal justice, and is reserved for those who refuse to cooperate.

First, there are amnesties. Many thousands of amnesties were granted, either for imprisoned FARC or FARC adjacent Colombians and for signatories of the Havanna Accords. These amnesties were offered to members who participated in FARC as combatants who were not tied to any violence directed against citizens. This was achieved by applying international humanitarian law (IHL), the laws of war, to FARC ex-combatants (Correa Flórez et al., 2022). IHL recognizes the legality of soldiers to fight, and kill, other soldiers. By applying IHL, the JEP essentially recognizes the legitimacy of the FARC, as IHL recognizes the legitimacy of soldiers. This effectively alters the FARC from terror group to rebel, combatant group in the eyes of the state. Contrast these Colombia machinations to the European treatment of unwanted, contentious citizens. The Colombian model expansively constructs legitimacy and belonging. It can be contrasted against the European practices of delegitimizing, abandoning, and even denationalizing their citizens as discussed above.

This section discusses the work of the JEP and sets it against the historical challenges faced in Colombia as regards peace and state consolidation. The purpose of these details is to invite consideration of how the Colombian case has parallels to European questions related to foreign fighters. These connections will be considered in the chapter's final section.

The JEP and Its Context

The JEP, born out of the 2016 Havana Peace Accords, began working in 2018. It is divided into three parts: an amnesty chamber, a restorative justice organ, and a punitive organ (which is applied where restorative means are rejected by the investigated parties). In the early years, the amnesty chamber carried most of the load, while the appeals and punitive organs sat quiet. Within a few years, however, the most innovative element of the JEP, the restorative justice organ proposing alternate sentences for cooperation with the tribunal, was up and running (Tarapués Sandino, 2020). This organ, the *Sala de Reconocimiento de Verdad, de Responsabilidad y de Determinación de los Hechos y Conductas* ("Chamber of Recognition" in English, for short) is designed to produce restorative justice.[14] Employing more than 100 sociologists as investigators, the work began by identifying the harms suffered during Colombia's 50-year conflict.[15] From these patterns, the Chamber of Recognition has constructed 11 "macro cases" based on its assessment of harms suffered during the conflict. These cases address patterns of harm and identify the most responsible perpetrators, who in some cases are FARC and in other cases are state actors. The facts of the cases are established in collaboration and cooperation between perpetrators and victims, with judges of the Chamber of Recognition acting as go-betweens.

[14] See Artículo 79 de la Ley 1957 (2019).

[15] Interviews with members of Grupo de Analysis de la Information (GRAI) February 2020, notes on file with author.

As of this writing, one case has been finalized, Case 01, related to kidnappings perpetrated by FARC. Seven individuals, all senior FARC commanders, have accepted responsibility and apologized to victims of the violence in public hearings.[16] It is hard to overstate the social importance of the narratives of apology, harm recognition, and contrition that these formal statements have made. In hearings before the FARC as well as in private fora, senior FARC officials have spoken publicly about the harm that certain FARC policies caused.

There remain, of course, significant challenges. The question of sanctions, for example, is still undecided. This is because the alternate sanction element of JEP's transitional justice mandate, arguably the most progressive and ambitious element in its toolkit aiming to facilitate social repair, is meeting obstacles generated both by defendants as well as the broader Colombian public (Liévano, 2024). The seven senior FARC leaders who accepted responsibility for kidnappings in Case 01 are still, as of this writing, waiting to learn what their alternate sanctions will comprise, where they will be carried out, and for how long. Can old men build schools, repair roads, and plant trees? Given that hundreds of assassinations are carried out every year in Colombia, can the JEP guarantee their safety, if they carry out reparative tasks in the remote communities where harm occurred? And can reparative tasks already undertaken count as part of 'time served'? From the other side, surveys indicate Colombians are dissatisfied when sanctions are reparative rather than punitive (Liévano, 2022). Can Colombians accept the sanctions JEP assigns?

The lesson from the JEP is not that transitional justice processes are simple, straightforward, or without challenge. Rather, the lesson the JEP provides is how antagonistic parties, after decades of existential conflict, can work together in a future-oriented process built around mutual recognition. Colombia's JEP was set up as part of the peace process following more than 50 years of civil war waged by the FARC. The FARC emerged in 1967, following a two-decade period of civil war called *La Violencia*. This was followed by a political compromise between the opposing political parties wherein they shared power, exchanging the presidency every four years, called *Frente National*. Locked out of power, many popular groups sought to assert control, including through violent means (Ronderos & Marín-López, 2022). Thus, the FARC and its five-decade

[16] JEP Auto No. 21, 26 January 2021.

struggle should be understood as part of a wider contestation for power and governance in a Colombian state that has arguably never consolidated control over all its regions and peoples (Lemaitre Ripoll, 2019; Pinzón, 2020).

In the period prior to the 2016 Havana Accords, far-reaching state initiatives to conquer the FARC had emboldened paramilitary forces, who often worked on behalf of the state or against the FARC. Studies of violence in Colombia indicate that paramilitary and government forces are responsible for the majority of Colombian violence (Fattal, 2018). Regardless, in the popular imagination, FARC bears the brunt of popular disdain for decades of violent conflict (García-Sánchez & Carlin, 2020). For regular Colombians, the FARC are terrorists and criminals and should not be the subjects of amnesties or non-punitive processes. In fact, harnessing these attitudes, the political right managed to sink the peace accords in the 2016 referendum, in a narrowly decided vote.

By recognizing the FARC's deep unpopularity, both for regular Colombians as well as for mainstream political parties, we can better understand how the example of transitional justice in Colombia might be applied to transitional justice for foreign fighters in Europe. Like the FARC, European foreign fighters are a deeply unpopular group which has also been harnessed for political gain. As with the FARC, it is possible to be curious about, and sympathetic to, the conditions which drove individuals to choose a path of violence while simultaneously condemning violence as a means of pursuing political goals. By examining the methods that the JEP has employed to legitimize elements of FARC existence and participation, while maintaining an insistence on retaining responsibility for violence, the JEP experience showcases the possibilities that can exist in addressing violent social actors outside of the securitized "war on terror" model which calls for the complete destruction of terror groups and the actors who populate them.

Transitional Justice for European Foreign Fighters

As discussed above, across Europe, as part of the "war on terror," states are suspending established rights protections in ways that disproportionately impact Muslims and racial minorities (Wacquant, 2009; Fadil, 2019). This creates an impasse between those who critique these measures as illiberal and impermissible in the name of rights, and those who argue for the need to expand our concept of risk, in the name of security. The fields of study that might assist us in navigating this impasse—security studies, terror studies, law, psychology, criminology, migration—are themselves divided by the impasse, which opens chasms within and between them. So far, there are few bridges.

The purpose of this chapter is to argue that liberal rights guarantees, currently marginalized as regards terror law in Europe, can return to the middle of European terror law practice by borrowing tools from a field that is designed to build bridges: transitional justice. Transitional justice addresses conflict and proposes "toolkits" designed to reconcile and reconstruct opposing sides (Quinn, 2009). Traditionally, transitional justice has been applied during or after violent conflict, as a means to end war or to sustain the peace (Elster, 2004). Emerging transitional justice scholarship considers "atypical" cases (Destrooper et al., 2023b) examining what transitional justice approaches might offer in cases of ongoing armed conflict, such as in Syria (Aboueldahab, 2018) or in cases of social contestation, such as affirmative action policies in the U.S. (Joshi, 2020). Transitional justice offers a means of compromise between opposing sides or ideas, and recognition of the legitimacy of the other is a necessary first step in all compromise (Margalit, 2013).

By setting the work of the transitional justice organ in Colombia, the JEP, in comparison with European responses to jihadi terror actors, this final section models how transitional justice tools might alter European approaches to jihadi terrorism. This is proposed in order to recenter liberal practices, which have been marginalized in relation to terror in Europe. The central ideological tool in the transitional justice tool kit is the recognition of the legitimacy of the other. The two examples considered in the first two sections show two sides of recognition. European treatment of Europeans participating in jihadi politics in the Levant rejects recognition of the rationales that drive this behavior. By contrast, the JEP in Colombia has traversed bitter rivalries and deep scores after 70 years of internecine war to extend the legitimacy codified for fighters under international laws of war to its own internal terrorists. This final section considers how recognition of the legitimacy of the other, postulated here as the basis upon which transitional justice practice is built, might impact European responses to homegrown jihadi terror actors.

The Transitional Justice Toolkit: Isolating Ideology

Transitional justice is rooted in liberal ideological constructions (Sharp, 2018). While transitional justice originated as a conceptualized temporary state of affairs designed to transition states from autocracy and/or violence to democracy and peace (Teitel, 2000), it has now been standardized and made uniform (Gissel, 2017). Central elements of this standardization include a focus on practices that meet rule of law mandates, as well as the participation of that state as partner rather than adversary (Destrooper et al., 2023a).

Part of the standardization of transitional justice is an insistence on the validity of its application wherever there is organized conflict. As a means of moving towards peace, transitional justice is no longer a practice applied post-conflict, but rather offers tools designed to move warring actors towards peace, cooperation, and a shared future. Unsavory bedfellows are par for this course, as transitional justice imagines collaboration for future peace between actors even while they are still actively engaged in conflict. This means that your enemies, who you may view as evil, subhuman, etc. due to how they have attacked using illegal violence, targeted civilians, or otherwise breached the norms of valid conflict, must become your partners in peace. Think of Hamas and Israel in their post 7 October 2023 conflict: each accuses the other side of unforgiveable atrocities. Yet each must deal with the other if peace is to be achieved (Margalit, 2013).

Transitional justice is grounded in compromise in place of absolute victory. Another way of saying this is that through the lens of transitional justice, compromise is victory. Transitional justice effectuates this by neutralizing, *i.e.*, not interrogating or engaging, actors' political beliefs or historical narratives. Participation in transitional justice practices does not require narrative movement in how groups represent their righteous struggles. Instead, and singularly, it requires cooperation with its own terms and tools. These tools consist of accountability, recognition, and disruption (Destrooper et al., 2023a). Because transitional justice looks beyond actors' ideological motivations, it has the potential to evade challenges based on ideology, motivation, and belief. In this sense, transitional justice isolates ideology, rendering it inapplicable to the present political problem.

Applying Transitional Justice in Colombia and Europe

Transitional justice practices begin by recognizing the legitimacy of the other side. We can therefore speak of transitional justice even in "aparadigmatic cases" where war is ongoing or there is no change in government regime (Destrooper et al., 2023a). Where negotiation between actors is ongoing, transitional justice becomes possible. This distinguishes, for example, current conflicts in Ukraine and Gaza (where even as cease fires are under negotiation, legitimizing recognition by the dominant/warring actors is missing) from the process underway at the time of this writing in Syria.

In Colombia, for example, the JEP has constructed an innovative procedure that begins by collecting victims' testimonies. Following the initial data gathering, the JEP employed criminologists and prosecutors to construct patterns of harm. The way of working, "macrocriminality" builds on little-tested theories of criminal law (Rojas Andrade & Merchán Duque, 2023). But by grounding its work in the suffering of the civilian population, the JEP sidesteps questions of perpetrator ideology. The JEP does not consider the rationale or comparative justifications behind kidnappings undertaken by FARC, for example. Similarly, it does not try to understand the securitization rationales that drove government-sponsored atrocities like the 'false positives' scheme, an extra-judicial killing program with more than 6000 recorded murders (Perry, 2022). Rather, the measurable suffering of the victims drives the process. This idea, that there is value in hearing, recording, and making someone accountable for victims' suffering, is a transitional justice trope. The JEP builds on this trope but challenges it as well by stepping away from strict, individual punitive accountablity.[17]

In practice, politically, this has real impact. It means that the leftist FARC guerillas may continue to call for resource redistribution and may represent their struggle as just and necessary. Likewise, the Colombian military may continue to exercise its police powers and insist on the righteous necessity of its cause. These political struggles can continue even as the transitional justice process advances. Neither of these political positions need impact the transitional justice process, because that process is not in opposition to either of them. Rather, so long as both parties

[17] This legalized concept of transitional justice is now the mainstream middle of transitional justice practice. See Gissel (2017).

continue to participate in transitional justice mechanisms, the transitional justice process—which includes recognition and accountability for harms, and disruption of the social processes which led to those harms, can continue.

If we view the question of terrorism in Europe through this transitional justice lens, we see that the absence of recognition and legitimacy for political views that are associated with terrorist manifestations makes transitional justice inapplicable in relation to European terror actors. European states have focused entirely on questions of ideology as they construct terror law as criminal offense. The harm that European terrorists commit, as constructed by terror law prosecutions, is often their belief system itself. This is not to say that terror does not manifest as violence, and that such manifestations should not be criminalized. Rather, to the degree that European terror processes reject the possibility of legitimate motives behind the ideologies they oppose—the "anti-knowledge" position as described by Stampnitzky (2013)—they render transitional justice processes or mechanisms impossible.

Transitional justice is both a mainstream mechanism for administering conflict, as well as a translation of liberal values into developmental social spaces (Destrooper et al., 2023b; Gissel, 2017; Sharp, 2018). By turning away from the kinds of engagement upon which transitional justice is based, European regimes demonstrate a turn from mainstream liberalism. The marginalization of foundational liberal beliefs—freedom of conscience; freedom from harmful discrimination—is reified in a European rejection of the kinds of mechanisms that would render transitional justice applicable to conflict in European societies.

Conclusion From the Middle to the Margins: Rights Protections and Dissent in Constitutional Democracies

At the time of writing, the liberal consensus is under threat. The central agent is the Trump regime in the U.S., but Europe is hardly immune. Right-wing populism drives some of this threat. Indeed, the racialization of terror law, when considered with mainstream rejections of multicultural European identities, crack-downs on migration, etc. is no longer a right-wing populist issue, but has moved decidedly to the political center. Moreover, the war in Gaza has broadened how terror is recognized and punished across Europe. Germany, based in an applied logic of support for Israel as *statsraeson,* has made critique of Israel illegal (Whittle, 2024). Journalist Masha Gessen saw their award from the Hannah Arendt Center recinded based on an article that compared Israel's treatment of Gaza to Jewish ghettos constructed in Nazi Germany (Gessen, 2023). When the documentary film *No Other Land*, produced by an Israeli/Palestinian partnership and documenting Israeli apartheid practices in the West Bank won an award, the German Minister of Culture explained that she was applauding only the Israeli member of the team (Oltermann, 2024). Denmark has sentenced individuals to prison for their responses to Hamas's October 2023 terror attack, or the wider war in Gaza, under the charge of "support for terror" (Grønning-Madsen & Wanigasuriya, 2024). One of these sentences is the one-month suspended prison sentence of a 16-year-old who wrote on a newspaper's website, in response to an article regarding bombs hitting Israel, "Yass. [Heart smiley face emoji]. [Palestinian flag emoji]"(Schropp, 2024). In other words, we live in a time when rights constructions considered central to liberal democracy are increasingly curtailed under an antiterror rubric.

The global war on terror asserts that terror laws navigate the space between different rights constructions. One is collective, the right to security. The other is individual, and comprises the core tenets of the liberal state, including the right to freedom of speech, conscience, association; the right to privacy; the right to be free from discrimination; and the right to life. These rights that in Arendt's parlance we have by right include a host of procedural rights, central among them the presumption of innocence. Yet in their response to terrorism, European states have criminalized and punished terror crime in ways that diverge from standard European criminal justice. European terror laws reach beyond typical criminal law subjects into administrative areas (prevention; citizenship revocation), intrude on protected rights (freedom of speech, belief, and religion) and disproportionately impact racial and religious minorities, *i.e.*, demonstrate bias. For these reasons, terror law practices have been widely critiqued as challenging rule-of-law norms and standards. The consequence has been to challenge rights protections for all Europeans.

Happily, there are tools, and available examples, to suggest how to counter this directional movement. This chapter has visited Colombia's innovative transitional justice instititution in order to model what tools that set ideology aside (transitional justice tools) can enable. The social, economic, and security impacts of FARC's 50-year rebellion impact Colombian society far more fundamentally than jihadi terror or foreign fighters have Europe, which is actually living in a time of declining terror activity, rather than increasing violence. For this reason, Colombia's example offers a template for what could be possible in Europe. Colombia has recognized (without agreeing with or somehow taking the side of) an internal enemy, and this recognition sets the stage for a shared future. Europe is seeking to remove, through Syrian camps or citizenship revocation, its enemy citizens. The impact of these practices is more far-reaching than the individuals lost to camps or removed from the polity. When citizenship rights are reduced for some, they are reduced for all; liberal rights guarantees are universal or they are non-existent. Colombia's practice shows there is another path.

References

Aboueldahab, N. (2018). *Writing atrocities: Syrian civil society and transitional justice, 21.* Brookings Institute. https://www.brookings.edu/wp-content/uploads/2018/04/transitional-justice-english_web.pdf

Ahmed, A. (2023). Decolonizing terrorism: Racist pre-crime, cheap orientalism, and the Taqiya Trap. In C. Cunneen, A. Porter, R. Webb, A. Deckert, & J. Tauri (Eds.), *The Routledge International Handbook on Decolonizing Justice* (Vol. 1, pp. 202–212). Routledge.

Ambos, K., & Peters, S. (Eds.). (2022). *Transitional justice in Colombia: The special jurisdiction for peace.* Nomos.

Andersson, A., Høgestøl, S., & Lie, A. C. (2018). *Fremmedkrigere: Forebygging, straffeforfølgning og rehabilitering i Skandinavia.* Gyldendal juridisk.

ANHA. (2024). Al-Hol camp administration confirms that ISIS children have become more extremist. *ANHA.* https://hawarnews.com/en/al-hol-camp-administration-confirms-that-isis-children-have-become-more-extremist

Anwar, T. (2022). Time will tell: Defining violence in terrorism court cases. *Security Dialogue, 53*(2), 130–147.

Arendt, H. (1973). *The origins of totalitarianism* (1st ed.). Harcourt, Brace, Jovanovich.

Baker, J. (2023, January 11). The Shamima Begum story. *BBC.* www.bbcpodcasts.com/listen/shamimabegum/

Bauböck, R., & Paskalev, V. (2015). Citizenship deprivation: A normative analysis. CEPS Papers in liberty and security in Europe. *CEPS.* 82.

Bell, C. (2009). Transitional justice, interdisciplinarity and the state of the "Field" or "Non-Field." *International Journal of Transitional Justice, 3*(1), 5–27.

Besnier, C., & Weill, S. (2019). Les filières djihadistes en procès: Approche ethnographique des audiences criminelles et correctionnelles (2017–2019). *Mission de Recherche Droit & Justice*.

Betts, T. A. (2022, July 13). Resolving the Detainee Dilemma: What next for the men, women & children of the Islamic state. *United States Department of State*. https://www.state.gov/resolving-the-detainee-dilemma-what-next-for-the-men-women-children-of-the-islamic-state-2/

Bolhuis, M. P., & van Wijk, J. (2020). Citizenship deprivation as a counterterrorism measure in Europe; Possible follow-up scenarios, human rights infringements and the effect on counterterrorism. *European Journal of Migration and Law, 22*(3), 338–365.

Cahn, O., & Alix, J. (Eds.). (2017). *L'hypothèse de la guerre contre le terrorisme—Implications juridiques*. Dalloz.

Carlson, K. B. (2023). Creating ontological outlaws: International criminal law and the contamination of liberal legal systems. *Hague Yearbook of International Law*.

Carlson, K. B. (2024). Ties that sever: Losing the right to belong in Denmark. *Law & Critique*. https://doi-org.ep.fjernadgang.kb.dk/https://doi.org/10.1007/s10978-024-09398-1.

Casey, C. (2021). Citizenship stripping, fair procedures, and the separation of powers: A critical comment on *Damache* v *Minister for justice*. *The Modern Law Review, 84*(6), 1399–1413.

Choudhury, T. (2017). The radicalisation of citizenship deprivation. *Critical Social Policy, 37*(2), 225–244.

Cooke, A. N., & Halberstadt, A. (2021). Adultification, anger bias, and adults' different perceptions of black and white children. *Cognition & Emotion, 35*(7), 1416–1422.

Correa, F., et al. (2022). Punishment and Pardon: The use of international humanitarian law by the special jurisdiction for peace in Colombia. *International Review of the Red Cross, 104*(919), 1199–1221.

Council of Europe. (2019). Withdrawing nationality as a measure to combat terrorism: A human rights-compatible approach? *Doc. 14790*.

Dagres, H. (2021, August 19). ISIS is defeated. What becomes of the "Cubs of the Caliphate" in Iraq? *Atlantic Council*. https://www.atlanticcouncil.org/blogs/menasource/isis-is-defeated-what-becomes-of-the-cubs-of-the-caliphate-in-iraq/

Destrooper, T., Gissel, L. G., & Carlson, K. B. (2023a). Introduction: transitional justice in aparadigmatic contexts. In T. Destrooper, L. G. Gissel, &

K. B. Carlson (Eds.). *Innovation and consolidation in transitional justice: Learning from aparadigmatic contexts* (pp. 1–21). Routledge.

Destrooper, T., Gissel, L. G., & Carlson, K. B. (Eds.). (2023b). *Transitional justice in aparadigmatic contexts: Accountability, recognition and disruption.* Routledge.

Duff, R. A. (2001). *Punishment, communication and community.* Oxford University Press.

Duffy, H. (2018). "Foreign terrorist fighters": A human rights approach? *Security and Human Rights, 29*(1–4), 120–172.

Elster, J. (2004). *Closing the books: Transitional justice in historical perspective.* Cambridge University Press.

European Court of Human Rights. (2022, September 14). *H.F. and Others v. France [GC].*

Fadil, N. (2019). The anthropology of islam in Europe: A double epistemological impasse. *Annual Review of Anthropology, 48*(1), 117–32. https://doi.org/10.1146/annurev-anthro-102218-011353

Fadil, N., Ragazzi, F., & de Koning, M. (Eds.). (2019). *Radicalization in Belgium and the Netherlands: Critical perspectives on violence and security.* Bloomsbury.

Fattal, A. L. (2018). *Guerrilla marketing: Counter in surgency and capitalism in Colombia*. The University of Chicago Press.

Flores, M. (2016). Foreign fighters involvement in national and international wars: A historical survey. In C. Paulussen, F. Capone, and A. De Guttry. Germany (Eds.), *Foreign fighters under international law and beyond* (pp. 27–47). T.M.C. Asser Press.

Garapon, A., & Rosenfeld, M. (2016). *Démocraties sous stress: Les défis du terrorisme global*. Presses universitaires de France.

García-Sánchez, M., & Carlin, R. E. (2020). The FARC in the public eye: Negotiation, integration, and political participation. *Journal of Politics in Latin America, 12*(3), 239–251.

Garland, D. (2002). *The culture of control.* Oxford University Press.

Gentleman, A. (2020, July 7). London-born twins face deportation to different countries. *The Guardian.* https://www.theguardian.com/uk-news/2020/jul/07/london-born-twins-face-deportation-to-different-countries.

Gessen, M. (2023, December 9). In the shadow of the Holocaust. *The New Yorker*. https://www.newyorker.com/news/the-weekend-essay/in-the-shadow-of-the-holocaust.

Gissel, L. E. (2017). Contemporary transitional justice: Normalising a politics of exception. *Global Society, 31*(3), 353–369.

Gopal, A. (2024, March 11). The open-air prison for ISIS supporters—and victims. *The New Yorker*. https://www.newyorker.com/magazine/2024/03/18/the-open-air-prison-for-isis-supporters-and-victims.

de Graaf, B. (2019). Foreign fighters on Trial: Sentencing Risk, 2013–2017. In N. Fadil, M. de Koning, & F. Ragazzi (Eds.), *Radicalization in Belgium and the Netherlands: Critical perspectives on violence and security* (pp. 97–130). Bloomsbury.

de Graaf, B., & Schmid, A. E. (Eds.). (2016). *Terrorists on trial: A performative perspective*. Leiden University Press.

Grønning-Madsen, N., & Wanigasuriya, B. A. (2024). Approval of terrorist actions: Have the Danish courts given due consideration to all applicable aspects in cases Linked to the Israel-Hamas conflict? *Bergen Journal of Criminal Law & Criminal Justice, 12*, 31–59.

Hamilton, C. (2019). *Contagion, counter-terrorism and criminology: Justice in the shadow of terror*. Palgrave Macmillan.

Ip, J. (2020). Reconceptualizing the legal response to foreign fighters. *International & Comparative Law Quarterly, 69*(1), 103–134.

Jones, S., et al. (2017). *Rolling back the Islamic state*. RAND Corporation.

Joshi, Y. (2020). Affirmative action as transitional justice. *Wisconsin Law Review, 1*, 1–48.

Kundnani, H. (2023). *Eurowhiteness: Culture, empire and race in the European project*. Hurst & Company.

Lacey, N. (2016). *In search of criminal responsibility: Ideas, interests, and institutions*. Oxford University Press.

Lafuente, J. (2016, October 4). Colombia dice "no" al acuerdo de paz con las FARC. *El País*.

Laine, T. (2017). Passing the buck': Western states race to denationalise foreign terrorist fighters. *Journal of Peacebuilding & Development, 12*(2), 22–35.

Lemaitre Ripoll, J. (2019). *El estado siempre llega tarde: la reconstrucción de la vida cotidiana después de la guerra*. Siglo Veintiuno Editores.

Lepoutre, J. (2020, August 5). Ghoumid and others v. France: The grey hole of nationality revocation. *Globalcit*. https://globalcit.eu/ghoumid-and-others-v-france-the-grey-hole-of-nationality-revocation/.

Liévano, A. B. (2022, March 14). First rift between colombia's peace tribunal and the victims. *JusticeInfo.Net*. https://www.justiceinfo.net/en/88737-first-rift-between-colombia-peace-tribunal-victims.html.

Liévano, A. B. (2024.). Colombia's JEP Unveils alternative sanctions but remains silent on punishment. *JusticeInfo.Net*. https://www.justiceinfo.net/en/130952-colombia-alternative-sanctions-silence-on-punishment.html.

Loyd, A. (2019, February 13). Shamima Begum: Bring me home, says Bethnal green girl who left to join isis. *The Times*. https://www.thetimes.com/uk/politics/article/shamima-begum-bring-me-home-says-bethnal-green-girl-who-fled-to-join-isis-hgvqw765d?region=global.

Margalit, A. (2013). *On compromise and rotten compromises*. Princeton University Press.

Midtbøen, A. H. (2019). Dual citizenship in an era of securitisation: The case of denmark. *Nordic Journal of Migration Research, 9*(3), 293–309.

Moaveni, A. (2019). *Guest house for young widows: Among the women of ISIS*. Random House.

Mohamedou, M. (2018). *A theory of ISIS: Political violence and the global order*. Pluto Press.

Naqvi, Z. B. (2022). Coloniality, belonging and citizenship deprivation in the UK: Exploring judicial responses. *Social & Legal Studies, 31*(4), 515–534.

Olasolo, H., & Ramirez Mendoza, J. M. F. (2017). The Colombian integrated system of truth, justice, reparation and non-repetition. *Journal of International Criminal Justice, 15*(5), 1011–1147.

Oltermann, P. (2024, February 27). German Minister says she clapped Israeli film-maker, not his Palestinian colleague, at Berlinale. *The Guardian*. https://www.theguardian.com/world/2024/feb/27/german-minister-says-she-was-only-applauding-israeli-filmmaker-at-berlinale.

Perry, J. (2022, August 5). Can the government police itself? Colombia's false positives scandal and its lessons for atrocity prevention. *The SAIS Review of International Affairs*. https://saisreview.sais.jhu.edu/colombia-false-positives-scandal-atrocity-prevention/.

Phillips, A. (2024, August 7). Shamima Begum loses final UK Court Bid over citizenship. *BBC News*. https://www.bbc.com/news/articles/cm2n8xv61x3o.

Pinzón, V. G. (2020). *Colombia: Between the dividends of peace and the shadow of violence*. German Institute of Global and Area Studies (GIGA).

Prener, C. (2023). Citizenship revocation and the question of proportionate consequences. *Statelessness & Citizenship Review, 5*(1), 112–117.

Quinn, J. R., (Ed.). (2009). *Reconciliation(s): Transitional justice in postconflict societies*. McGill-Queen's University Press.

Ragazzi, F. (2016). Suspect community or suspect category: The impact of counter—Terrorism as "Policed Multiculturalism." *Journal of Ethnic and Migration Studies, 42*(5), 724–741.

Ramraj, V. V., Hor, M., Roach, K., & Williams, G. (Eds.). (2012). *Global anti-terrorism law and policy* (2nd ed.). Cambridge University Press.

Razack, S. (2008). *Casting out: The eviction of Muslims from western law and politics*. University of Toronto Press.

Richardson, H. C. (2025, February 4). Letters from an American. https://heathercoxrichardson.substack.com/p/february-4-2025.

Rojas Andrade, G. A., & Merchán Duque, M. (2023). *Investigación Macrocriminal y Enfoque Restuarativo En La Justicia Transicional*. Bogotá: Tirant lo Blanch.

Ronderos, S., & Marín-López, D. (2022). Rebels at war, criminals in peace: A critical approach to violence in Colombia. *Rethinking Marxism, 34*(1), 99–115.

Rothmaier, K. (2019). Germany and its returning foreign terrorist fighters: New loss of citizenship law and the broader german repatriation landscape. *ICCT*.

Sayyid, B. S. (2004). *A fundamental fear: Eurocentrism and the emergence of Islamism*. Zed Books.

Sayyid, B. S. (2022). *Recalling the caliphate: Decolonization and world order*. Hurst Publishers.

Schropp, J. (2024, December 20). Terrorstøtte med emojis og hashtags: Hvad skal der til for at blive terrorsympatisør? *Kristeligt-dagblad*. https://www.kristeligt-dagblad.dk/danmark/terrorstoette-med-emojis-og-hashtags-hvad-skal-der-til-blive-terrorsympatisoer.

Seemann, A. (2020). Citizen outcasts: The penalty of "Loss of Civil Rights" during the Norwegian treason trials, 1945–1953. *Scandinavian Journal of History, 45*(3), 360–383.

Sharp, D. N. (2018). *Rethinking transitional justice for the twenty-first century: Beyond the end of history*. Cambridge University Press.

Stampnitzky, L. (2013). *Disciplining terror: How experts invented 'Terrorism'.'* Cambridge University Press.

Stonebridge, L. (2024). *We are free to change the world: Hannah Arendt's lessons in love and disobedience*. Hogarth.

Tamir, Y. (1995). *Liberal nationalism*. Princeton University Press.

Tarapués Sandino, D. F. (2020). El Tribunal Para La Paz y Las Salas de Justicia de La JEP Como Órganos Jurisdiccionales Sui Generis. *Universitas, 69*, 1–20.

Teitel, R. G. (2000). *Transitional justice*. Oxford University Press.

Tripkovic, M. (2021). Transcending the boundaries of punishment: On the nature of citizenship deprivation. *The British Journal of Criminology, 61*(4), 1044–1065.

UN Security CouncilSC Resolution 2178. (2014). https://main.un.org/securitycouncil/en/s/res/2178-%282014%29

Vedaschi, A., & Arianna, C. (2019). *Citizenship revocation in Italy as a counter-terrorism measure*. https://verfassungsblog.de/citizenship-revocation-in-italy-as-a-counter-terrorism-measure/

Wacquant, L. (2009). *Punishing the poor: The neoliberal government of social insecurity*. Duke University Press.

Weill, S. (2020). Transnational Jihadism and the role of criminal Judges: An Ethnography of French Courts. *Journal of Law and Society, 47*(S1), S30-53.

Whittle, H. (2024, November 6). Germany passes controversial antisemitism resolution. *DW*. https://www.dw.com/en/germany-passes-controversial-antisemitism-resolution/a-70715643.

Williams, Z. (2023, March 22). Ham-Fisted but Humane: The BBC's podcast about Shamima Begum raises vital questions. *The Guardian*. https://www.theguardian.com/commentisfree/2023/mar/22/shamima-begum-bbc-podcast-im-not-a-monster.

Wood, G. (2017). *The way of the strangers: Encounters with the Islamic state*. Random House.

CHAPTER 11

Conclusion. Applying the Middel/Margins Model to International Law and the Rules-Based International Order

Kerstin Bree Carlson

Introduction

This book project began before Russia's 2022 invasion of Ukraine, and as it was being finalized, Israel's destruction of Gaza was approaching its two-year point. One of the many charges leveled against these two wars is that they indicate a marginalization of the rules-based international order (also sometimes referred to the international legal order, ILO). This can be seen in Russia's drive for territorial empire, a clear violation of the United Nations Charter, as well as Israel's genocidal campaign against Palestinians, violating established tenets in the laws of war. While the rules-based international order has always suffered challenges, the events that have transpired over the past few years have moved the dial of

K. B. Carlson
Roskilde University, Roskilde, Denmark

K. B. Carlson (✉)
The American University of Paris, Paris, France
e-mail: carlson@ruc.dk

M. Robin et al. (eds.), *The Changing Fights and Fighters of Contemporary War*, https://doi.org/10.1007/978-3-032-05518-7_11

the conversation significantly. Where do current events and conversations place the rules-based international order between middle and margins?

The conclusion considers this question through two lenses. First, after laying out challenges to the rules-based international order within the wider field of war studies, it revisits the chapters in this volume to assess how their topics contribute to arguments regarding the changing standing of that order. It finds that chapters articulate, lean on, or seek to expand notions embraced by a rules-based international order. Second, it argues that a rising jurisprudence driven by countries from the global south (the margins) is reimagining a middle for the rules-based international order. It briefly visits several cases brought by countries from the global south asserting the concepts and practices of the rules-based international order, including in circumstances where the states involved do not stand to gain from their involvement. With these two lenses, the conclusion applies the book's argument to its own chapters, as well as to an emerging international legal jurisprudence, demonstrating the value of the margins/middle model for war studies and social science more generally.

Contesting Margins and Middle: International Law & the Rules-Based International Order

One legacy of the Second World War is an international, rules-based order designed to help maintain peace and promote human rights (Sloss, 2022). It features a series of international institutions, where the United Nations is the first among equals. The UN's chief purpose is to preserve peace, as war is outlawed except in self-defense. Complementary institutions and organizations provide spaces for discussion regarding how antagonism and disagreement should be managed (Klabbers, 2015). The power of international law, like all law, lies in its potential to offer alternate venues to force and violence (Cotterrell, 1995). We want states to submit their grievances to a court rather than fight them out on a battlefield, or carry them out against civilian bodies (Walzer, 2015). International law is built on consent: in principle, states are only obligated to obey what they consent to. This starts with state engagement with the International Court of Justice (ICJ). States can consent generally (compulsory jurisdiction), or on a case-by-case basis, usually byspecific treaties that recognize ICJ jurisdiction over disputes arising under the treaty. Only a minority of the world's states (74)[1] have consented to general jurisdiction before the ICJ. This list excludes most of the states that are members of the UN Security Council—the U.S. withdrew its general consent after the ICJ ruled against it as regards its support for an armed group in Nicaragua,[2] and China and Russia never gave such consent. Even states that have consented to jurisdiction have at times modified their consent when they felt the law was against them, like the U.S. in 1986 after the *Nicaragua* case or Australia, after East Timor achieved statehood (it modified its consent to remove ICJ jurisdiction over maritime issues). Nevertheless, even states that are skeptical of the ICJ tend to recognize the court sufficiently to participate in cases where it determines it has jurisdiction over them (Mégret, 2022). In this way, the categories created, actors recognized, and institutions implicated by the rules-based international order become unavoidable subsets of war studies.

The rules-based international order has always been imperfectly realized. Rules are not followed by all participants at all times, and rules are not evenly applied to all participants in all situations. Regardless, the power of the rules-based international order has been to construct a middle, where action, aggression, and disagreement could be debated and litigated, and to relegate those states who elect not to participate or comply to the margins. Since the Second World War, there have always been individual rogue regimes, like North Korea and, for a time, Albania. These regimes put their states on the margins of the rules-based international order by declining to participate or recognize that order. But there have also been states who found themselves relegated to the margins based on the behavior of their regimes. This was often, though not exclusively, due to internal action, like South Africa's apartheid regime or Iraq's murderous campaign against its Kurds. In these instances, states did not contest the legitimacy of the rules-based international order but rather found themselves sanctioned under it.

Especially where sanctions relate to the manner in which a regime is treating some section of its citizenry, the path from the margin to the middle is written in the institutions and organizations of the international legal order itself. Bring your territorial dispute before the ICJ and heed its

[1] https://www.icj-cij.org/declarations (accessed 14 March 2025).

[2] Military and Paramilitary Activities in and Against Nicaragua, Nicaragua v United States, Merits, Judgment, (1986) ICJ Rep 14, ICGJ 112 (ICJ 1986).

determination; analyze your military conduct via the categories outlined in the Geneva Conventions, and outlaw illegal conduct—this has been the middle for the rules-based international order for several decades. The distinction between middle and margins in the rules-based international order has traditionally been as simple as whether one recognized and employed the tools, institutions, and categories created by the rules-based international order. Thus, to take the most notorious example, the United States, a habitual violator of rules as agreed, nonetheless has not heretofore been considered a rogue state under the rules-based international order because it has always applied the categories and insisted upon the legitimacy of the rule-based order even while breaking the rules.[3]

As an analytical lens, the rules-based international order works within a war studies framework, offering a corollary to that frame. Several chapters in this volume take up the rules-based international order directly, either in terms of its definitions, its application, or its actors. One of the most fundamental bulwarks of the international legal order is its imagined distinction between civilian and military objects, logics, and actors. For example, the Geneva Conventions construct two categories, combatants and non-combatants, with a series of distinctions regarding what is permissible in relation to either group. In Chapter 7, Marie Robin considers how conceptualizations regarding who is a "fighter" in jihadi groups are challenging this foundational distinction. Robin shows how jihadi groups broaden the category of war's violence to include speech, information, and ideology as weapons of war, which in turn broadens the category of which actors should be considered warriors (or combatants, in the language preferred by the rules-based international order). Likewise, Amelie Theussen's Chapter 4, examining the geographically layered battlefield that comprises modern warfare, also articulates challenges to the rules-based international order's war logic, which insists that war must not be "everything, everywhere all at once" but rather contained to particular military spaces. This, too, can be understood as an element of the distinction between combatants and non-combatants at the heart of modern rules regarding international relations.

The question of a distinction between civilian versus combatant *logics* is taken up in Arthur P.B. Laudrain's Chapter 5, where he examines

[3] The second term of US President Donald Trump and his extreme "America First" policy may alter assessments of the United States' position within or outside the rules-based international order; at the time of writing, it is too soon to say.

how states seeking to grow their military acumen have leveraged civilian cyber capacities to win military victories. Laudrain considers attacks that range from the arguably still civilian (economic and political) to technical meddling all the way to the fully militarized (Israel's pager attack on Hezbollah). Laudrain's chapter shows how "middle ground states" are seeking to increase their military might by challenging strict distinctions between civilian and military methods and arenas. Likewise, Troels Burchall Henningsen's Chapter 3 builds on challenges to the rules-based international order with his consideration of an emerging incidence of proxy warfare. Proxy warfare challenges a central logic of the rules-based international order, which is the foundational role played by sovereign states. The logic of the rules-based international order is that sovereign states are the central actors in that order: only they may make or change rules, for example. Proxy wars challenge these structures by obfuscating goals and responsibilities in connection to violence. Henningsen's chapter examines regional drivers in Africa and the Middle East to theorize the rise in proxy warfare beyond what great power, state sovereignty theories can offer.

Other chapters address the rules-based international order more tangentially, though no less significantly. Two chapters consider the actors implicated within systems working under the rules-based international order. In Chapter 8, Vicky Karyoti examines drone operators' status in relation to other military professionals to argue that drone operators exist in a grey zone because they are in many ways not recognized as military professionals. This matters, of course, because the rules-based international order recognizes categorical distinctions between combatants and noncombatants that impact their rights (the right to kill, enjoyed by combatants) and privileges (the privilege not to be targeted, for non-combatants). Karyoti examines what the relevant criteria for professionalism in the military is, before concluding that drone operators meet these criteria. Karyoti's chapter challenges our understanding of how we define military professionals especially as the tasks that a professional military performs evolve. In Chapter 6, Jacqueline G. Burns examines women's participation in peace to contrast formal and informal processes. G. Burns shows how the increasingly informal practice of war has opened spaces for women's participation that have not been possible in the peace processes following more traditional forms of warfare; this analysis, beginning with categories of formal/informal, operates in the shadow of the rules-based international order.

Finally, chapters not directly addressing the rules-based international order or the actors impacted, either directly or in response to it, take on concepts or theories that are in dialogue with that order. In Chapter 9, Patrick Mello examines the variance in countries' military responses to the Islamic State (IS) in order to argue that internal political structures, rather than geopolitical constructions, best explain that variance. Mello's chapter is a reminder that rules-based is not for international orders alone; internal orders and their rules also have important impacts. In Chapter 10, Kerstin Bree Carlson contrasts challenges to liberalism evidenced by European treatment of terror actors with the transitional justice model Colombia is applying to its terror actors. Since liberalism underwrites the rules-based international order, Carlson's argument that applying a transitional justice model to European terror prosecutions would re-liberalize them is in dialogue with the rules-based international order as it is understood and applied. And in Chapter 2, the chapter that opens the book, Chiara Libiseller and Lukas Milevski argue for a greater focus on empiricism. Libiseller and Milevski's focus on actors' intentions and actions, rather than prefabricated war studies concepts, can also be seen in relation to the rules-based international order, which permits great variety in individual state ideology, structure and function, so long as there is a realm where common understanding is recognized. International treaties, the currency of the rules-based international order, represent one such realm.

Invoking International Law in Pursuit of Peace: Examples from the Global South

The rules-based international legal order is built on treaties between states: these comprise the most explicit "rules" of the order. In the event of disagreement or breach, the central international dispute resolution mechanism available to states is the International Court of Justice (ICJ), the world's oldest international court. Its current iteration arose after World War II, but its roots reach back to the nineteenth century, when international peace architects imagined the possibility of offering states an alternate to disputes on the battlefield.

Presently the ICJ, together with the state-to-state international law it applies, is enjoying a moment. For the better part of a century, the ICJ quietly addressed cases that interested only a small cadre of international lawyers. Flashy international criminal tribunals, starting with Nuremberg in 1946 and moving on to the UN tribunals for Yugoslavia and Rwanda

(1993 and 1994), followed by the International Criminal Court (ICC) (2002), took most of the oxygen in the room as far as international law was concerned. A court's court, the bulk of the ICJ's jurisprudence concerns questions of its own jurisdiction. This jurisprudence is itself not extensive: the ICJ has heard fewer than 200 cases over its history. Contrast this number with the more than 160 indictments the UN's Yugoslavia tribunal processed during its three decades of work, as an indication of the missing urgency and excitement related to the ICJ's work.

This staid impression of the ICJ was challenged when South Africa brought claims against Israel under the Genocide Convention in late 2023. In January 2024, the world seemed to stand still as it awaited the ICJ's ruling, a new level of attention and publicity for the court (McIntyre & Plan, 2024). On 26 January, when the ICJ issued provisional measures finding that it is "plausible" that Israel is committing genocide and ordered Israel to adhere to its responsibilities under the Genocide Convention but stopped short of ordering the ceasefire that South Africa requested, there was widespread celebration (Milanovic, 2024). South African, Palestinian, and Israeli state representatives all fêted the ways that the ICJ had recognized elements of their arguments; international law scholars and commentators rejoiced in the near unanimity and strong rhetoric produced by the court (Chotiner, 2024). It was left to a small minority, beginning with the citizens of Gaza still living under siege, to decry the ways that the court's ruling brought no immediate mitigation of the deadly realities of contemporary life in Gaza (Humaid, 2024).

South Africa was able to bring a claim against Israel, a state with whom it shares no borders and no particular connection, due to the *erga omnes* jurisdiction that is included in the Genocide Convention. The Genocide Convention was enacted in 1948 and has been signed by/acceded to by 153 countries.[4] Genocide is called "the crime of crimes" because of its collective significance; it concerns the destruction of a people. Emerging from the horrors of the Holocaust, genocide's legal definition hinges on demonstration of an intent to destroy a group in whole or in part. The Genocide Convention makes all states who are parties to it responsible for the prevention of genocide anywhere in the world. To do so, it recognizes *erga omnes* jurisdiction, which allows any member state to charge any other, and makes the ICJ the necessary adjudicator.

[4] Convention on the Prevention and Punishment of the Crime of Genocide, Dec. 91,948, S. Exec. Doc

Even though the Genocide Convention enables any member state to bring a case against any other though its *erga omnes* jurisdiction, this potential has only recently been exploited. South Africa's 2023 case against Israel was only the second *erga omnes* application of the Genocide Convention; the first was Gambia's case against Myanmar, opened in 2019. The other applications of the Genocide Convention have been between warring states: *Bosnia v. Serbia*, *Croatia v Serbia*, and the recently opened case of *Ukraine v Russia*. These previous iterations of the Genocide Convention, where claims of violations under the Convention accompany more standard elements of warfare, represent what can be called "lawfare," the use of law as a means of waging war. The subjective position of the parties in these cases may partially help explain why concluded cases brought under the Genocide Convention have so far never resulted in a finding of genocide by the ICJ. The difficulty of demonstrating genocide under the standard articulated in the ICJ's two concluded genocide cases (brought by Bosnia and Croatia against Serbia) has led many scholars to decry the ICJ's application of law as so strict and impossible to meet that it contravenes the purpose of the Genocide Convention, which is to ensure that genocides do not recur (Behrens & Henham, 2013; Carlson & Gissel, 2024; Howse, 2024). This strict standard presents a high bar that Gambia, South Africa, and Nicaragua may have difficulty surmounting in the cases they have brought, all of which are ongoing and where resolution is likely years away.

The particularities of establishing genocide under international law are not the subject of this conclusion. Rather, what is more significant for our discussion is who is bringing these cases: specifically, that they are being mounted by countries in the global south. Moreover, these countries' invocations of the rules-based international order—here the Genocide Convention's injunction "never again!" and concomitant *erga omnes* jurisdictional tools which enable any country to invoke it—reassert the principles that ground that order. Instead of charging genocide against a sworn enemy, the three cases briefly summarized here address a wrong in the world in which the filing state has no stake beyond its commitment to established treaties. These cases are therefore significant both because they re-engage a once central and now increasingly marginalized series of commitments, represented by the rules-based international order, as well as because this movement back towards center from periphery is being effectuated by states that have traditionally been marginalized (global south). These cases therefore showcase middle/margins movement both of ideas as well as actors.

Genocide Convention Cases: Addressing the Purpose of the Rules-Based International Order

As stated above, the ICJ, the UN's court which hears claims between states, has only concluded two genocide cases to date, and has never held a state responsible for genocide. This has contributed to discussions of the Convention as a "failure" (Burns, 2018). This is notwithstanding the many genocide findings produced by international criminal courts in cases against individuals, including individuals acting in conflicts that the ICJ has found not to be genocidal.[5] There is thus a kind of tension emerging in international law between dynamic institutions applying and finding genocide (international criminal courts) and the grandparent of international law, the ICJ. It is this tension that states of the global south are putting to use to advance rules recognized by the international legal order.

The first state to do so was Gambia, which brought a case against Myanmar in 2019 under the Genocide Convention. The case resulted from a particular set of circumstances. First, Gambia itself had undergone regime change from an authoritarian regime to a democracy, with a peaceful transfer of power in 2017 (Mendy, 2025). Second, the newly appointed Minister of Justice, Abubakarr Tambadou, had worked for years in the prosecutor's office at the UN Tribunal for Rwanda, i.e., he had been professionally trained in one of the dynamic international criminal law institutions whose jurisprudence challenges the ICJ's, at least in terms of the applicability of finding genocide under law. Finally, a serendipitous last-minute switch of ministers found Tambadou substituting for one of his colleagues on a state visit to Bangladesh. Tambadou reports that when he saw the conditions Rohingya refugees were living under at Cox's Bazar, he was reminded of his experience in Rwanda

[5] This fracture at international law is the topic of an amicus curae (friend of the court) brief submitted to the ICJ by six countries in the Gambia v. Myanmar case. These six countries—Canada, Denmark, France, Netherlands, Germany and the United Kingdom—filed a brief encouraging the ICJ to consider jurisprudence from international criminal court findings of genocide. This brief was filed prior to South Africa's case against Israel, which case none of these six countries support. For discussion, see Carlson & Gissel, 2024.

(Durmaz, 2019). Moved to act, Tambadou began investigating what measures he and his office could take, with the result being a filing against Myanmar under the Genocide Convention before the ICJ.

In its submission, the Gambia requested the ICJ rule on provisional measures while awaiting the final determination of genocide. Rulings at the ICJ take years. The ICJ's January 2020 ruling on provisional measures, finding Gambia's claim of genocide "plausible" and ordering Myanmar to follow its obligations under the Genocide Convention,[6] is in legal terms "a win" for Gambia and the Rohingya (Milanovic, 2020). The practical implications for Rohingya refugees are unfortunately minimal. ICJ orders are unenforceable. Additionally, an order to follow legal obligations one had even before the order is issued is arguably not much of an order. For the oppressed Rohingya, the case brought by Gambia has so far made few improvements beyond bringing attention to their plight and tarnishing the reputation of once-fêted leader, Aung San Suu Kyi.

This first use of *erga omnes* jurisdiction, built into the Genocide Convention but never applied in its 70-year history, was nevertheless significant and boundary breaking (Carlson & Gissel, 2020). It paved a way for new applications of international law to pressing humanitarian crises, as we can see in states' attempts to use the ICJ to address Israel's destruction of Gaza.

Questions of Israel's occupation of Palestine have been the subject of ICJ jurisprudence prior to South Africa's 2023 case under the Genocide Convention. In 2002, the ICJ produced an Advisory Opinion advising that Israel's internal border wall was illegal, as were Israeli settlements in the West Bank.[7] This was reiterated in a further ICJ Advisory Opinion on 19 July 2024.[8] These cases attracted little attention outside of international law and politics circles, however, a significant contrast to the contentious reception to South Africa's case in late 2023. On 7 October 2023, Hamas fighters breached the boundary between Gaza and Israel, raiding nearby towns and attacking a music festival, killing 1200 Israelis and taking hundreds hostage. In response, Israel attacked Gaza, first

[6] Application of the Convention on the Prevention and Punishment of the Crime of Genocide, Gambia v Myanmar, Provisional measures, ICJ GL No 178 (ICJ 2020).

[7] Legal Consequences of the Construction of a Wall in the Occupied Palestinian Territory, Advisory Opinion, ICJ GL No 131 (ICJ 2004).

[8] Legal Consequences arising from the Policies and Practices of Israel in the Occupied Palestinian Territory, including East Jerusalem, Advisory Opinion (ICJ 2024).

bombing relentlessly followed by a ground invasion. While international law permits self-defense,[9] the rules-based international order specifies rules of engagement that require protection of civilians. In the immediate aftermath of 7 October 2023, Israeli actions in Gaza produced thousands of civilian deaths; approximately half of them were children.

South Africa acted quickly. While Israel and its allies continued to insist that Israel was acting only within its rights, South Africa gathered evidence of Israeli army crimes and their resulting harm. In November 2023, South Africa filed a case before the ICJ alleging Israeli activity in Gaza was prohibited under the Genocide Convention. South Africa additionally requested that the ICJ should pronounce preliminary measures which would include a ceasefire. After two days of oral hearings in January 2024, the ICJ ordered provisional measures. Interpretations of the significance of this order vary. On the one hand, the ICJ condemned Israeli's actions in strong terms. The issuance of a provisional order was itself a repudiation of Israel's position, given that the ICJ can only exercise jurisdiction (i.e. issue an order) in a case where a plausible finding of violations of the Genocide Convention exists. On the other hand, the ICJ stopped short of ordering a ceasefire in Gaza. Instead, as in the *Gambia v. Myanmar* case, the ICJ's provisional order instructed Israel to comply with the tenets of the Genocide Convention. Given that Israel is already obligated to do exactly this, one could question the legal significance of such an order (Carlson, 2024b).

In the months that followed, as Israel continued its brutal campaign in Gaza, South Africa approached the ICJ again, repeating its request that the court order a ceasefire as a provisional measure. The opinion produced by the ICJ in April 2024 was much more diffuse than the January 2024 order, with fifteen ICJ judges producing five different texts. Beyond the majority opinion and a dissenting opinion, three judges submitted "declarations," which sought to articulate what the majority opinion was arguing (Carlson, 2024a). To put it another way, the judges at the ICJ disagreed as to what the ICJ had ordered. For some, the majority opinion ordered a ceasefire, since compliance with the terms of the order could only be achieved with a ceasefire. For others, the order merely reiterated

[9] The UN Charter's Article 2 permission of self-defense does not, however, apply in circumstances of occupation; here a stricter, human rights-based standard (like one applied in domestic policing circumstances) applies. See discussion in Akande & Tzanakopoulos, 2021.

the instructions the ICJ had earlier produced ordering Israel to comply with the Genocide Convention.

In October 2024, South Africa filed a 750-page Memorial to the ICJ in support of its complaint against Israel. As of this writing, 14 other countries have joined the complaint in support of South Africa's case, most of whom are from the global south.[10]

The first country to join South Africa's case, Nicaragua, also filed its own complaint under the Genocide Convention in March 2024. In this case, the defending state is not Israel but rather Germany, accused of violating the Genocide Convention for its arms sales to Israel and defunding of UNRWA. On April 8 and 9, 2024, the two sides were heard in oral arguments before the ICJ. On 30 April 2024, the ICJ declined to issue provisional measures, which essentially would have ordered Germany to stop weapons sales to Israel.[11] The case, however, is still ongoing; it is only the initial request regarding provisional measures which has been denied.

State Disputes and the Requirement of Participation: Applying the Standards of the Rules-Based International Order

Gambia, South Africa, and Nicaragua's claims under the Genocide Convention are flashy and have received extensive attention, but they are not the only instances of important challenges of the middle/margins divide seen recently in international law. One decade-long, under the radar application of the international legal order can be seen in the jurisprudential efforts of the Democratic Republic of Congo (DRC). Conflict has roiled DRC since the 1990s. The violence that took place

[10] Those countries are: Nicaragua (intervention request submitted on 8 February, 2024); Belgium (intention declared on 11 March); Ireland (intention declared on 27 March); Colombia (intervention request submitted on 5 April); Libya (intervention request submitted on 10 May); Egypt (intention declared on 12 May); Cuba (intention declared on 22 June); Mexico (intervention request submitted on 28 May); Palestine (intervention request submitted on 3 June); Spain (intervention request submitted on 28 June); Türkiye (intervention request submitted on 7 August); Chile (intervention request submitted on 13 September); Maldives (intervention request submitted on 2 October); Bolivia (intervention request submitted on 9 October). See https://unric.org/en/south-africa-vs-israel-14-other-countries-intend-to-join-the-icj-case/ (accessed 30 June, 2025).

[11] Alleged Breaches of Certain International Obligations in respect of the Occupied Palestinian Territory (Nicaragua v. Germany), Request for the Indication of Provisional Measures Order

between 1998–2003 claimed more than six million lives: the largest wartime loss of life since the Second World War. Though fought on the terrain of DRC, the conflict involved at least 11 countries and is referred to as Africa's World War. At the time of writing, violence has been flaring again, driven by many of the same actors for the same reasons.

In 1999, DRC turned to the ICJ for relief. It brought a claim against Rwanda, Burundi, and Uganda for illegal acts of war on its territory. In 2005, the ICJ held for DRC in its case against Uganda.[12] The ICJ found that Uganda's military actions in DRC violated principles of non-use of force as well as the principle of non-intervention. It also found Uganda liable for violations of human rights including killing, torture, and plunder, and ordered Uganda to pay reparations.[13] It dismissed DRC's claims against Rwanda and Burundi, however, since it found that it did not have jurisdiction over them.[14]

Following this judgment, for more than a decade, the two sides negotiated how much Uganda should pay. These negotiations ultimately failed, and DRC took Uganda back to the ICJ. In 2022 the ICJ determined that Uganda must pay DRC USD 325 million in reparations.[15] While the award represented much less than the USD 11 billion DRC requested, the judgment is still quite significant. There are two central reasons for this. First, because the ICJ has not traditionally issued awards regarding reparations (Desierto, 2022). The ICJ's determination that Uganda must pay DRC USD 65 million each year over the next five years represents a new and significant avenue for international law. Second, because even though ICJ decisions are not enforceable, Uganda has been paying, so far at least.

The ICJ judgments, and DRC and Uganda's work under them, also reveal a critical missing aspect of international law: an agreement of cooperation between states like Rwanda in the international legal order. Following the 1994 genocide, and under the leadership of Paul Kagame,

[12] Armed Activities on the Territory of the Congo (Democratic Republic of the Congo v. Uganda), Judgment, I.C.J. Reports 2005, p. 168 (19 December 2005).

[13] Id para 345.

[14] Activités armées sur le territoire du Congo (nouvelle requête: 2002) (République démocratique du Congo c. Rwanda), compétence et recevabilité, arrêt, C.I.J. Recueil 2006, p. 6 (3 February 2006).

[15] Activités armées sur le territoire du Congo (République démocratique du Congo c. Ouganda), réparations, arrêt, C.I.J. Recueil 2022, p. 13 (9 February 2022).

Rwanda has strategically deployed international interest, assistance, and assets without signing on to many of the broader rules-based modes of interaction like jurisdiction before the ICJ (Carlson, 2022). Rwanda has not consented to ICJ jurisdiction.[16] Therefore, for DRC to bring a claim against Rwanda before the ICJ, Rwanda must either agree, or the DRC must make a claim covered by a treaty that gives the ICJ jurisdiction. This is why the case the DRC won against Uganda in 2005, which led to a reparations ruling in 2022 and money being paid by Uganda to DRC, failed against Rwanda. Uganda has consented to compulsory ICJ jurisdiction, and Rwanda has not. Attempts the DRC made to bind Rwanda by asserting violence committed on its territory violated treaties that Rwanda is a party to also failed.

With Rwanda out of reach of the ICJ, the DRC turned to another instrument of the international legal order, the International Criminal Court (ICC), for relief. The ICC has jurisdiction over atrocity crimes committed in member states. Rwanda is not a member of the ICC, but DRC is. Therefore, crimes committed on its territory can be investigated by the ICC. The ICC has been investigating atrocities in DRC since 2004. Several of its judgments have concerned violence committed by individuals in DRC. In 2019, it found a commander in M23, the group associated with current upswings of violence in DRC, funded by Rwanda, guilty of crimes against humanity.[17] In 2023, the DRC made its second request to the ICC to investigate atrocity crimes committed by M23. The prosecutor has acknowledged the request; time will tell if DRC is able to obtain recognition of criminal acts committed by individual actors through ICC processes.

Judgments by the ICC implicate individuals; judgments by the ICJ implicate countries. For DRC, eventual indictments by the ICC against individual warriors financed by Rwanda may provide little more than symbolic justice, and even these are not yet pronounced. Regardless, the story of the DRC's decades-long creative applications of international law tells its own story regarding how interlocutors in the global south are engaging the rules-based international order, moving it back to the middle.

[16] https://www.icj-cij.org/declarations

[17] Ntaganda, ICC-01/04–02/06–2359, Judgment (July 8, 2019). See discussion in (Carlson, 2019).

Chagos Islands: Using the Master's Tools to Dismantle the Master's House

The final example the conclusion considers is the recently decided colonial claims regarding the Chagos Islands. When the UK granted Mauritius its independence in 1968, it separated the Chagos Islands in order to retain control over them. It leased the largest island, Diego Garcia, to the U.S. for a military airbase. Between 1965–1973, thousands of Chagosians were forcibly deported from the islands. In the decades since, Mauritius as well as Chagosians and their allies have been agitating for recognition of rights abuses against them as well as the return of Chagos to Mauritian control (von Massow, 2024).

In 2010, the U.K. declared the waters surrounding the Chagos Islands a marine protected area over which it had sovereignty. Mauritius brought suit against the U.K. under the United Nations Convention on the Law of the Sea (UNCLOS) and won.[18] Following this recognition, the UN General Assembly asked the ICJ to issue an advisory opinion regarding the legality of the separation of the Chagos Islands from Mauritius. In 2019, the ICJ held that this separation was in violation of international law and that the Chagos Islands should be returned to Mauritian control. Although the U.K. initially rejected this ruling it eventually succumbed to international pressure and recognized the judgment (Vyawahare, 2025).

International law draws its legitimacy from its claim to universalism, which is both procedural (unbiased application) as well as substantive (rules all would, and do, agree to). TWAIL ["Third World Approaches to International Law"] scholarship challenges this claim to universalism by showing how states in the global south are more likely to be victims of the international legal order than progenitors of it. Like Audrey Lorde in her famous 1984 essay, many TWAIL scholars assert that "the master's tools will never dismantle the master's house."

Over the past several years, however, states in the global south have been challenging TWAIL's central precepts. South Africa's genocide case against Israel filed before the International Court of Justice in late 2023 has solidified an emerging trend of progressive, boundary-pushing uses of international law by countries who historically have been marginalized by it. In cases before the ICJ and the ICC referenced above,

[18] Chagos Marine Protected Area Arbitration (Mauritius v. United Kingdom), UN Permanent Court of Arbitration, 18 March 2015.

states from the global south are making bold, strategic international law claims. More significantly, many of these cases are not obviously self-serving (such as African government referrals to the ICC, permitting those states to outsource punishment of challengers), but rather in application of the universal, universalizing rationales articulated by and for these international law tools.

Conclusion

International law is built on the useful fiction of sovereign equality between states. Critical international law and security scholars, however, have long described international law as a tool by and for powerful states applied to insure and legitimize existing power imbalances (Anghie, 2007; Orford, 2006). Critical scholars challenge the possibility that international law might present a tool by which less powerful states could participate equally as players in an international system. For these theorists, international law is a method to enforce their marginalization, rather than a middle to which states might aim or aspire.

A series of international law innovations by countries from the global south challenges this assessment. The most well-covered of these examples is South Africa's genocide case against Israel at the ICJ. Although this case has made global headlines, and for a moment turned the hitherto sleepy ICJ into an exciting, much-discussed international judicial organ, South Africa's use of the ICJ to challenge Israel's conduct of hostilities in Gaza is one example of a larger trend where states from the global south have been engaging with and applying international law.

This concluding chapter has briefly reviewed several recent cases before the ICJ brought by countries in the global south, which apply established law expansively. As the chapters in this volume have done, the conclusion has interrogated how fluidity and movements between core and periphery can advance our understanding of war and the actors and spaces in which it is enacted. In the case of international law, countries long seen to be marginalized in the international system are positioning themselves in an arguably middle space. Domestic justice ministries, aided by international lawyers, are the fighters in these spaces; courts are the battlefields. Whether these cases elevate, or hollow out, the reach, power, and content of international law remains to be seen. Will adoption from the margins shore up the middle, or contribute to marginalizing it?

Bibliography

Akande, D., & Tzanakopoulos, A. (2021). Legal: Use of force in self-defence to recover occupied territory. *European Journal of International Law, 32*(4), 1299–1307.

Anghie, A. (2007). *Imperalism, Sovereignity and the making of international law*. Cambridge University Press.

Behrens, P., & Henham, R. (Eds.) (2013). The criminal law of genocide: International, comparative and contextual aspects.: Ashgate Publishing, Ltd.

Burns, R. (2018, December 18). Genocide: 70 years on, three reasons why the UN convention is still failing. *The Conversation*. http://theconversation.com/genocide-70-years-on-three-reasons-why-the-un-convention-is-still-failing-108706

Carlson, K.B. (2019, July16). Why the Ntaganda Judgment Shows That the ICC Has Found Its Footing. *The Conversation*. http://theconversation.com/why-the-ntaganda-judgment-shows-that-the-icc-has-found-its-footing-120433.

Carlson, K.B. (2022). The justice laboratory: International criminal law in Africa. London/Washington D.C.: Chatham House/Brookings.

Carlson, K.B. (2024a, May 30). Productive ambiguities? The International Court of Justice on Israel's Military Operation on Rafah. *Justice in Conflict*. https://justiceinconflict.org/2024/05/30/productive-ambiguities-the-international-court-of-justice-on-israels-military-operation-on-rafah/.

Carlson, K.B. (2024b, February 1). Rights without remedies: The failure of the international court of justice to order a ceasefire to stop alleged genocide in Gaza. *Justice in Conflict*. https://justiceinconflict.org/2024/02/01/rights-without-remedies-the-failure-of-the-international-court-of-justice-to-order-a-ceasefire-to-stop-alleged-genocide-in-gaza/.

Carlson, K.B. & Gissel L.E. (2020, January 14). Why the Gambia's Plea for the Rohingya Matters for International Justice. *The Conversation*. https://theconversation.com/why-the-gambias-plea-for-the-rohingya-matters-for-international-justice-129365.

Carlson, K.B. & Gissel L.E. (2024, January 19). What is genocide? Six Western countries want a broader application of the law—Experts Unpack Why It Matters. *The Conversation*. http://theconversation.com/what-is-genocide-six-western-countries-want-a-broader-application-of-the-law-experts-unpack-why-it-matters-221153.

Chotiner, I. (2024). *January 27*. The Importance of the I.C.J. Ruling on Israel.

Cotterrell, R. (1995). Law's community: Legal thought in sociological perspective. Oxford: Clarendon Press.

Desierto, D. (2022, February 14.) The international court of justice's 2022 reparations judgment in DRC v. Uganda: "Global Sums" as the New Device for Human Rights-Based Inter-State Disputes. *EJIL Talk*. https://www.ejiltalk.org/the-international-court-of-justices-2022-reparations-judgment-in-drc-v-uganda-a-new-methodology-for-human-rights-in-inter-state-disputes/.

Durmaz, M. (2019, December 11). Abubacarr Tambadou: The Man Taking on Myanmar's Aung San Suu Kyi. *TRT World*.

Howse, R. (2024, January 12). Opinion: How the international court of justice can hold Israel accountable in Gaza. *Los Angeles Times*.

Humaid, M. (2024, January 26). "This court is a failure": Palestinians in Gaza decry ICJ'S interim ruling. *Al Jazeera*. https://www.aljazeera.com/features/2024/1/26/this-court-is-a-failure-palestinians-in-gaza-decry-icjs-interim-ruling.

Klabbers, J. (2015). *An introduction to international organizations law*. Cambridge University Press.

Lorde, A. (2018). *The master's tools will never dismantle the master's house*. Penguin Books.

McIntyre, J., & Plan, A. (2024, January 31). The ICJ goes viral: Transparency and sensationalism in South Africa v. *Israel. Opinio Juris.*. https://opiniojuris.org/2024/01/31/the-icj-goes-viral-transparency-and-sensationalism-in-south-africa-v-israel/

Mégret, F. (2022, March 12). Russia's non-appearance before the ICJ against Ukraine: Of not so vanishing vanishing acts and their vanishingly thin justification. *EJIL Talk*. https://www.ejiltalk.org/russias-non-appearance-before-the-icj-against-ukraine-of-not-so-vanishing-vanishing-acts-and-their-vanishingly-thin-justification/.

Mendy, A. (2025, March 13). Post-dictatorship Gambia: A slow march to democratic stability? *Center for Democracy and Development*. https://www.cddwestafrica.org/blog/post-dictatorship-gambia-a-slow-march-to-democratic-stability/.

Milanovic, M. (2020). *January 23*. ICJ Indicates Provisional Measures in the Myanmar Genocide Case. https://www.ejiltalk.org/icj-indicates-provisional-measures-in-the-myanmar-genocide-case/

Milanovic, M. (2024, January 26). ICJ Indicates Provisional Measures in South Africa v.. *EJIL Talk* https://www.ejiltalk.org/icj-indicates-provisional-measures-in-south-africa-v-israel/.

Orford, A. (2006). *International law and its others*. Cambridge University Press.

Sloss, D. L. (2022). Introduction: Preserving a rules-based international order. In D. L. Sloss (Ed.), *Is the international legal order Unraveling*? (pp. 1–34). Oxford University Press.

von Massow, S. (2024). Resurrected colonial courts and the decolonization of the Chagos archipelago. *Verfassungsblog*. https://doi.org/10.59704/a6721139bcf5c6a6
Vyawahare, M. (2025, May 30). UK signs Deal handing over Chagos to Mauritius, but tensions remain. *Mongabay*.
Walzer, M. (2015). Just and unjust wars: A moral argument with historical illustrations. Fifth edition. New York: Basic Books.

Index

M. Robin et al. (eds.), *The Changing Fights and Fighters of Contemporary War*, https://doi.org/10.1007/978-3-032-05518-7

GPSR Compliance
The European Union's (EU) General Product Safety Regulation (GPSR) is a set of rules that requires consumer products to be safe and our obligations to ensure this.

If you have any concerns about our products, you can contact us on

ProductSafety@springernature.com

In case Publisher is established outside the EU, the EU authorized representative is:

Springer Nature Customer Service Center GmbH
Europaplatz 3
69115 Heidelberg, Germany

www.ingramcontent.com/pod-product-compliance
Ingram Content Group UK Ltd.
Pitfield, Milton Keynes, MK11 3LW, UK
UKHW020933180926
475692UK00003B/4
9783032055170